Higher Education
and its Communities

SRHE and Open University Press Imprint
General Editor: Heather Eggins

Current titles include:

Catherine Bargh *et al.*: *Governing Universities*
Catherine Bargh *et al.*: *University Leadership*
Ronald Barnett: *The Idea of Higher Education*
Ronald Barnett: *The Limits of Competence*
Ronald Barnett: *Higher Education*
Ronald Barnett: *Realizing the University in an age of supercomplexity*
Neville Bennett *et al.*: *Skills Development in Higher Education and Employment*
John Biggs: *Teaching for Quality Learning at University*
David Boud *et al.* (eds): *Using Experience for Learning*
Etienne Bourgeois *et al.*: *The Adult University*
Tom Bourner *et al.* (eds): *New Directions in Professional Higher Education*
John Brennan and Tarla Shah: *Managing Quality in Higher Education*
John Brennan *et al.* (eds): *What Kind of University?*
Anne Brockbank and Ian McGill: *Facilitating Reflective Learning in Higher Education*
Stephen Brookfield and Stephen Preskill: *Discussion as a Way of Teaching*
Sally Brown and Angela Glasner (eds): *Assessment Matters in Higher Education*
John Cowan: *On Becoming an Innovative University Teacher*
Heather Eggins (ed.): *Women as Leaders and Managers in Higher Education*
Gillian Evans: *Calling Academia to Account*
David Farnham (ed.): *Managing Academic Staff in Changing University Systems*
Sinclair Goodlad: *The Quest for Quality*
Harry Gray (ed.): *Universities and the Creation of Wealth*
Andrew Hannan and Harold Silver: *Innovating in Higher Education*
Norman Jackson and Helen Lund (eds): *Benchmarking for Higher Education*
Merle Jacob and Tomas Hellström (eds): *The Future of Knowledge Production in the Academy*
Mary Lea and Barry Stierer (eds): *Student Writing in Higher Education*
Elaine Martin: *Changing Academic Work*
Ian McNay: *Higher Education and its Communities*
David Palfreyman and David Warner (eds): *Higher Education and the Law*
Craig Prichard: *Making Managers in Universities and Colleges*
Michael Prosser and Keith Trigwell: *Understanding Learning and Teaching*
John Richardson: *Researching Student Learning*
Stephen Rowland: *The Enquiring University Teacher*
Yoni Ryan & Ortrun Zuber-Skerritt (eds): *Supervising Postgraduates from Non-English Speaking Backgrounds*
Maggi Savin-Baden: *Problem-based Learning in Higher Education: Untold Stories*
Peter Scott (ed.): *The Globalization of Higher Education*
Peter Scott: *The Meanings of Mass Higher Education*
Anthony Smith and Frank Webster (eds): *The Postmodern University?*
Colin Symes and John McIntyre: *Working Knowledge*
Imogen Taylor: *Developing Learning in Professional Education*
Peter G. Taylor: *Making Sense of Academic Life*
Susan Toohey: *Designing Courses for Higher Education*
Paul R. Trowler: *Academics Responding to Change*
David Warner and Elaine Crosthwaite (eds): *Human Resource Management in Higher and Further Education*
David Warner and Charles Leonard: *The Income Generation Handbook* (2nd edn)
David Warner and David Palfreyman (eds): *Higher Education Management*
Diana Woodward and Karen Ross: *Managing Equal Opportunities in Higher Education*

Higher Education and its Communities

Edited by
Ian McNay

The Society for Research into Higher Education
& Open University Press

Published by SRHE and
Open University Press
Celtic Court
22 Ballmoor
Buckingham
MK18 1XW

email: enquiries@openup.co.uk
world wide web: www.openup.co.uk

and 325 Chestnut Street
Philadelphia, PA 19106, USA

First published 2000

A catalogue record of this book is available from the British Library

ISBN 0 335 20734 0 (hb)

Library of Congress Cataloging-in-Publication Data
Higher education and its communities / edited by Ian McNay.
     p. cm.
   'The chapters in this collection have been developed from papers prepared
for, and presented at, the 1999 Annual Conference of the Society for Research
into Higher Education in Manchester'—Acknowledgements.
   Includes bibliographical references and index.
   ISBN 0–335–20734–0
   1. Education, Higher—Social aspects—Great Britain—Congresses.   2.
Community life—Great Britain—Congresses.   I. McNay, Ian.   II. Society for
Research into Higher Education. Conference (1999 : Manchester, England)

LC191.9.H54   2000
378.1′03′0941—dc21   00–037512

Typeset by Graphicraft Limited, Hong Kong
Printed in Great Britain by St Edmundsbury Press, Bury St Edmunds, Suffolk

Contents

The Editor and Contributors

Patrick Ainley is Reader in Learning Policy, School of Post-compulsory Education and Training, University of Greenwich, UK, and convenor of the FE/HE network of the Society for Research into Higher Education.

John Brennan is Director of the Centre for Higher Education Research and Information at the Open University, UK.

Kevin Brosnan is Teaching Fellow in Academic Innovation, University of Stirling, UK.

Anne Corbett is a journalist and research student at the London School of Economics, UK.

Rosemary Deem is Professor of Educational Research and Director of the University Graduate School at Lancaster University, UK.

Eric Gilder is a professor at the Lucian Blaga University of Sibiu (Romania) and Reviews Editor of the UNESCO journal, *Higher Education in Europe.*

Yvonne Hillier is a senior lecturer in the Department of Continuing Education, City University, London, UK.

Carolyn Jackson is a lecturer in the Department of Educational Studies, University of York, UK.

Rachel Johnson is a research associate in the Department of Educational Research, University of Lancaster.

Maurice Kogan is Professor Emeritus of Government and Social Administration at Brunel University, UK and Director of the Centre for the Evaluation of Public Policy and Practice.

Ann Lahiff is a senior lecturer in the School of Post-Compulsory Education and Training, University of Greenwich, UK.

Janice Malcolm is a senior research fellow in the School of Continuing Education, University of Leeds, UK.

Ian McNay is Professor of Higher Education and Management, and Head of the School of Post-Compulsory Education and Training, University of Greenwich. He chairs the Research and Development Committee of SRHE.

Nick Nelson is Senior Research Fellow in the School of Education, University of Leeds, UK.

Su-Ann Oh is a doctoral student in the Department of Educational Studies, at Hertford College, University of Oxford, UK.

Julia Preece is a lecturer in the School of Education, University of Surrey, UK, and convenor of the Eastern European network of SRHE.

Tarla Shah is Projects and Development Officer in the Centre for Higher Education Research and Information at the Open University, UK.

David Smith is Senior Research Fellow in the School of Education, University of Leeds, UK.

Penny Tinkler is a lecturer in the Department of Sociology, University of Manchester, UK.

Judith Watson is consulting partner in the research agency, Sustainable Findings, and a former Senior Research Fellow, School of Post-Compulsory Education and Training, University of Greenwich, UK.

Edwin Webb is Reader in English and Education, School of Post-Compulsory Education and Training, University of Greenwich, UK.

John Wyatt is Senior Visiting Research Fellow in the Centre for Institutional Studies, University of East London, UK.

David Yeomans is Principal Research Fellow in the School of Education, University of Leeds, UK.

Miriam Zukas is Chair of the School of Continuing Education, University of Leeds, UK.

Acknowledgements

The chapters in this collection have been developed from papers prepared for and presented at the 1999 annual conference of the Society for Research into Higher Education in Manchester. I am grateful to many presenters who allowed me to choose from a much wider range. The criteria for inclusion in a collection like this concern balance and fit; there were many quality contributions that it has not been possible to include. A list of relevant sessions and presenters at the conference is given in the appendix.

I am grateful to the editors and publisher – Blackwell – of one of the Society's journals, *Higher Education Quarterly*, for permission to include Maurice Kogan's stimulating piece. It also appeared in *Higher Education Quarterly*, 54(3). Further thanks for support go to colleagues in SRHE and at the University of Greenwich, and, finally, to my PA, June Washer, who sorted out many problems, especially those where new technology proved, again, less than perfect.

Introduction

1

Community: A Diverse Conceptualization and Realization

Ian McNay

The word 'community' has become one of the most overused and abused terms in the English language. With disregard for the sense of common attachment traditionally inherent in the idea, the word is applied with little restraint to just about any geographic locale that happens to be embraced by political boundaries. This leads to such oxymorons as the labelling of suburban commuter polities as 'bedroom communities'.

However, colleges and universities may be no better when it comes to the jargonistic use of community. Can an individual really find community as a solitary member of an 18,000 student institution? This is a dubious proposition.

(Cortes 1999: 12)

This collection explores some interpretations of community within higher education. There could be many: over 40 per cent of UK universities include the word in their mission statement (Davies and Glaister 1996). That ranked it ahead of concepts such as learning, scholarship, knowledge, excellence, society or the economy. Cortes was putting community in opposition to diversity and arguing that campuses are divided since people find community identity in smaller units, possibly Polanyi's 'academic neighbourhoods' (Polanyi 1958), or other affinity groups. Those issues of identity, affinity, locality recur throughout the chapters here.

Community is a reassuring word, like motherhood and apple pie, carrying a sense of belongingness. As Raymond Williams says (in Emmett 1982), it is 'warmly persuasive' and 'never used unfavourably'. Yet it has sometimes had a bad press by association. Margaret Thatcher, denying the existence of society, saw community as a useful concept and grasped one of its underlying characteristics: of interdependence of its members. Thus it was where care could be exercised, so that the government could delegate, or abdicate, responsibility for care of its citizens. There was, of course, a short-lived community charge to pay for this. More recently, during discussion of the 1999 Crime and Public Protection Bill there was a proposal to rename the probation service the 'Community Punishment and Rehabilitation Service'. So, not only care, but also control; again, those two concepts recur here.

This distortion of the concept of community into a delivery framework for government policy can be seen also in higher education where the 'community of scholars' became responsible for implementation of policy for higher education aimed at 'serving the economy more effectively' (Department of Education and Science 1987). When things went awry, the defect was always with implementation, not with the policy, echoing other areas of provision such as health, welfare and prisons.

More recently, government agency initiatives such as Higher Education Reach-out to Business and the Community (HEROBAC) have set HE institutions within a wider community that they exist to serve (Higher Education Funding Council for England 2000). They are, by implication, not part of it, and neither is 'business' which was added to the original formulation. This 'hinterland' community can be local or regional, or European/international. The national level is underplayed. Yet national need was postulated as the reason for nationalizing both the polytechnics and further education colleges that had been nurtured by local communities. So had the civic universities, who lost that commitment after 1945 as the University Grants Committee (UGC) homogenized universities and student grants allowed the development of campus-based provision that took young people away from their community roots. Perhaps the national identification is muted because of the devolution debate. It comes through, though, in the parallel debate on citizenship with its emphasis on common standards and obligations.

The source of the concept

For Mellor (1991), community is one of the key words in sociology that have 'diffuse meanings because they relate to a set of central values in society, which, if scrutinized, would lose much of their precision and would look more like myths' (p. 289). Such terms are 'imbued with contradictory and emotionally charged beliefs'. 'Community', in particular, carries 'high flown notions', what Emmett (1982) calls 'a commitment to romanticism'. John Wyatt's chapter links the two concepts.

The history that Mellor traces, of its use in urban sociology, has parallels in higher education. Tönnies (1955) developed the concept, *Gemeinschaft*, and related it to locality, to meetings of minds and to blood ties with rituals, traditions and 'natural' authority (of men). This contrasts with *Gesellschaft* (society, or association) where social relationships derive from economic organization with more extrinsic drives. Meetings of minds and economic imperatives may be in opposition in higher education, as Su-Ann Oh shows.

The assumption that communities were small was set in opposition to Marxist larger-scale organization. They were local, not central or corporate; personal and collegial, not bureaucratic (McNay 1999). The 'blood tie' concept remained in studies of the Jewish ghetto and on ethnic groups in large cities (Wirth 1969). In those cities, though, locality remains important as people organize their daily life despite politicians (as professionals in higher education do, despite senior management; McNay 1995). The political raises its head in such communities when there are threats to them, for example from 'development' involving demolition of homes and dispersal of people when bypasses, motorways or shopping centres are proposed. Affinity communities may also strengthen themselves by active resistance to oppression which transforms, as with gays or black groups, into positive promotion, with pride, of a particular common identity.

Those ascriptions of meaning – of common interest groups, internal and external, of geographical locations small and large – are here in this collection, as is the theme of threat and collective response. There is also some treatment of the range of other communities that higher education institutions serve, based on geography, identity or affinity.

Content organization

The first main section of the book starts with a view from history through literature. Newman's (1873) *Idea of a University* is often referred to nostalgically and ignorantly by many who yearn for a golden age of universities as communities. They omit from their vision his omission of research from a university mission. They may also not realize the reality of nineteenth-century English universities – the Scots were different. John Wyatt reveals some of this by reviewing contemporary representations as more modern concepts of universities began to emerge through a succession of value shifts in Victorian society. Maurice Kogan then sweeps vigorously and rigorously through concepts of academic communities, the role and identity of individuals within them, the processes that operate within them, and their relationship with the wider world. In doing so he introduces themes that later chapters pursue. We might usefully ask how far the three precepts with which he ends operate for institutions we know.

As anyone knows who has moved house, especially to smaller settlements, acceptance as members of communities can take time. For many academics, it involves study for and success in a PhD. Penny Tinkler and Carolyn Jackson look at that element in the gatekeeping process governing entry to membership of academic communities: the PhD examination. They uncover a variety of conceptions and practices in relation to this certification of citizenship. Janice Malcolm and Miriam Zukas argue that, after entry, a sense of community identity is only partial. References to research communities are frequent, to teaching communities rare (though learning communities are coming up fast). Yet most academics spend more time teaching than researching; certainly the imbalance of funding is towards teaching. Malcolm and Zukas argue that developing as a full citizen with a professional identity is best done by support to situated learning linked to a discipline 'neighbourhood' since role expectations are conditioned by local cultures and particular knowledge bases.

The next two chapters move the focus from the staff to the collective institution. Rosemary Deem and Rachel Johnson explore how far universities as communities are fragmented or divided: hierarchically by the distancing of managers from the managed; by disciplines, especially as leaders within disciplines move to more corporate management roles or compete with others for resources, and by gender in approaches to inclusion or exclusion and gender-based solidarities (or communities?). John Brennan and Tarla Shah also explore a possible threat to the academic community and its values, this time from 'outside the walls', in the approaches to quality assurance and accountability that government adopts on behalf of the wider community. Both chapters have optimistic views about the fundamental robustness of academic values at the collective level.

Perhaps the threat comes through individuals. Su-Ann Oh considers a possible canker in the academic community in the UK and China. The different opportunities that staff have to pursue externally funded work, and to profit from it carry two risks: of divisiveness because of inequalities of opportunity and reward; and of an undermining of fundamental values of autonomy and openness that, for some, are defining characteristics of universities. She also shows how far the collective ethic is prevalent in the two systems: individuality in the socialist market economy of China may be legitimated and find less contentious expression since the campus community does not provide 'home comforts' in the way that some UK universities do. In the UK case, reflecting the wider polity, the question is posed as to whether the need is greater for a freedom of information Act than it is for one to protect privacy.

The chapters in Part 1, then, examine external influences on the internal community. Part 2 looks from the inside to the outside as universities renew their relationship with their location and the people in the neighbourhood so that David Blunkett's experience is rarer:

> Higher education has also meant a great deal to me personally. In the community in which I grew up, it was unheard of for anybody to enter higher education, and in too many communities that remains the case. It is one of the reasons why I take the widening participation agenda so seriously. Higher education opened up significant new opportunities for me. It lifted my sights and raised my expectations. The learning I undertook, and the friendships I formed at university, have been of enduring value to me. These are things I want not only for my family, but for many thousands more of our people, particularly my constituents and those in similar areas of our nation.
>
> (Blunkett 2000: 32)

First, Julia Preece looks at a group of learners developing a sense of self through which they understand better their cultural community and their adopted locational community as well as their collective identities as women.

The geographical boundaries of 'community' stretch to embrace the region in contemporary constitutional debates. The learning region is part of the discourse that links lifelong learning to economic development, though social progress is rarely mentioned. The idea featured within the Dearing Report as part of its flawed analysis of incremental evolution of higher education provision (National Committee of Inquiry into Higher Education 1997). With devolution to the national states in the UK and the establishment of Regional Development Agencies there is a debate on where strategic planning of post-compulsory provision should be done. The debate is longstanding (McNay 1991). Judith Watson and her colleagues argue that it is underinformed and vitiated by the failure to see such provision as a whole, with movement of people *within*, rather than *between* discrete sectors.

Next in Part 2 comes the Community; European, that is, and with a capital C, where the region has a strong identity within policy. Anne Corbett, however, focuses at Community level, though issues of sovereignty and subsidiarity bubble below her narrative. She adopts an historical perspective on policy-making as leaders of the community sought to develop a community identity among some of its citizens, using initiatives in higher education to promote mobility for mutual understanding. Governance of the Community is an important issue in developing a commonality of identity and yet, as she shows, the frictions and fractures are always there as special interests compete with attempts at common, collective approaches. Much like a university or college community, really.

Part 2, like the previous one, ends with a paired comparison of two countries: France and England in the context of European Community policy on, among other things, lifelong learning and regionalism. Yvonne Hillier considers learning in the workplace community in the two countries, indeed within two regions, given the regional emphasis in the EU on employment and education policies. In France, there is a law and a levy on employers to fund employees' learning; yet there seems to be little by way of policy or strategy and the universities are disengaged. In England, there is neither a law for older workers nor a levy, but the policy of targets for workforce achievement, and the existence of vocational qualifications with currency in the academic community have promoted a greater exchange between the two parts of the remit of the Department for Education and Employment. A regional development strategy, as anticipated in the chapter by Watson *et al.* has, therefore, something to build on, and a European scheme, similar to Erasmus as outlined by Anne Corbett, could help to develop further schemes for the full citizenship role for people in their local, regional and national communities.

Ruth Finnegan (1994) was one of the first people to explore new meanings of community in higher education in a period of mass provision and of moves away from full-time campus-based models. She saw the Open University as an open community given the multiple community identities of its students and staff. For her, in the Open University, the higher education experience had become, 'not a lengthy commitment to some permanent academic community but a set of opportunities which people can move into and out of as suits their needs at different times' (p. 183).

She saw communications technology as helping to 'recover' community in this new world. In Part 3, two chapters explore this vision of a future. Edwin Webb and Ann Lahiff analyse discourse within a set of programmes using computer-mediated communications. They argue that there is a learning community represented by these. One could ask whether, as with Finnegan's examples, a more appropriate term would be learning group – are those in attendance in classrooms communities? Networks, I would also accept, but my view is that, just as towns lost community coherence as they grew, so too have universities in a mass era. As, then, Web-based communications close distance in the wider world and allow affinity groups to develop in electronic 'sites', so too in higher education. But we still have some way to go before a new way of being in a virtual community emerges when common 'sites' in space and time are removed. Lahiff and Webb focus on learning in groups; Kevin Brosnan's focus is the organization and his review reveals that Information and Communication Technologies (ICT) can be used not only for development, but also for control, in the new managerialism discussed by Deem and Johnson.

Eric Gilder's chapter brings a final optimism for the future. Drawing examples from three countries rarely highlighted in analyses of higher education, he puts a case for the continuing relevance of more traditional views of learning communities, of communities of scholars and centres of liberal values and thought in wider communities where poverty, war and recent oppression provide a setting often hostile to the exercise of freedoms of challenge, of disputation, of difference. Perhaps, in the modern world, we recover our sense of common identity and common cause only when facing a common external threat. If so, the continuous crises provoked in some HE systems augur well for internal community solidarity, at least for those who share known, common values.

There is still more to investigate: our field of enquiry is in constant flux. The students who feature in this collection are not in the mainstream. Some who are may find different ways of transferring identity to new communities after the disruption of moving into higher education and away from the community that nurtured them (Hoggart 1958). The authors in Barnett (1994) explored some student-focused issues, but the roles of students' unions, of halls of residence, of societies based on affinity – cultural, religious, sporting, whatever – are rarely touched upon. And, do those who move away from their alma mater in the diaspora after their degree is awarded, look back and feel some identity with that community? Perhaps that is another conference . . . and another book.

References

Barnett, R. (ed.) (1994) *Academic Community: Discourse or Discord?* London: Jessica Kingsley.

Blunkett, D. (2000) *Modernising Higher Education – Facing the Global Challenge.* Speech given at the University of Greenwich, 15 February. London: DfEE.

Cortes, C.E. (1999) Building community from communities: diversity and the future of higher education, *Metropolitan Universities*, 9(4): 11–18.

Davies, S.W. and Glaister, K.W. (1996) Spurs to higher things? Mission statements of UK universities, *Higher Education Quarterly*, 50(4).

Department of Education and Science (1987) *Higher Education: Meeting the Challenge.* London: HMSO.

Emmett, I. (1982) Blaenau Ffestiniog, in A. Cohen (ed.) *Belonging*, pp. 205–9. St John's Newfoundland: ISER/Memorial University of Newfoundland.

Finnegan, R. (1994) Recovering 'academic community': what do we mean?, in R. Barnett (ed.) *Academic Community: Discourse or Discord?* London: Jessica Kingsley.

Higher Education Funding Council for England (2000) *Higher Education Reach-out to Business and the Community Fund*, Circular 00/50. Bristol: HEFCE.

Hoggart, R. (1958) *The Uses of Literacy.* Harmondsworth: Penguin.

McNay, I. (1991) Cooperation, coordination and quality in employer and education partnerships: a role for the regions, in P. Raggatt and L. Unwin (eds) *Change and Intervention: Vocational Education and Training.* London: Falmer Press.

McNay, I. (1995) Universities going international: choices, cautions and conditions, in P. Blok (ed.) *Policy and Policy Implementation in Internationalisation of Higher Education.* Amsterdam: EAIE.

McNay, I. (1999) Changing cultures in UK higher education: the state as corporate market bureaucracy and the emergent academic enterprise, in D. Braun and F-X. Merrien, *Towards a New Model of Governance for Universities? A Comparative View.* London: Jessica Kingsley.

Mellor, R. (1991) Community and urban life, in P. Worsley (ed.) *The New Modern Sociology Readings.* London: Penguin.

National Committee of Inquiry into Higher Education (1997) *Higher Education in the Learning Society* (Dearing Report). London: NCIHE.

Newman, J.H. (1873) *The Idea of a University.* Oxford: Clarendon Press.

Polanyi, M. (1958) *Personal Knowledge: Towards a Post-critical Philosophy.* London: Routledge & Kegan Paul.

Tönnies, F. (1955) *Community and Society.* London: Routledge.

Wirth, L. (1969) Urbanism as a way of life, in R. Sennett (ed.) *Classic Essays on the Culture of Cities.* New York: Appleton Century Crofts.

Part 1

The Academic Community

2

Persistent Ghosts: Romantic Origins of the Idea of University Communities

John Wyatt

Isaiah Berlin (1999: 1), in his analysis of the roots of romanticism, warned that what he called 'the greatest single shift in the consciousness of the West' has left us with a legacy of conflict. We are caught between its intellectual and emotional inheritance and other opposing sets of intellectual structures. Using works of imaginative literature, I want to convey some of the nineteenth-century's romantic bequest of ideas on the nature of the university. The setting, nineteenth-century England, is narrow, because although there was a relatively rapid increase in chartered institutions in the second half of the century, in the first half there were few institutions of university status: Oxford, Cambridge, the London federation of King's and University Colleges, and Durham. Narrowness has one advantage, enabling us to concentrate on a system emerging slowly and, unlike European instances, in a non-revolutionary political context.

If readers knew only of English university life through novels of the nineteenth century, even those written after the Royal Commissions of the 1850s, they would assume that only two ancient confessional universities existed, both in an unreformed condition. This would be an error, for, even before the reforming Acts of Parliament made siginificant changes to the two universities' constitutions and curricula, there were reforms brought about by their own members (see Brock and Curthoys 1997; Rothblatt 1968). Similarly, there would be little or no appreciation of two external shaping forces particularly affecting the new universities: the Scottish experience of the Enlightenment and its impact on its ancient institutions, and the effects of German initiatives (Ashby 1967).

Romanticism's attitudes were never unidirectional in respect of attitudes to institutions, whether they were governments, Churches or universities. The opposing positions of a Blake and a Burke or Coleridge exemplify a conflict of ideas about old institutions, on one hand rejecting decayed agents of repression, on the other appreciating them as the incarnation of ancient historical values set against new materialism. As the century progressed and romanticism itself changed in England, the university became the battleground for such oppositions, at first in theology (which had its own literature) and then on broader educational issues. In this, as in other instances of the tensions within the ranks of intellectuals attempting to repel industrialism and utilitarianism, public debate was realized in works of imagination which made a drama out of a crisis and created images of heroes and (a few) heroines in situations where tension could be illustrated. There was a notable evolution of such images. In simple terms, there was a breakpoint about the middle of the century when a new literature of university life emerged, seeing Oxford and Cambridge not as the arenas for the repression of youth, but as nurseries for the renewal of the nation. There are certain themes which appear to haunt discussion of the university in society during two centuries.

The university as an ideal community

The two English confessional universities at the beginning of the nineteenth century represented for many intellectuals an entrenched hierarchical society at odds with the new romantic spirit. This spirit promulgated the idea of youth awakening to maturity rather than submitting to ancient traditional discipline. In the radical novel, *The Adventures of Hugh Trevor* by Thomas Holcroft (first published in parts from 1794 to 1797), the young hero enters Oxford with the expectation that he will find an ordered society: 'A band of seers living in fraternity, governed by one universal spirit of benevolence, harmonised by one vibrating system of goodness celestial' (p. 74). As in his subsequent picaresque journey through experiences with other pillars of the establishment, the Church, politics and the law, Hugh Trevor finds reality sadly out of sorts with the ideal. Students are coarse, gluttonous, and debauched; the tutors are no better. As Turl, a poor student (often in the early nineteenth-century campus novel the voice of revelation), tells him, the tutors' role is 'To watch and regulate the tufts of caps, the tying of bands, the stuff and tassels of which gowns are made, to reprimand those who wear red or green and to take care that the gownsmen assemble at proper times and to hear prayers gabbled over as fast as tongues can give them utterance . . .' (p. 82).

The sense of ancient reactionary institutions falling into decay was not confined to the radical novelists. Oxford and Cambridge had a reputation in the eyes of the rising middle classes for indiscipline and lax care of young men, confirmed eventually in mid-century by the reports of the Royal Commissions. In 1852, the Royal Commission on Oxford regretted that not only had the university dragged its feet in collaborating with the Commission, but also discipline amongst undergraduates was disturbingly slow to improve.

> The grosser exhibitions of vice, such as drunkenness and riot have in Oxford, as in the higher classes generally become rare. The intercourse with their tutors has, in many cases, become more confidential

and more frequent . . . There still remains, however, much to be done . . .
Of existing evils the most obvious are sensual vice, gambling, in its
various forms and extravagant expenditure . . . In the villages round
Oxford . . . the opportunities to vice are too abundant. Gambling is
carried on in the University, as elsewhere, in such a manner as to make
it extremely difficult of detection . . . Driving, riding and hunting are . . .
causes of great expense. Of these amusements the most expensive is
hunting. It seldom costs less than four guineas a day.

    (Royal Commission, 1852 quoted in: Maclure 1986: 67)

Despite the evidence of corruption in the ancient halls and the feeding of
an exciting savour of scandal to the new middle class by novelists, there
remained in the public mind an idea that the university community ought
to be something better than a nursery where the rich late adolescent could
work out his destiny while sowing wild oats, perhaps even a model of an
ideal community. German philosophers such as Johann Fichte, Wilhelm
von Humboldt, and F.W. Schelling conveyed a very elevated role for the
university in the nation: 'The human race fulfils its destiny by an uninter-
rupted and steady progress . . . The University, however, is the institution
expressly devised to secure the non-interruption and steadiness of that
progress . . . it is the most important and the most holy thing which the
human race possesses' (Turnbull 1926: 263).

 In the English setting the ambitions for the university were less extremely
formulated, but a continuing theme was the concept of self-governance, a
kind of ideal state where rank was allocated by academic talent and not by
birth or political influence. Less well known than the often quoted lines of
Wordsworth on his carefree days as an undergraduate at Cambridge is the
evocation in Book IX of *The Prelude* of the College he remembers as a
model of the well ordered state:

> Nor was it least
> Of many debts which afterwards I owed
> To Cambridge and an academic life
> That something there was holden up to view
> Of a republic, where all stood thus far
> Upon equal ground, that they were brothers all
> In honour; as of one community –

    (1979: Book IX 1805, lines 226–32)

Note Wordsworth's use of the key word 'community', a term which was
progressively used to convey a romantic vision of a better-ordered society
(Plant 1974). A 'community of scholars' or 'community' began to displace
the words, 'the spirit of association', the last found, for instance, in political
novels such as Disraeli's *Sybil* (1845). The distrust of the mechanical factory-
led organization of people and the decay of ancient forms of authority
combined with a romantic historicism encouraged a quest for a new form
of ordering the way that people might live in life-enhancing groups.

In respect of the two ancient universities, the idea that they could retain and renew something valuable from an old order, where equality rested on talent, gained strength during the period when reform threatened their independence. Brock and Curthoys (1997) illustrate how Oxford's stubborn resistance to government interference, signalled by the rejection of Robert Peel as a candidate for one of the university Parliamentary seats, began to earn credit for the university as a defender of freedom in the eyes of liberal thinkers.

It is impossible to discuss the idea of academic community without a reference to Newman, not only his *Idea of a University* (Newman 1873) but also in his autobiographical material (Newman 1895). Rather than repeat the scores of articles and books on the first, which, after all, was not re-garded with much interest on publication (Brock 1996: 67), I shall briefly illustrate the kind of personal attachment to an Oxford community found in his reminiscences about his student days at Trinity College and then as a don at Oriel. The college, he wrote, 'is the shrine of our best affections, the bosom of our fondest recollections, a spell upon our after-life, a stay for the world-weary mind and soul, wherever we are cast, till the end comes' (Rothblatt 1997: 295). His personal investment in college life emerges tragi-cally as he remembers, in his exclusion from Oxford, that 'there used to be much snapdragon growing on the walls opposite my freshman's rooms there, and I had for years taken it as the emblem of my own perpetual residence even unto death in my own University' (Newman 1895: 237). Years before he had written a poem about the snapdragon, then the symbol of humility (Beer 1993: 144). This combination of monastic virtues and monastic tenure for life makes membership of the Oxbridge common room, junior or senior, a special privilege far beyond the external world's com-mon definition of a place of work. The sense of a place set apart dominated English thinking about the university and its special role in the nation.

The undergraduates in fiction were not immune to the experience of something which distinguished the college as a community. Again, it is a combination of two romantic features, historicism and the belief that envir-onment has a moulding effect on character. In Thackeray's novel *Pendennis* (published 1848–50), despite the hero's cool attitude to the studies of the university, he is immediately attracted by the college 'with its pretty foun-tain playing, the tall chapel windows and the hall with its tapering lantern and oriel windows' (Thackeray 1994: 205–6). Even more, the serious hero, Robert Elsmere in Mrs Humphrey Ward's 1888 novel of that name, is moved by history: Oxford 'laid its old irresistible spell; the sentiment haunting its quadrangles, its libraries, and its dim melodious chapels, stole into the lad's heart . . .'. It is the unbroken line of history, 'the continuity, the complexity of human experience, the unremitting experience of the race, the stream of purpose running through it all' (Ward 1987: 50–1) which binds the young scholar to a lifetime commitment to learning.

The university may have entranced the young Robert Elsmere initially, but it is the college rather than the university that is prominent in the novel and in other literature and may go some way to explain the dominance of the category 'college' in English discussion of higher education. Even at the end of the twentieth and beginning of the twenty-first century, the word seems to take precedence in labelling what are now much larger organizations (Keen and Warner 1989). It is again an instance of the persistent idea of the Oxbridge model that has made the term stand as a mark of something better than 'school', 'institute' or 'academy'. Rothblatt asserts that the Oxford of the 1860s was not the inspiration for Newman's *Idea of a University*, but the college life he had lived forty years before was, for it affected how he felt and added 'well-being to being'. 'The idea of a university is cerebral. The idea of a college is a state of mind' (Rothblatt 1997: 294).

The student estate

It was barely possible to consider at the beginning of the nineteenth century the notion of a class or estate of students, except perhaps in German novels of youth in times of trial. Goethe's Young Werther (1774) and Schiller's characters in the drama *The Robbers* (1781), for instance, were popular in England, but examples of young men passing through a rite of passage in novels with an English university setting are less deeply involved in storm and stress. One reason was that the number of students at Oxford and Cambridge for the first decades of the nineteenth century was fairly stable, and in some years even declining; moreover, it was only a small proportion of the population (Stone 1974). Furthermore, it was a group of young men restricted by religious tests to the established Church. As *Hugh Trevor* (1794–97) illustrated, Oxford was socially condemned by many as an unsuitable place for youth (Holcroft 1973). Many middle class and some aristocratic parents sent their offspring to Scottish universities to avoid the moral dangers of unreformed Oxbridge.

When reforms of the two universities began to appear on the public agenda, particularly during the openly discussed Commissions of Enquiry in the 1850s, a remarkable literary interest increased, but remained stubbornly locked into narratives about the unreformed university. For years there circulated light skits on university life (Curthoys and Day 1997). Thackeray's *Book of Snobs* (1848) is perhaps the best written of the genre with its keenly observed class distinctions of dress and behaviour at Oxbridge.

One example was still in print in 1982, *The Adventures of Mr Verdant Green – an Oxford Freshman*. The pen-name of the author, Cuthbert Bede, indicates a north-eastern origin; he was an alumnus of the new Durham University, although, following the fashion for campus novels, he portrays the Oxford scene. Paradoxically, at the moment of the greatest changes to Oxford, Cuthbert Bede chooses to present the life of an unreformed Oxford where the students spend money, drink, gamble and fight the Town. The college authorities are cardboard figures of repression.

A far more polished and penetrating novel, although still celebrating an Oxford or Cambridge of the 1830s, was Thackeray's *Pendennis*. In a later novel Thackeray places a hero, Henry Esmond, in the university of the late seventeenth/early eighteenth century where he indulges in typical student pleasures. Arthur Pendennis studies, or rather for the most part does not study, in the 1830s or 1840s at a university for which Thackeray invented the word 'Oxbridge'. The examination system has been instituted, although it is an irritation to young bloods rather than an inspiration to work. The hero thoroughly indulges in student gambling, drinking and horse riding, eventually 'ploughing' his exams and he is rusticated. This much is like the career of Verdant Green, a celebration of youthful spirit, but there is a progression in this novel. *Pendennis* is a bridge into a new kind of imaging of student life. It is in the tradition of the *Bildungsroman*, for the hero begins to reform and, after a tearful confession to his relatives, retakes his examinations successfully.

After a decade or so of the infusion into Oxford and Cambridge of the moral seriousness of Thomas Arnold and the Rugby-trained cadres, then the developing interest in Christian Socialism, new fictions of the universities emerge. Tom Brown proceeds to Oxford with the confidence of having done well at Rugby School, but he is not tried and tested in the adult world. Hardy, his perplexing contemporary, a poor servitor, explains to Tom that at Oxford, despite the opportunities for sport and for reading, there is a 'vacuum of time' leaving a man with the difficult, disturbing process of 'looking more or less into his inside' (Hughes 1864: 46) – a full-bodied romantic notion. Tom does not consider that he has much to learn from introspection, after all he is a Rugbeian. He begins a student career of eating well, drinking, fighting in the town, and, most important, participating in manly sports. Spending the money he does not have, he descends into moral swamps, even taking the extra slippery step of kissing a barmaid!

Tom Brown at Oxford, however, is much more than another *Verdant Green*. It is the occasion for interesting insights into what a university might be at its best according to Christian socialist ideals. Hardy, in just wrath at a piece of deceit by one of their peers, exclaims:

> 'I shouldn't get so furious, Brown, if I didn't care about the place so much. I can't bear to think of it as a kind of learning machine, in which I have to grind for three years to get certain degrees which I want. No! This place – and Cambridge and our great schools are the heart of dear old England. A low standard up here for ten years may corrupt half the parishes in the kingdom.'
>
> (Hughes 1864: 74)

Hardy is both a serious scholar, who eventually gains a fellowship, and an excellent sportsman. A second influence on the reformed Tom Brown is the shadowy figure of Grey, again not a wealthy student, but an earnest Christian who is able to enrol Tom in his social work with the poor in Oxford and in London.

Two new elements enter the genre with this novel. One is an emerging sense of what a university education is for. Study is no longer derided. Hardy, for instance, demonstrates an ingenious system for revising classical history – a surprising digression in a Thackeray plot. There is also a shift away from the traditional accounts of student escapades. The experience of the peer group at Oxford is now an essential component, particularly in the by-now officially approved but non-curricular modes of earnest discussion and athletic pursuits, reinforcing the aesthetic environment and the living history of old quadrangles.

The second is the note sounded in the quotation from Hardy's exhortation about the damage that might be done by immoral behaviour. Of course, Hardy spoke in the context of the education of the clergy, still in the 1860s a major activity of Oxford and Cambridge. The influence of the great universities on the nation becomes a predominant argument for their status as special communities in public speeches, biographies and in fiction. The scholar's vocation has become, in English terms, what Fichte earlier in the century had dreamt: 'The most widely extended survey of the active advancement of the human race in general, and the steadfast promotion of that advancement' (Fichte 1848: 217–18).

The muscular community

The association of athleticism and the idea of student career is traceable, like much of the romantic idea of a university, to German sources, but mutated in English institutions. Here I use Ashby's (1967) biological metaphor to describe the change in forms of ideas as they adapt to different cultures. The new public school ethos of muscular Christianity, developed in post-Arnoldian Rugby, had already spread to the universities. The student culture became one of hearty athleticism associated with strong moral purpose, with masculinity, and with patriotism. Christopher Wordsworth, the poet's nephew, was to be one of the initiators of the university cricket match in 1827 and of the boat race in 1829. In 1911, Max Beerbohm combined rowing with romance (in the amorous sense) in a high moment of comic sentiment in *Zuleika Dobson: An Oxford Story* and the nostalgic market was created for the film *Chariots of Fire* to be popular some seventy years later.

Hardy in Hughes's Oxford novel expresses the values that university games can encourage. They rest on control and moral duty:

the muscular Christian has hold of the old chivalrous and Christian belief that a man's body is given to him to be trained and brought into subjection, and then used for the protection of the weak, the advancement of all righteous causes, and the subduing of the earth which God has given to the children of men . . .

(Hughes 1864: 113)

Alton Locke is the story of a poor self-educated tailor. He visits his rich cousin at Cambridge and watches with admiration the May Bumps racing. The smooth teamwork of the oarsmen moves him to patriotic tears because the undergraduates represent the achievements of the nation at Gibraltar, at Quebec and in the building of British industry and the creation of colonies all over the world: 'that grim, earnest stubborn energy, which since the days of the old Romans, the English possess of all the nations of the earth' (Kingsley 1908: 161–2). These last two quotations show many elements of Victorian romanticism: a linking with history, a sense of national destiny and, through restraint and physical control, a strong masculinity.

The excluded

These accounts of student life would be incomplete if some reference were not made to the outsiders, those such as the self-taught and women who were not part of the privileged resident university.

The reality of the reforming zeal of some members of the ancient universities to educate the new industrial masses is underplayed in the fictional literature, although it can be discovered in the work of, for instance, Mrs Humphry Ward. Both Oxford and Cambridge were involved in establishing the new universities and, particularly with the founders of London University, in the development of adult education on a part-time basis. The Scottish experience of Mechanics Institutes and their enthusiastic promulgation by Scottish university alumni such as Lord Brougham and George Birkbeck developed, with the participation of influential Oxbridge dons, into long-lasting institutions such as the Workers' Educational Association and the Settlement movement in the industrial cities (Kelly 1970). A particularly good example of 'out-reach' by Oxford-educated men is in the late nineteenth-century novel *Robert Elsmere*, by Mrs Humphry Ward (1987). The eponymous hero takes his Oxford tutor to the institute for adults that he has established in the parish in which he works and studies. There he teaches natural history and arranges a small museum for specimens collected by the men and gives Sunday afternoon readings from Shakespeare and the classics.

A reading of the few literary works which include characters who struggled to teach themselves leaves one with the impression of an ambiguity which may be a dilemma at the heart of romanticism. Typical of these literary figures are two opposed men in the widely read *Excursion* by William Wordsworth, published in 1813. The poem's central figure, the Wanderer, has little formal schooling at his simple home in Scotland, but a minister gave him books and some mathematical instruction. The young Wanderer saves his meagre wages to buy a copy of Milton's works and practises trigonometry as he looks after his herds. Scholarship does not change his life. Turning down a post as teacher, he returns to the mountain paths and the fields as an itinerant hawker. The opposing figure, called the Solitary, is also self-taught. Through a series of family tragedies, he becomes an embittered man dallying at first with the French Revolution and then retiring into solitary gloom. His reading is dangerous – the work of the atheist, Voltaire. Learning has led him into despair, not out of it.

In novels of social criticism such as those of William Godwin, Elizabeth Gaskell and of Charles Kingsley (to take three examples chronologically), there are self-taught figures admired for their hard work and perseverance against terrible odds, but, in almost all cases, the account of their lives carries qualifications.

Godwin's *Caleb Williams* (1794) is about a clever young man who acts as secretary to a rich landowner. The young student's Achilles heel is his curiosity, the very quality that enabled him to learn quickly. It is the uncontrollable need to know about his employer's hidden secret that causes a long, bitter struggle, imprisonment, and an end in suffering for both men.

Even in a sympathetic writer about the poor, such as Elizabeth Gaskell, there is a strange uncertainty about autodidacts such as Job Leigh in *Mary Barton* (1848). Job is a self-taught natural historian, but, despite the high level of his achievement, the author's tone is one of faint amusement at his learning. *Alton Locke* (1850) is a more sustained account of this phenomenon. Significantly, the dean of a Cambridge college both encourages and discourages the poor tailor. He advises him to study science as the appropriate modern subject for a writer with aspirations, but discourages him in his wish to enter Cambridge. Alton, asserts the Dean, would be better catered for as a working man in St Mark's Anglican Teacher Training College.

The most searing depiction of exclusion is Thomas Hardy's *Jude the Obscure* (1896). Jude follows almost the same learning path as Wordsworth's Wanderer of eighty years before, being helped at first by a clergyman and then struggling on self-taught. His ambitions are academic and he aims to enter Christchurch University (Oxford). He is curtly rejected by a letter from the head of the college which he wishes to join. In a drunken response he writes on the walls of the college what might well be romanticism's rebuff to conventional learning: ' "I have understanding as well as you: I am not inferior to you; yea, who knows of such things as these?" – Job xii 3' (Hardy 1985: 169).

It is as if the questions at the heart of romanticism are asked by this poor aspirant learner. Is the natural man best left to live the natural life? Does an education dry up the natural springs of grace that romanticism had vigorously promulgated?

The position of women in higher education as portrayed in the texts deserves a much longer review, but the same haunting question for some romantic writers can be discerned. I select from a mid-century (1847) poem, Tennyson's *The Princess, a Medley*, as an instance of the dilemma. The story within a story about a woman's college in an imaginary land, later simplified in a Gilbert and Sullivan operetta, *Princess Ida*, was a difficult publication for Tennyson. He was aware of contemporary initiatives in women's higher education with the founding of Oberlin College in the United States and the Queen's and Bedford Colleges in London in 1848 and 1849. Careful emendation of first drafts of the poem were made to make it acceptable to the public. A king allows his daughter to set up a collegiate type of university in a remote corner of his kingdom where men are not allowed. The college is, perhaps not surprisingly, very Oxbridge, with deans and Amazonian bulldogs and proctors. The curriculum appears totally open, 'Whatsoever can be taught and known', but medicine and anatomy are not permitted in order to comply with contemporary views of feminine propriety. The botanical and geological sciences, however, are considered appropriate for women students. A geological expedition to study a mammoth fossil takes place:

> Hammering and clinking, chattering stony names
> Of shale and hornblende, rag, and trap and tuff,
> Amygdaloid and trachyte.

> (Tennyson 1950: 186)

Women could be imagined in a man's world, particularly if they avoided Greats and chose new subjects. *The Princess* touches on some questions for the romantic educationalist. Was the education of women in the same way as men entirely desirable? Are there subjects, such as in aesthetic and scientific fields, which are more appropriate for women than the male curriculum of ancient history and languages?

The Victorian question of whether there are distinct sex-related divisions in higher learning is illuminated by an extraordinary example: the involvement of John Ruskin in the practical affairs of Whitelands College, a teacher training college for women founded by the Anglican National Society in Chelsea. As well as persuading William Morris and Burne Jones to design the college's chapel windows and the reredos, Ruskin established a prize, but not in the usual form of a competition for academic performance. Romantically, the students would elect 'the likeablest or the nicest girl of the year'. She would be a May Queen and receive a cross designed by Ruskin himself with a set of his works. A May Day ceremony evoking a medieval rustic idyll with maypole dancing would be performed on the occasion of the election. And so it came to pass. Even today the ceremony takes place in the same way, with the 'equal opportunity' addition of May Monarchs when so elected, a remarkable persistence of a ghost of late Victorian romance (Cole 1981).

The academic leaders of the tribe

The don appears in an ambiguous light in the imaginative literature of the nineteenth century, as does the university lecturer or professor in recent detective and thriller dramas and novels. In our own time, the university lecturer is portrayed either as a clever crook, a dusty eccentric useful for ingenious solutions to mysteries, or as a Machiavelli of the campus. The

romantic ambiguity about learning dies hard. Perhaps too the Old Testa-
ment suspicion of the fruits of the Tree of Knowledge is perennial. In the
early nineteenth century, as already illustrated, the dons are stereotyped
as relics of an ancient system. As late as Tennyson's *Princess*, there remains
more than a whiff of old and corrupt common room. The young undergraduates tell their lady companions about their Oxbridge tutors:

> . . . and one
> Discussed his tutor, rough to common man
> But honeying at the whisper of a lord,
> And one, the Master, rogue in grain,
> Veneered with sanctimonious theory . . .

> (Tennyson 1950: 167)

Tom Brown at Oxford two decades later (1864) demonstrates that Oxford
dons were changing. Hardy, the poor sizar, graduates well (although one of
his examiners snootily notes his lack of polish in Latin translation). He
becomes a fellow and sets new standards in teaching. The redirection of the
teaching relationship – earnest, hard working and concerned about the
moral welfare of students – arrives in England long after the German thinkers of the beginning of the century had proposed a high purpose for the
university teacher. Schelling (1996) asked the University of Jena in 1802,
'Who is to set the student on the right road?' His answer was truly romantic.
First the student must follow 'his own good genius', and second, 'those who
because of the nature of their own special fields are unmistakenly committed to a universal view of human knowledge' (p. 8). Schelling meant the co-
ordinating, unifying teachers of philosophy, but he might well have been
forecasting the institution of Oxford Greats. That Victorian project, also
concerned with a unified curriculum, was aimed at the education of men,
whom their tutors and the nation saw as preparing first to be gentlemen
and next to lead Empire (Jenkyns 1997: 513). This new relationship of
tutor and student depended on the milieu in which the student was taught,
the special community, the college. As Beer (1993) says, the Victorians
found the Oxbridge college gave security and made sense in a world which
was rapidly changing and full of contradictions.

One of the best ways to see the change of the duties of the Oxbridge
tutor from distant disciplinarian to moral and social guide is to focus on the
phenomenon of the reading party. Arthur Hugh Clough's long poem, *The
Bothie of Tober-na-Vuolich*, is a romance about a group of Oxford students on
a reading party with their tutor (significantly named Adam) in the Scottish
Highlands (Clough 1968). In that romantic return to Nature they discuss
with their wise and patient mentor their awakening manhood. The hero
falls in love with a Scottish girl who seems to be a natural in every sense:
untutored, but, because of her upbringing, close to Nature in the remote
Highlands, a deeply sensitive thinker.

The tutor is at hand to guide Philip as he tortuously discovers what he
ought to do. Adam is the good *in loco parentis*; once attached to a man he is

a resource for life. Clough, like Newman, but for different reasons, was eventually an exile from Oxford, having been one of its favoured sons. His poem has hidden levels of criticism about the alma mater at a time of great change. Phelan (1999) has carefully and skilfully analysed the connection betwen the innovative metre of the poem and the controversial reform of the Oxford curriculum. Clough's fable stands as a pointer to the new Oxbridge where the reforming don becomes a foundation for, if not a pillar of establishment England and Empire. Philip and his wife, after he has graduated with a first, go off to New Zealand to raise sheep.

Despite the arrival of the new men, the images of the academic remain mixed. In George Eliot's *Middlemarch* (published 1871–72) there is a famous creation and a warning to all dedicated scholars. The heroine, Dorothea Brooke, is 'educated from the toy box of history', a provincial woman's poor share of learning. She is, however, a clever and serious-minded woman who consents to marry a scholar, Casaubon, a student of the new (German-inspired) historical studies of religion, because she believes she can be a handmaiden to his great cause. Casaubon, however, is the most damaging kind of researcher. His great work on the myths of civilization will never be finished because he is so buried in the detail. He is, it is true, not a university tutor, but he is university trained and a researcher at continental universities. Casaubon's chief failing as a husband and as a man is a reflection of his obsessive work. In George Eliot's striking image of light and dark, he is portrayed 'with his taper before him he forgot the absence of windows, and in bitter manuscript remarks about other men's notions about the solar deities, he had become indifferent to the sunlight' (Eliot 1994: 192). Casaubon's learning had dried up his humanity and made other people's lives arid, even after death. His binding will made it difficult for his widow to remarry the true romantic genius, the artist, Casaubon's nephew. There is much more to add on Eliot's observations of the new educated classes of the second half of the century, not least about Lydgate, a new man, a scientist, continental trained and with practical concerns about public health.

One final example of the ambiguous depiction of the Oxbridge don is from Mrs Ward's 1888 novel *Robert Elsmere*. The hero, whom we have already met soaking up the atmosphere of his Oxford college and as a teacher-priest, undertakes a theological and social pilgrimage to find what he should do in troubled England. Two interesting characters have a serious influence on his decisions. One is a Casaubon-like figure, his Oxford tutor Edward Langham, an ascetic who is very controlled in the application of his intelligence, in complete contrast to the young woman with whom he falls in love, the artistic professional singer Rose, Robert Elsmere's sister-in-law. He feels but he cannot act in this relationship:

> he could not be simple; he could not be spontaneous. His lectures became dry and his scholarship bare . . . and degenerated into the microscopic study of texts. The victim of that critical sense which says

No to every impulse and is always relentlessly and yet hopelessly, seeing
the future through the neglected and outraged present.

(Ward 1987: 56)

A dreadful warning for all researchers.

There is an even more destructive force at work in Robert's milieu. It is
the local squire, Wendover. A university educated man both in England
and in Germany, he is a destructive critic of theology. His magnificent
library is at Robert's disposal but his personal influence is deeply disturbing
for Robert's faith. In the end, Wendover is his own destroyer, suffering
from some undefined degenerative mental state, brought on by study and
Faustian thirst for ultimate knowledge. Sparrow (1967: 20–1) comments on
the alleged portraits of Oxford worthies in this novel.

Revenants laid to rest?

To be relevant for our present condition the study of nineteenth-century
images must say more than 'here are the roots of our dilemmas', although
tracing intellectual roots is a valuable way of beginning to comprehend
contemporary contradictions. A good case has been made by Cuthbert (1996)
for acknowledging the lessons to be learnt from a study of modern campus
novels and for the role of humour in understanding the academic workplace.
What remains and what do we want to remain in these massified and
multiversity times of the romantic ideas of academic communities?

First, there is a strong continuing claim for a privileged status for the
special academic community, despite the fact that groups of highly educated men and women now work in very different and even competing
'communities'. Even in the nineteenth century the presence of other institutions which could carry out some of the functions of the universities were
part of the discussion of the nature of a university. In all technologically
advanced countries, commercial and government enterprises have their
own research institutions and now there is the growing global presence of
other ways of learning without the need to leave your computer. If the
universities are to claim special privileges, such as academic freedom and
the right to make their own decisions about governance and about teaching
and research, the idea of community requires redefinition in the context of
large organizations and progressively intrusive government.

The work of Bauer exploring the notion of a 'space of action' for higher
education institutions (Bauer *et al.* 1999: 281) and the redefinitions by
Barnett (from 1990 onwards), for instance, encourage the view that new
sinewy arguments can be made with internal and external authorities to
convince the paymasters about the essential link between ownership and
governance of the universities and how they teach and research. The
romantic ghost that should be laid to rest is that there is one idea of a
university and that it is a place set apart. Alternatively, Coleridge's judgement
that an institution should contain the principle of progress and the principle

of permanence (Rothblatt 1997: 293) remains as the foundation of an academic community which can flourish, change and yet retain the order necessary for research and study.

In the case of the public role of the academic, the debate is now inevitably swallowed up in the complex larger issue: the position of the intellectual in modern society, a society which produces media personalities and experts at a greater rate than scholars. What should be borne in mind in battling through the problems of defining a role for the academic tribe is that their position in the eyes of the rest of the world may not be as prestigious or even as neutral as the academics think it is. A salutary experience is to read the final chapter of Noel Annan's study *The Dons* (1999), which is about the ups (and more) the downs of the reputation of academics in the final decades of the twentieth century. The dreadful images of Casaubon and Wendover may be over one hundred years old, but Malcolm Bradbury's History Man or David Lodge's Professor Zapp, to quote two modern novel characters, cannot be dismissed as literary fancy.

Finally, much discussion of the university is still based on the assumption that the university's chief function is with young people newly out of school, neglecting the vital reality of the make-up of the modern university. Increasing numbers of students come to university to study full or part time long after leaving school. The image of the university student has changed from Tom Brown, but there is still a fixed idea of romantic youth in the drama and novel and perhaps in the minds of policy-makers. In the 'real world' of university planning, concentration on the university as finishing school neglects so many; for instance, the large numbers in postgraduate studies, again full and part time. The nineteenth-century romance with athleticism is (perhaps) remote, but the continuing popularity of the notion of a university as a playground for the enlargement of the personality of the young or the theatre for delayed adolescence is not dead.

The concentration of the nineteenth-century writers of campus novels on the idea of national power strengthened by muscular Christianity is not a likely revenant, but the concentration of modern governments on the link between national greatness and prosperity and the university is alive and kicking, sometimes to the exclusion of other civilized values of higher education.

The nation that grasps a new romanticism, that continues to treat its varied learners as human beings as well as students, recognizes that learning is the engagement of all levels within the university, and demonstrates a zest for lifelong learning (and does not interpret this phrase merely as retraining employment casualties for a second job) will be the nation that more than survives the changing times. It will redefine 'community', as each age must do.

References

Annan, N. (1999) *The Dons.* London: HarperCollins.
Ashby, E. (1967) The future of the nineteenth-century Idea of a University, *Minerva*, VI(1): 3–17.

Barnett, R. (1990) *The Idea of Higher Education*. Buckingham: SRHE and Open University Press.

Bauer, M., Askling, B., Marton, S. and Marton, F. (1999) *Transforming Universities*. London: Jessica Kingsley.

Beer, J. (1993) *Romantic Influences, Contemporary, Victorian, Modern*. London: Macmillan.

Berlin, I. (1999) *The Roots of Romanticism*, edited by H. Hardy. London: Chatto & Windus.

Brock, M.G. (1996) The intellectual and the university: an historical perspective, *Reflections on Higher Education*, 8: 66–81.

Brock, M.G. and Curthoys, M.C. (eds) (1997) *The History of the University of Oxford: Nineteenth-century Oxford*, Vol. VI, Part 1. Oxford: Oxford University Press.

Clough, A.H. (1968) *The Poems of Arthur Hugh Clough*, edited by A.L.P. Norrington. London: Oxford University Press.

Cole, M. (1981) *Whitelands College May Queen Festival*. London: Whitelands College Monograph.

Curthoys, M.C. and Day, C.J. (1997) The Oxford of Mr Verdant Green, in M.G. Brock and M.C. Curthoys (eds) *The History of the University of Oxford: Nineteenth-century Oxford*, Vol. VI, Part 1. Oxford: Oxford University Press.

Cuthbert, R. (ed.) (1996) *Working in Higher Education*. Buckingham: SRHE and Open University Press.

Eliot, G. (1994) *Middlemarch*. London: Penguin (first published 1871–72).

Fichte, J.G. (1848) *The Popular Works of Johann Gottlieb Fichte*, translated by W. Smith, section LIV. London: Chapman.

Holcroft, T. (1973) *The Adventures of Hugh Trevor*. Oxford: Oxford University Press (first published 1794–97).

Hughes, T. (1864) *Tom Brown at Oxford*. London: Macmillan.

Jenkyns, R. (1997) The beginning of Greats 1800–1872, in M.G. Brock and M.C. Curthoys (eds) *The History of the University of Oxford: Nineteenth-century Oxford*, Vol. VI, Part 1. Oxford: Oxford University Press.

Keen, C. and Warner, D. (1989) *Visual and Corporate Identity*. Banbury: HEIST.

Kelly, T. (1970) *A History of Adult Education in Great Britain*. Liverpool: Liverpool University Press.

Kingsley, C. (1908) *Alton Locke, Tailor and Poet*. London: Nelson (first published 1850).

Maclure, J.S. (1986) *Educational Documents*, 5th edn. London: Methuen.

Newman, J.H. (1873) *The Idea of a University*. Oxford: Clarendon Press.

Newman, J.H. (1895) *Apologia Pro Vita Sua*. London: Longmans (first published 1865).

Phelan, J.P. (1999) Radical metre: the English Hexameter in Clough's *Bothie of Toper-Na-Fuosich*, *The Review of English Studies*, New Series, 50(198): 166–87.

Plant, R. (1974) *Community and Ideology: An Essay in Applied Social Psychology*. London: Routledge & Kegan Paul.

Rothblatt, S. (1968) *The Revolution of the Dons*. Cambridge: Cambridge University Press.

Rothblatt, S. (1997) An Oxonian idea of a university, in M.G. Brock and M.C. Curthoys (eds) *The History of the University of Oxford: Nineteenth-century Oxford*, Vol. VI, Part 1. Oxford: Oxford University Press.

Schelling, F.W.J. (1996) *On University Studies*, translated by J. Morgan. Athens, OH: Ohio University Press (first delivered as a lecture 1802).

Sparrow, J. (1967) *Mark Pattison and the Idea of a University*. Cambridge: Cambridge University Press.

Stone, L. (ed.) (1974) *The University in Society*, Vol. 1. Princeton, NJ: Princeton University Press.

Tennyson, A. (1950) *The Princess: a Medley*, in *Collected Poems of Tennyson*. London: Macmillan.

Thackeray, W. (1994) *Pendennis*, edited by J. Sutherland. Oxford: Oxford University Press (first published 1848–50).

Turnbull, G.H. (1926) *The Educational Theory of J.G. Fichte*. London: Hodder & Stoughton.

Ward, H. (1987) *Robert Elsmere*, edited by R. Ashton. Oxford: Oxford University Press (first published 1888).

Wordsworth, W. (1979) *The Prelude: 1799, 1805, 1850*, edited by J. Wordsworth, M. Abrams and S. Gill. New York: Norton.

3

Higher Education Communities and Academic Identity

Maurice Kogan

In thinking and talking about such categories as community we enter the realm of moral philosophy. There has always been a moralizing descant in the discussion of higher education, and much of the most distinguished writing has been normative rather than empirical in its base. One of the problems I wish to tackle here, however, is the current belief that politically initiated moralities can improve the purposes and working of higher education. One commentator once described higher education studies as a paradigmal mess. One might also say that it is an area that suffers from an overload of unclarified and competing values.

Sometimes, indeed, the higher education scene seems to resemble a morality play. At one time, a limited number of institutions in western Europe called universities, catering for a limited number of people, were clear that they should engage in the disinterested search for truth, within the rules set by the 'Republic of Science', and teach the new generation of able young people how to engage in the same pursuits. Now, however, new preoccupations and new moralities are to be observed. Universities, originally organized so as to assert minimal influence over the disciplines, have a whole range of institutional roles concerned with the advancement of what is in essence social and public policy: new employment legislation, collective research work directed to economic development, quality assurance, equal rights, internationalization, and relations with the community. We also have new professoriats – professors of quality and the professors of lifelong learning, for example – which owe their origins to policies rather than to the development of knowledge, although they may recruit knowledge from the disciplines and produce new subject shapings as did business studies, town planning and social work before them.

I do not deplore these developments but refer to them to make a point about the current rhetoric about community. Some functions of higher education arise from its internal dynamics, knowledge systems and logic. Others are in response to external demands or from interaction between the two. At minimum, the external demands ought to be reconcilable with the internal dynamics of higher education. And when they acquire academic status, as such subjects as business studies and planning did much earlier, that must come with a body of knowledge based on analysis and empirical material, rather than on public or social concern with issues.

Yet whilst the academy must have what Martin Trow once called its private life, higher education has social obligations which start with the proper performance of the academic tasks of teaching, promoting learning and the creation and testing of knowledge – and without them higher education is preaching or journalism or consultancy – and then go on to work with values and groups outside its walls. My concern here is with specifying how a proper balance can be achieved between the two and how to define the relationship so that it might stand up in both logic and operation. In such an exercise there should be no holds barred. Good causes are often advanced by the employment of rhetoric. But as academics and intellectuals, we ought to know what we are doing and to be able to distinguish between rhetoric and a case built on reality, including the fact that people and institutions may share values and functions but also have different ones.

To pursue this end, I begin by noting the already slippery uses of the word 'community'. In 1955, one commentator noted 94 definitions of it (Hillery 1955), and 'its definition has continued to be a thriving intellectual pastime of sociologists'. It has been used to describe a type of collectivity, in which a group may share territory or social ties – ethnic, religious, academic or professional – or a social relationship or sentiment (Azarya 1985). If its use has always been loose, it has become so promiscuous as to deprive it of meaning. We now have a gay community, who may, for all I know, loathe each other, and we have, if not a criminal community then a criminal fraternity. The use of the word 'community' in discussions of higher education courts two problems. First, it is a 'warm glow' word which implies good relations when they may not exist or may not even be necessary for good working. Secondly, it obfuscates the need for close analysis of roles within and beyond education in which the relationships may be that of dependency or exchange or a hard business of establishing *quids* for *quos*. Its use is no substitute for hard work in stating and making connections. Similarly, phrases such as 'peer review' assume relationships which may often be in no sense between peers. Just watch a senior academic group reviewing a research project or team.

I now take up three related themes. I first discuss the different communities of academics, and the extent to which they lend support to the advancement of individual academic identity. These include the academic communities of the invisible colleges and their modes of internal governance by elites. I consider the communitarian implications of the changing pattern of institutional management. Then, I consider the relationship of academics and their institutions to the wider world of society and the economy.

The communities of academics and academic identity

First, then, the internal communities of academics. What are the forces making for academic development? We must reckon with two broad possibilities. For development to be strong it must be firmly rooted in the intellectual self-confidence of the disciplines and subject areas to which the academics belong, that is, the context in which a sense of academic identity flourishes. In a confident academic system, new knowledge is generated through accepted processes of discovery and testing, and through following the logic of the issues being tackled. And evidence is always in fugue with theory development.

But the internal communities of academics must have as their starting point the nature of those who inhabit them. Here we come to the fertile territory opened up long ago by R. Burton Clark (1983) and more recently pursued by Jussi Välimaa (1995) and Mary Henkel (Henkel 2000).

Mary Henkel takes up from communitarian moral philosophy key concepts of academic identity which depict, first, the *distinctive individual* who has a unique history, who is located in a chosen moral and conceptual framework, and who is identified within a defined community or institution by the goods that they have achieved. It is to that setting that the individual looks for the esteem and recognition so important to the academic. These three elements of individual identity must be what makes an academic an effective professional. They are strengthened and matured through the processes of professional education and experience.

But the distinctive individual is also an *embedded individual*. They are a member of communities and institutions which have their own languages, conceptual structures, histories, traditions, myths, values, practices and achieved goods. The individual has roles which are strongly determined by the communities and institutions of which they are a member.

Thus we have and need a notion of *professional identity* which is both individual and social, so that people are not only stronger because of their expertise and their own moral and conceptual frameworks, but also performing a range of roles which are strongly determined by the communities and institutions of which they are a member.

All of this is compatible with both professional creativity and freedom and observation of social needs. The constituents of professionality sit at odds with the kinds of behavioural directions and prescriptive frames laid down by recent government-inspired actions and policies.

I should mention the place of students within the concepts attributed to community. At least one former colleague and some, if a minority, of those interviewed in a recent evaluative project would maintain that 'there is no difference between faculty and students – all are learners'. We all hope that we will enable students to acquire the knowledge and intellectual skills that we should have. We may well learn from students' life experiences. But do we not have a different starting point in our acquired knowledge and capacity to handle it and are our obligations not quite different? This illustrates quite well the danger of cosy ascriptions of community that eschew differentiation and definition.

External academic communities

These conceptualizations of identity give us a basis from which to reconcile individual academic autonomy and responses to widening circles first within academe and then outside it. The notion of embeddedness helps us to recognize that academics do not inhabit an intellectual and moral solipsism. Within the university there are collegial clusters, increasingly yielding power to wider university concerns, initiatives and control. Collegia also develop bureaucratic functions and behaviour – in developing and regulating the curriculum, for example (Kogan 1998), and need not always be suffused with communitarian goodwill.

Increasingly, however, as Henkel notes in her recent book (Henkel 2000), the individual academic becomes dependent on the institution for their place within a system in which resources are tight, workloads are becoming heavier and quality demands more pressing. Indeed, there is a mutual dependence because the institution depends upon individuals for its reputation and income and its nature depends on the balance of power and the quality of the exchange relationships established.

External threats, challenges and regulation have in some respects strengthened communities within institutions through requiring more coherence in the curriculum, even pride in performance within the total quality assurance (TQA), or emerging research groups in new university departments. At the same time, communitarian values are not only strengthened but also challenged by competitive pressures and the stresses caused by extra and multiple burdens.

There are the external academic connections which may more fittingly be described as communities than the internal institutional connections. At the deepest level, as Becher (1989) has shown, there are links between disciplinary cultures and forms of knowledge. In them people are bound together by shared values, expertise and standards rather than the obligations of shared tasks. These are represented by the invisible colleges of the subject areas and disciplines.

The sources of academic power and honour, however, including the award of professorial title, seem now more able to draw on other sources and reference points than that of the core subject areas. I refer here, for example, to titles mysteriously appearing on the names of institutional leaders without any disciplinary or subject record of note. Leaving aside that aberration unknown in other countries, for the most part we rely on judgements made outside our own institutions for legitimizing professorial and readership titles, for the award of research grants and for the more esteemed forms of publication as well as election to the principal honorific societies.

Barnett (1992: 7) elaborates these connections:

> One . . . conception of quality . . . is based on the expression of the tacit conceptions of value and propriety in the academic community. Its reflection in peer review contains the implicit claim that the conversations of the academic community are self-justificatory . . . On this conception, it is the character and quality of the continuing interactions of its members that is at issue rather than any end-point or definitive outcome.

He continues:

> there is something valuable about the idea of the academic community . . . Despite the disciplinary divisions of academics and their activities, there lies an unwritten but universal code tying every member of the academic community together. That higher level commonality is founded . . . on a 'culture of critical discourse' (Gouldner 1979).
>
> (1992: 66)

We could usefully consider whether academic conversations can rest wholly on self-justification, unless the point being made is that they must be true to academic values and only then can usefully enter a wider world of usage and relevance.

Lesser minds have added that:

> Academics do not share a discipline base; their tasks are complex, loosely defined. If we define a professional as one who possesses esoteric knowledge shared only with others in the same profession, physicists, historians, sociologists are not in the same profession. But . . . they share conditions, status and functions. A shared belief in such values as the need to demonstrate the evidence and logic behind statements, or an altruistic concern for one's students, might bond together otherwise disparate groups into one profession.
>
> (Kogan, Moses and El-Khawas 1994: 28–9)

Some time ago, Trow (1974) noted that at one time an academic could expect to be hospitable to a member of their institution or of their subject area from within the whole universal discipline, but that was now impossible to sustain. Now more powerful forces than size affect the integrity of anything that can be called an academic community. Institutional leaders are now more likely to be of a managerial than academic cast, and are set apart by salary, car, house. Within institutions, anything that Barnett or Newman or Minogue might identify as the intrinsics of academic life are at minimum paralleled and in some places overwhelmed by the increased power of administrators – often drawn from academic ranks – who advance systemic rather than academic values and pursuits.

Are we still within the definition of a community? I think so. There is an assumed affinity of value, of accordance with norm-driven power, and when, for example, our work is reviewed, of shared task. Academic collegiality may not always be represented by sweetheart behaviour – my impression is that those closest to each other in subject interests are more likely to be critical of and competitive with each other than with those in other or adjacent areas. Fraternal relationships can include those on the Cain and Abel model – but subject connections do entail some assumption of collectivity and of communal bonding.

There are interesting differences in assumptions of community between subject areas. In our recent evaluation of the impact of the Foresight initiative (Henkel *et al.* 2000), it was noticeable how academics in a 'hard' area referred quite often to the 'materials community', and indeed showed evidence of shared commitments not only to their academic substantives but also to ways of ensuring collective thinking about ways of making stronger connections with the world of application.

What place do the activities of academic elites have in the shared values of an invisible college? In principle, the concept of an elite with its connotations of separateness does not sit comfortably with the softer and more collegial style of a community. Kogan and Hanney (2000) detected four potential sets of academic elites or leaders. They were quite different from each other and the only groups that would figure in academic communities were the academic elites proper – the Fellows of the British Academy and the Fellows of the Royal Society – and we can all decide for ourselves how far they feel part of a community or whether their separateness is stronger than their collegiality.

The connection between them and the apparently different world of the co-opted elites is also significant. These are academics who become part of an elite by virtue of government appointment to some position of power. The connection between them and the 'real' academic elite is far stronger in the natural sciences than in the humanities or social sciences. But there are fascinating connections between these leadership groups which we have described as that of tectonic plates (a phrase also used by Barnett) and denoting the power generated by the movements of otherwise disconnected entities. Thus the statuses awarded and the decisions made by the academic elites create access to power and resources which are allocated by the co-opted elites. If we take them together with institutional leaders – themselves a heterogenous group – we can see that the notion of an integrated academic community is likely to be illusory. We all defer to our own subjects and disciplines outside our institutions, but, beyond that, connections are hardly communitarian.

The relationship of academics and their institutions to the wider world

So far I have been doing what HE analysts do best: writing about the inner workings of academe. When considering the relationship of academics and their institutions to the wider world of society and the economy we get into a different world of policy declaration and institutional hopes and boasts. The relationships are difficult to define and to operationalize, let alone fashion into any sense of there being a shared community.

Let me first bring out the negative aspects of this interface and then move on to some more affirmative if aspirational aspects.

In all relationships there is a need for separateness – the assertion of identity – as well as connectiveness. In the classic modes of higher education there is a particularly strong case for separateness on grounds of the need for freedom to think the unthinkable action and to bear witness to the truth and independent theory. In this view, HE's didactic purposes are not primarily instrumental but, as Barnett construes Newman, would be more than 'useful' and not confined to the particular (Barnett 1990) which the division of labour seems to some extent to demand. Barnett also quotes Minogue (1973) who argues that academic enquiry is not intended to provide solutions to social problems.

We need not take sides on this issue, but simply note that universities are a social artefact which can indeed fill any purpose that society sets for them. If the assumptions of Newman and Barnett sustain a parsimonious definition of what constitutes academic activities we could quite easily go on to argue that universities can do more than pursue academic activities and that, indeed, their access to wide forms of expertise makes it a waste for them not to do so. Certainly in some of our lifetimes, say forty years ago, Oxford and Cambridge have combined high academic ideals and performance with the more instrumental functions of training the ruling classes and providing a finishing school for chaps up for amateur dramatics and the hunt. Look now how well their business schools are doing, though established in the teeth of opposition.

Moreover, it is not just academics in materials or medicine but many forms, too, of the humanities and the social sciences that need and to some extent feed on the common experiences of humanity. Some of us have spent our working lives in forging such links, not wholly or mainly out of altruistic motives, but because without those contacts we have no reality base on which to work.

But does that make us part of a community that we share with them? At minimum we need to have a negotiated order, but might not our worth to them reside in difference rather than close concomity? Do industrial leaders want universities to mimic them, or do they pay for something different? How often has one heard from part-time masters students that they benefit most from courses because they can pursue their work interests but in a totally different setting and from perspectives that apply critique or bring new constructs to their working lives?

We ought to be leary about the rhetoric that is being applied to higher education as Newman's vision fades and new non-academic tasks derived from the social and economic agenda appear as part of the Faustian bargain that we have had to strike. Yet I do not side with the solipsist side of the argument. Universities must be part of the working world, but that does not mean that they form part of a community with it except in very local and special senses. Our major civic universities to some extent owed their genesis and early sustenance to local business and civic connections, and though some of that connection could be onerous and obtrusive, both sides benefited. One has to say, however, that once a Manchester or Sheffield reached its international status those links became tenuous. The story of polytechnic incorporation was one of successful breakaway from what they regarded as an oppressive relationship with local authorities (Kogan and Hanney 2000).

Connection and involvement remain essential, on terms which are not best described as those of a community. What precepts can one lay down for the connection?

- All universities must start with ensuring that their distinctive missions and competences are strong so that they can enter into negotiation and partnerships from a position of strength. Universities at their best, however, promote multiple missions.
- Universities' relations with external bodies and sponsors should be based on rigorous negotiation of who will get what in return for what. An exchange relationship entails a more useful metaphor than does that of a community. It can be used to successfully empower groups external to the university without weakening the university's position.
- Establishment of external connections must always stand the test of being compatible with the academic functions and standing of the university which is primarily entrusted to its academic components.

Thus I see individual identity, its institutional and subject settings and the world outside the university as separate but linked entities, giving each other support not by the assumed sharing of values implied by 'community' but through negotiation and exchange.

References

Azarya, V. (1985) 'Community', in A. and J. Kuper (eds) *The Social Science Encyclopedia*. Routledge & Kegan Paul.
Barnett, R. (1990) *The Idea of Higher Education*. Buckingham: SRHE and Open University Press.
Barnett, R. (1992) *Improving Higher Education*. Buckingham: SRHE and Open University Press.
Becher, T. (1989) *Academic Tribes and Territories: Intellectual Enquiry and the Culture of Disciplines*. Milton Keynes: SRHE and Open University Press.
Clark, B.R. (1983) *The Higher Education System: Academic Organization in Cross-national Perspective*. Los Angeles: University of California Press.
Gouldner, A. (1979) *The Future of Intellectuals and the Rise of the New Class*. London Macmillan.

Henkel, M. (2000) *Academic Identities and Policy Change in Higher Education*. London: Jessica Kingsley.

Henkel, M., Hanney, S., Kogan, M., Vaux, J. and von Walden Laing, D. (2000) *Academic Responses to the UK Foresight Programme*. Uxbridge: Centre for the Evaluation of Public Policy and Practice, Brunel University.

Hillery, G.A. (1955) Definitions of community: areas of agreement, *Rural Sociology*, 20.

Kogan, M. (1998) Academic and administrative interface, in B. Little and M. Henkel *Changing Relations between Higher Education and the State*. London: Jessica Kingsley.

Kogan, M. and Hanney, S. (2000) *Reforming Higher Education*. London: Jessica Kingsley.

Kogan, M., Moses, I. and El-Khawas, E. (1994) *Staffing Higher Education: Meeting New Challenges*. London: Jessica Kingsley.

Minogue, K. (1973) *The Concept of a University*. London: Weidenfeld & Nicolson.

Trow, M. (1974) Problems in the transition from elite to mass higher education, *Policies for Higher Education*. Paris: OECD.

Välimaa, J. (1995) *Higher Education Cultural Approach*. Studies in Education Psychology and Social Research, Research Studies Series 315, University of Jyväskylä, Finland.

4

The PhD Examination: An Exercise in Community-building and Gatekeeping?

Carolyn Jackson and Penny Tinkler

The British PhD has faced increasing scrutiny in recent years as a result of concerns over PhD completion rates (Hockey 1991; Collinson and Hockey 1995; Booth and Satchell 1996) and questions about the structure of the doctoral programme (Burgess 1997). Increased scrutiny in these domains has occurred alongside investigations at a micro level into key aspects of the doctoral programme, most notably the supervision of PhDs, the relationship between supervisor and student (Hockey 1997; Delamont *et al.* 1998) and doctoral research cultures (Delamont *et al.* 1997a). Despite the gradual yet increasing recognition that the doctoral process is a valuable area for research enquiry, one central component of this process – the PhD examination – has received little attention. Anecdotal accounts, often within student guidebooks, provide some valuable insights into aspects of the PhD examination process (Burnham 1994; Delamont *et al.* 1997b; Graves and Varma 1997) and signal the variability of this crucial part of the doctoral programme. However, little is known about the detail and diversity of the British PhD examination process. Furthermore, despite the fact that successful completion of a PhD is increasingly a prerequisite for entry into academic posts, little attention has been afforded to the role of the PhD examination in the academic world. Set in the context of an increasing number of students undertaking PhD research (Higher Education Statistics Agency 1996/7), this chapter focuses on the PhD examination process in Britain and its relationship to, and role within, academia.

In the midst of concerns about 'the loss of an academic community' and the subsequent re-examinations of whether a single 'academic community' ever existed (Barnett 1994; Finnegan 1994), there has been increased attention to alternative ways in which 'community' can be defined and can be seen to exist within the contemporary academic world. Barnett, for example, refers to community as interchangeable with 'coherence of endeavour' (1994: 4). Finnegan also proposes an alternative conception of an 'open academic community', one that is 'based not on contiguity, but on joint *interests* or on a sense of *belonging* together' (1994: 187, emphasis in original). The use of the term 'sense' is important here because communities are as much about perceptions of shared interests as they are about actual common concerns. Finnegan further argues that individuals can belong to multiple communities such that 'academic community' becomes a 'relative and multifaceted affair' (p. 188).

The argument presented in this chapter is that the PhD examination can be seen as playing a role in relation to a number of communities and networks within the academic world. In the chapter we focus upon three main communities which the PhD serves: the institutional community, the professional community and the knowledge community. First, the PhD, and in particular the doctoral examination, can be seen as one of the ways in which universities are tied into a broader community of higher education institutions with common aims, interests and relations of interdependence. Indeed, the PhD is a defining feature of a British university. Secondly, the doctoral examination process plays an increasingly important part in the constitution and monitoring of a professional academic community. Fulton (1996) argues that despite at least four 'axes of differentiation' including distinctions between disciplines, academics do share certain common interests. These common interests stem from the 'regulations and structures which relate to the occupation of higher education teaching as a whole, and [which] are mirrored by trans-disciplinary unions and associations' (p. 159). Fulton also suggests that, 'from the viewpoint of the general public, there can be little doubt that the single profession has a perceived reality' (p. 159). Relatedly, the PhD examination is also key to the construction of the idea of a community of academics, and can be seen as a ritualistic performance of community. Thirdly, the PhD examination serves specific knowledge communities in that it monitors standards within a particular field and is increasingly a prerequisite and preparation for acceptance into that field of knowledge.

The organization and conduct of PhD examinations are also revealing about the operation of various academic communities and they are particularly illuminating about gatekeeping practices. A gatekeeper, as Becher (1989) reminds us, is a person who 'determines who is allowed into a particular community and who remains excluded' (p. 60). Although there has been some research on academic gatekeepers, attention has focused primarily upon their roles as referees, editors, and as members of appointment panels (Becher 1989; Spender 1981; Weiner 1996). The significance of doctoral examining as a gatekeeping practice has not been the subject of scrutiny. Becher (1989) describes how the 'tribes of academe . . . define their own identities and defend their own patches of intellectual ground by employing a variety of devices geared to the exclusion of illegal immigrants' (p. 24). Although Becher does not include doctoral examinations in his study, we would argue that these examinations have an important place amongst a tribe's repertoire of strategies as well as serving the interests of a broader community of professionals.

Delamont (1996) argues that research on higher education suffers from the problem of familiarity: as 'insiders' of the system being researched, researchers take for granted many of the features of that system. Delamont suggests, therefore, that one of the key tasks of researchers of higher education is 'to make the familiar strange' (p. 147). This chapter attempts to make the PhD examination process 'strange', and thereby to bring into focus and subject to critical gaze many aspects of the PhD examination process hitherto taken for granted.

Furthermore, the chapter aims to challenge the assumption that what is familiar is also standard. Frequently, lecturers and those responsible for producing staff development and training materials generalize about the PhD examination process in ways that deny or marginalize the diversity of policy and practice in British universities. Moreover, when talking about their experiences of examining, academics seem to ignore the fact that they themselves are a common factor in these examinations, and that this has implications for how examinations are conducted.

This chapter is organized around two key features of the examination process that are particularly pertinent to a discussion of communities: (i) the organization of the examination, and (ii) the conduct of the viva voce and related issues about purpose and experience. The discussion draws upon five main sets of data. First, we draw upon institutional policy data concerning the PhD from 20 British universities (11 'old' and 9 'new'[1]) (see Tinkler and Jackson 2000). Secondly, we draw upon questionnaire data relating to the PhD examination process from four perspectives, namely the perspectives of: (i) external examiners (54), (ii) internal examiners (46), (iii) supervisors (42), and (iv) candidates (88).[2] Responses were drawn from lecturers and previous PhD students at two (old) universities in the north of England. The lecturers were all based in arts, humanities or social sciences departments. Candidates had been based in arts, humanities, social sciences or science departments.

Organization of the PhD examination process

The PhD examination is arguably one of the most formal and explicit gatekeeping processes operating within academia. Whilst a PhD certainly does not guarantee access to an academic post, increasingly a lack of one bars the path of most would-be academics. Selection of gatekeepers or PhD examiners is, then, a crucial component of the examination and gatekeeping process. The operation of the selection process is particularly revealing about the role of the examination within academic communities and vice versa. University policy suggests that the PhD examination process is an important way in which individual institutions present themselves to, and are perceived by, the broader higher education community. The PhD examination is also key to the establishment of the principles of common standards and a common currency in qualifications, both of which act to constitute and monitor the HE community.

Policy stipulations about the criteria by which examiners should be selected are particularly revealing about the institutional significance placed on the relationship between the doctoral examination and the higher education community. Regulations around the choice of examiners can be categorized under three headings. Those that relate to: (i) academic credentials, (ii) experience, and (iii) 'independence'. Emphasis on the 'independence' of the external examiner is a common feature of university policy and it is of particular relevance to our reflections on the role of the PhD examination in academic communities.

An examination of policy reveals that independence is an extremely vague principle which is operationalized in different ways in different institutions. Indeed, there appears to be no common consent as to what independence is or how it should be regulated. Rules around independence operate at different levels, as they relate to the examiner's relationship to the institution, the department and the individual. Independence of the external examiner is a criterion that featured strongly in the documentation of all, bar one, of the universities in our sample. This independence is 'guaranteed' in one or more of the following three ways. First, by rules regarding the period that must have elapsed since the external examiner had any formal attachment to the university. Second, by regulations that stipulate how frequently individuals can be allowed to examine at an institution. Third, by rules which govern whether, and under what conditions, a candidate's supervisor can act as an examiner.

Arguably, the objectivity and impartiality of the examiner are the qualities being sought through these procedures, and seven of the nine new universities state this explicitly. Whilst the aims of independence and objectivity appear to be common amongst the universities, the ways in which institutions operationalize these goals highlight the relative and slippery nature of these concepts. Although institutions usually state that external examiners must be 'independent' of the institutions at which they examine, only two of the old universities provide clarification, compared with all of the new universities. Institutions which provide such detail usually state that the external examiner must not have been employed by the university during the last three years, although in the case of one university this period is six years. A frequency clause, which sets out how often an external examiner can examine within a particular department or university before they become overly 'familiar' with it and the people in it, is also stipulated at four institutions. Conceptions of how much contact leads to familiarity are, not surprisingly, variable, with institutions offering very different specifications as guarantors of independence: these can range from twice in five years, to once or twice a year.

Regulations about whether the supervisor can act as an examiner are the third guarantor of independence amongst our sample institutions, but once again policy does differ considerably. Interestingly, only five institutions unambiguously state that the supervisor cannot act as an examiner; more usually university policy states that supervisors cannot 'normally' be appointed as an examiner and in most cases guidance is provided about exceptions to this rule.

We can identify three possible aims of regulations around 'independence': (i) the fostering of impartiality, (ii) the preservation of common academic standards, and (iii) the making and performance of community. Each of these aims raises interesting questions relating to communities.

Attempts to foster impartiality by stipulating acceptable formal relations between an individual and either a department or an institution do not engage with the organizational features of academic life, more specifically the ways in which communities transcend and cross-cut the department and/or university. An individual's discipline or knowledge community, for example, is widely viewed as particularly important to academics and the focus of considerable loyalty (Becher 1989; Fulton 1996).

Common academic standards, whilst perhaps recognized as being nothing more than notional by many within academia, must nevertheless be sought within higher education.[3] 'Common standards' both derive from, and are the product of, common interests and provide a sense of a shared project amongst institutions in higher education. They are also necessary for the establishment of a common currency in qualifications. Indeed, the PhD serves as a common currency amongst higher education institutions with important implications for the recruitment of lecturing staff and their position within the academic world and wider society. The utilization of external examiners is the method employed for attempting to obtain a degree of interinstitutional consistency in terms of standards. In terms of the PhD, the adoption of the external examiner system is also linked to concerns to gain validation and also status from the broader higher education community for the institution's research degrees and the candidates who are awarded them.

Rules about independence can also be interpreted in terms of the production and performance of community. In this instance, two communities are served simultaneously: the institutional community and the community of professional academics. Interinstitutional reliance and reciprocity can be interpreted as mechanisms which serve to reinforce the web of interdependence which contributes to the formation of institutional and professional communities. That the decision to award or withhold the PhD and entrance to academia depends largely on an examiner external to the candidate's institution, reinforces the notion that the PhD examination process is part of the gatekeeping function *of,* and *for,* a broader academic community or communities. Linked to this, the use of an external examiner can be seen as part of the performance of community. The perceived role of the viva as a ritualistic practice linked to a rite of passage can be interpreted as an important part of this performance.

Institutional policy provides the framework within which individual lecturers or supervisory teams organize the doctoral examination. The processes by which examiners are selected, within the context of university policy stipulations, are illuminating about the organization of knowledge communities, in particular the networks within these, and gatekeeping practices. These processes also show how members of knowledge communities act as representatives of a broader professional community.

Questionnaires sent to lecturers (relating to the most recent examination in which the respondent was involved) and to candidates reveal, not surprisingly, that supervisors are key to the selection of appropriate examiners. Candidate questionnaires reveal that area of specialism is the most frequently cited of the reasons listed for choosing an external examiner (91 per cent of cases). Other reasons include the supervisor knowing the examiner personally (43 per cent), the supervisor's recommendation (37 per cent), and that the examiner is 'known to be fair' (28 per cent). The importance of the examiner's area of specialism is to be expected and is a key way in which a knowledge community is operationalized within the examination process. The importance of 'known to be fair' reflects the assumption that gatekeeping is an arbitrary practice. The relationship between the supervisor and the examiner is clearly important in the selection process, and in the following we address briefly one specific aspect of this relationship, namely the gender dimension.

Questions concerning the gendering of roles within the PhD examination revealed that women were marginal in the roles of examiner (internal and external) and supervisor. Even though 47 per cent of the candidates were female, 76 per cent of external examiners, 79 per cent of internal examiners and 82 per cent of supervisors were male. The lower proportion of women relative to men serving as external examiners was, however, consistent with the preponderance of men in senior academic posts. Higher Education Statistics Agency data reveal that of the 31,003 men and women holding senior academic grades (full time and part time) in 1997/98, approximately 17 per cent were women (Higher Education Statistics Agency 1997/8). These findings show that men are the principal gatekeepers in doctoral examinations, as they are in other areas of academic life (Brookes 1997; Ramazanuglo 1987).

Whilst the proportion of male and female examiners and supervisors is consistent with the gender composition and hierarchy of academia, the gender relationships between examiners, supervisors and candidates cannot be explained solely with reference to this. Our data are suggestive of more complex gender dynamics operating in the context of the PhD examination. Our questionnaire data, which related to 222 PhD examinations across Britain, revealed that men were more likely than women to serve as external examiners of male or female PhD candidates. However, these data also revealed that women were more likely to act as external examiners for female than for male candidates; questionnaires revealed that 40 per cent of female candidates were examined by women compared with only 10 per cent of male candidates. Our data also revealed a relationship between the gender of the supervisor and that of the external examiner: 44 per cent of women supervisors used female external examiners compared with 19 per cent of male supervisors. These data suggest that supervisors utilize networks in gender-specific ways to select examiners, and/or that they draw upon gendered networks. The importance of networks to the selection of examiners is evident from data revealing that in 75 per cent of cases the supervisor knew the external examiner personally.

Conduct, purpose and role of the viva

Having examined issues related to the set-up of the doctoral examination, we consider another important feature of the PhD examination process: the viva voce or oral examination.

Questions frequently asked of the viva are whether it: (i) serves a purpose in the examination of the candidate, (ii) is of ritualistic value, or (iii) is defunct. One could also ask whether the viva does, or does not, have a role to play *vis à vis* academic communities and, if so, which communities. Is the viva key to academic gatekeeping and, if so, in what ways? In order to address these questions, we look first at the significance attached to the viva within institutional policy and then examine the views, perceptions and experiences of lecturers and PhD candidates.

The viva is a compulsory part of the PhD examination process at all of the 20 institutions in our survey. At one institution, policy is unequivocal that an oral examination must be taken. More usually, subject to the authorization of an appropriate senate committee, the viva can be waived owing to exceptional conditions. In these cases an alternative, usually written, examination is stipulated. The insistence on an oral or alternative examination suggests that the PhD examination process does have two essential components: submission of the thesis and a further examination. The fact that many institutions stipulate that one cannot fail a PhD outright without undertaking a viva or alternative examination is evidence of this. Arrangements for posthumous vivas that are set out in the policy of seven institutions, all new universities, provide a further and fascinating illustration of this principle.

Although the importance of the viva is postulated either explicitly or implicitly at all the universities in our sample, there are some significant inconsistencies in policy concerning the viva which suggest a certain ambiguity about its role. For example, if the viva is an integral component of the PhD examination, it would follow that one could fail the PhD on the basis of an unsatisfactory oral examination. This is actually the case in 60 per cent of our 20 institutions (9 new, 3 old). At the remaining institutions, examiners do not seem to have the option of failing a candidate on the basis of their viva performance. A further inconsistency that emerges in policy concerns the point at which the examiners' provisional decision may be released to the candidate. If, as most institutions suggest, the viva is integral, the decision would seem to be dependent on performance in the viva, and this would not be available until after the viva. Only four institutions stipulate that this should be the case. Furthermore, although rules which prohibit the release of a decision until after the viva suggest that the oral is central to the PhD examination process, only one of these universities entertained the idea that a candidate might fail the viva. Policy statements reveal diversity and also inconsistency. The latter indicates that the function of the viva is often ambiguous and that it is not straightforwardly concerned with the examination of the doctoral candidate.

Questionnaires distributed to candidates at two universities support the impression that the role of the viva is not necessarily or exclusively linked to the examination of the candidate but that it may also be ceremonial, celebratory and confirmatory. Our results revealed that 32 per cent of candidates were informed of the examiners' decision at the start of the viva.[4] These data, and data concerning the effect of the viva upon examiners' perceptions of the candidates' work, indicated that the viva was not, in the majority of cases, the site of decision-making. In 74 per cent of cases the viva served merely to confirm the examiners' opinion of the candidate. Where the viva did influence the examiners this did not necessarily alter the examiners' decision. The exceptions were usually cases where the candidate was borderline. In the majority of cases, therefore, the viva merely served to confirm a decision made on the basis of reading the thesis. Although the work of confirmation is less obviously a gatekeeping strategy than is an examination or test, it is still a necessary and important component of monitoring access to academic communities. Where the results of the examination were given to the candidate at the beginning of the viva, the viva served neither an examination nor a confirmation role. In these instances the viva was attributed a different role (one also shared, in part, by vivas which had examination and confirmation functions).

Responses from lecturers to a question about how they perceived the role of the PhD viva produced an interesting, diverse range of answers. Significantly, only a minority of respondents (6 per cent) regarded the viva as totally redundant although even these often added 'except in cases of . . .'. More usually, academics cited a number of roles for the viva, most of which were related to the location of the candidate within three key academic communities. These roles included: monitoring access to the professional community; upholding common standards across institutions, the profession and within knowledge communities; providing advice to facilitate the (successful) candidate's entry into, and establishment within, the professional community and the knowledge community; acting as a meaningful rite of passage.

The majority of academic respondents attributed various examining and advisory functions to the viva. These measures can be interpreted as gatekeeping mechanisms that ensure that only appropriately skilled people can enter the professional community. The PhD in itself is not enough to secure access to the professional community but it is increasingly a prerequisite for entry. Typical responses were that the viva: ensures authenticity; checks the candidate's understanding; clarifies areas of weakness; tests the candidate on their knowledge of the broader literature (the relevant subdiscipline field and how they are placed within it); tests oral skills; checks that the candidate can 'defend' their thesis and thereby show ability to work within a framework which prioritizes debate, competition and individualism; decides between 'referral' and 'fail'. Related to these monitoring mechanisms, a few respondents also mentioned that the viva served to ensure standardization across institutions and to check the quality of supervision: 'an opportunity for the external to meet and "check" on the candidate (*and* the supervisor as well)'.

A number of respondents claimed that the viva should provide (successful) candidates with experience and information. This provision would seem to facilitate the entrance and establishment of candidates in knowledge communities and in the academic profession. One of the most common responses in this category was that the viva offered an opportunity for the candidate to receive guidance on the publication of their thesis. Publishing is of considerable importance for shaping disciplines and their research agendas (Spender 1981). It is also crucial to the development of academic visibility and credibility and is, therefore, an essential feature of establishing oneself within a knowledge community as well as within the professional community. In her examination of the processes that are instrumental in determining the publication of research, Spender (1981) identifies gatekeepers as a primary obstacle to publishing. We suggest that the role of the PhD examiners, especially the external examiner, also serves an important role in fostering or inhibiting the budding academic's attempts to get their work published.

The viva was also described by a few respondents as serving a ritualistic purpose as a rite of passage which marks and celebrates the transition of the candidate from one status to another, higher one: 'perhaps most important, especially in successful cases, as a rite of passage'; 'the viva . . . disrupts what is often a protective relationship . . . but at the same time it should provide the student with confidence that he/she has been able to produce a finished piece of research that has met the wider canons of scholarship within the relevant discipline.' In this last quote, the candidate is described as moving from the relative security of their relationship with the supervisor to a position of acceptance within a broader knowledge community. This quote also neatly encapsulates the idea that the examiners can act as arbiters of what constitutes 'the wider canons of scholarship'.

The mystery that surrounds the viva undoubtedly contributes to its perceived role as a rite of passage. The mystery also contributes to the viva's gatekeeping function in that the arbitrary nature of the process is not open to inspection and is, moreover, seemingly too diverse to categorize. Although there is no standard form of viva in British universities, the data from our institutional policy survey (Tinkler and Jackson 2000) and our questionnaires support the idea that the viva is generally a private affair and that postgraduates rarely get an opportunity to observe a viva.[5] Our questionnaires to academics (about their latest involvement in a PhD examination) and candidates revealed that in 64 per cent of cases only the examiners and candidate were in attendance. In 27 per cent of cases the supervisor was also in attendance. Only rarely was there a chairperson (4 per cent) or observer (6 per cent). Given that very few PhD students have the opportunity to attend a viva prior to their own, it seems important to consider how students are prepared for the oral examination. Although most PhD candidates in our survey did receive some guidance about the viva, this was often limited and derived from narrow pools of experience. The most often cited source of information was the supervisor (89 per cent), followed by fellow students (57 per cent), 'grapevine stories' (55 per cent), their own experiences of upgrading (23 per cent) and, in a minority of cases, a mock viva (11 per cent). The reliance on information from supervisors deserves further attention. As with lecturers whom we questioned about examining, our questionnaire to supervisors revealed that only 37 per cent had received any formal training, and of these academics only 10 per cent had received specific guidance on preparing students for the doctoral examination. Supervisors generally relied heavily on their own experience and also on advice from colleagues in preparing their students for a viva. Our questionnaire data also suggest that, even after being successfully examined for a doctorate, candidates are not always clear about how the examiners' decision was made because the candidate does not usually have access to the examiners' reports.

The mystery which surrounds the viva is also fostered by the lack of standardization. Our questionnaires to candidates revealed considerable diversity in the content and tone of the oral examination. This arose partly from variations in institutional policy but also, importantly, from the different perspectives and practices of examiners and also group dynamics in the viva. Questionnaires to academics revealed that they generally received very little formal training regarding the PhD examination process – 92 per cent of academics had received no formal training for examining a PhD thesis. A substantial number claimed also not to have received any guidelines from the institution at which they were examining (12 per cent of external examiners and 34 per cent of internal examiners). Although roughly three-quarters of academics claimed to have received some informal training, this usually consisted of their own experience of being examined for a PhD or of advice from colleagues. The reliance on one's own experience and that of colleagues suggests that different styles of examining are communicated generationally, that is, from one generation of academics to another, and also disseminated laterally via colleagues. Recently, there has been increased interest in discipline cultures and socialization processes (Delamont *et al.* 1997a). The PhD examination can be seen as one of the earliest informal lessons which an aspiring academic receives on gatekeeping.

Given that the viva is a gatekeeping mechanism which serves various academic communities, it is perhaps useful to reflect upon the influence of the viva on the candidate's interests and future ambitions. Although the viva generally did not disrupt pre-existing career ambitions, 19 per cent of candidates reported an increased desire to work in academia while 16 per cent reported a decreased desire to seek work in academia. For 39 per cent of candidates the viva increased their wish to work in the field of their PhD while 9 per cent reported the opposite effect.

Conclusion

We have argued that the PhD examination can be seen as playing a role in relation to a number of different communities within the academic world: the institutional community, the community of professional academics and the knowledge community.

The PhD, and in particular the doctoral examination process, can be seen as one of the ways in which higher education institutions are tied into a broader community with common tasks, interests and relations of interdependence. We have identified at least three ways in which this occurs. First, educating postgraduates to PhD standard is a common practice of higher education. It is therefore one of the activities which defines the higher education institution and which binds institutions together as fulfilling a common role in society and, more specifically, in the education system. Secondly, the PhD serves as a common currency amongst institutions of higher education with important implications for the recruitment of lecturing staff and their status in the academic world. Thirdly, the process by which the PhD is awarded is a mechanism by which institutions are brought together into relations of interdependence as each institution is dependent on others within the community for validation of (i) the quality of the education services which they provide, and (ii) the standard of the candidate's work and competence.

The PhD examination also has an important role to play in relation to knowledge communities in that it (i) monitors standards within the field, and (ii) is increasingly a prerequisite and preparation for entry into a knowledge community. The role of the PhD examiner in advising a candidate on the publication of work is particularly important given the significance of publishing to visibility and validation within a knowledge community. Likewise the examiner is important as mentor or referee for the successful doctoral candidate. Finally, the PhD examination can be seen as instrumental in gatekeeping the professional community, as possession of a PhD is, increasingly, the common academic standard for entry into the occupation of university lecturer.

Notes

1. We use the term 'new' university to refer to those given the status of university under the Further and Higher Education Act 1992, and the term 'old' university to refer to those with the status of university prior to 1992.
2. We received responses from 71 lecturers relating to external examining, 66 lecturers relating to internal examining, and 61 lecturers relating to PhD supervision.

Whilst all of these responses were analysed in relation to questions about training for examining or supervision, not all of these lecturers had experience of examining a PhD or supervising a PhD to completion. As such, the figures reported here are those that did have examining or supervisory experience at PhD level.

3. The problematic nature of the notion of 'common standards' is illustrated by Johnston's (1997) analysis of examiners' reports submitted within Australian PhD examinations, and in other academic activities such as refereeing articles for academic journals (Spender 1981). Although most academics are wary of making claims regarding 'common standards', there is still, as Weiner (1996) points out, an assumption that 'academic excellence' is transparent.

4. It is beyond the scope of this chapter to discuss differences between disciplines in any detail. However, it is worth noting that 47 per cent of candidates in the arts, humanities or social sciences were informed of the examiners' decision at the start of the viva compared with only 15 per cent of candidates in the natural sciences.

5. Two of the 20 institutions in our policy survey, and one of the institutions included in our questionnaire survey, had public examinations (Tinkler and Jackson 2000).

References

Barnett, R. (1994) Recovering an academic community: above but not beyond, in R. Barnett (ed.) *Academic Community: Discourse or Discord?* London: Jessica Kingsley.

Becher, T. (1989) *Academic Tribes and Territories: Intellectual Enquiry and the Culture of Disciplines.* Milton Keynes: SRHE and Open University Press.

Booth, A. and Satchell, S. (1996) British PhD completion rates: some evidence from the 1980s, *Higher Education Review*, 28(2): 48–56.

Brookes, A. (1997) *Academic Women.* Buckingham: SRHE and Open University Press.

Burgess, R.G. (1997) The changing context of postgraduate education in the United Kingdom, in R.G. Burgess (ed.) *Beyond the First Degree: Graduate Education, Lifelong Learning and Careers.* Buckingham: SRHE and Open University Press.

Burnham, P. (1994) Surviving the viva: unravelling the mystery of the PhD oral, *Journal of Graduate Education*, 1(1): 30–4.

Collinson, J. and Hockey, J. (1995) Sanctions and savings: some reflections on ESRC doctoral policy, *Higher Education Review*, 27(3): 56–63.

Delamont, S. (1996) Just like the novels? Researching the occupational culture(s) of higher education, in R. Cuthbert (ed.) *Working in Higher Education.* Buckingham: SRHE/Open University Press.

Delamont, S., Atkinson, P. and Parry, O. (1997a) Critical mass and doctoral research: reflections on the Harris Report, *Studies in Higher Education*, 22(3): 319–31.

Delamont, S., Atkinson, P. and Parry, O. (1997b) *Supervising the PhD: A Guide to Success.* Buckingham: SRHE and Open University Press.

Delamont, S., Parry, O. and Atkinson, P. (1998) Creating a delicate balance: the doctoral supervisor's dilemmas, *Teaching in Higher Education*, 3(2): 157–72.

Finnegan, R. (1994) Recovering 'academic community': what do we mean?, in R. Barnett (ed.) *Academic Community: Discourse or Discord?* London: Jessica Kingsley.

Fulton, O. (1996) Which academic profession are you in?, in R. Cuthbert (ed.) *Working in Higher Education.* Buckingham: SRHE/Open University Press.

Graves, N. and Varma, V. (eds) (1997) *Working for a Doctorate.* London: Routledge.

Higher Education Statistics Agency (1996/7) *Student Records 1996/97.* Cheltenham: HESA.

Higher Education Statistics Agency (1997/8) *Resources of Higher Education Institutions 1997/98.* Cheltenham: HESA.

Hockey, J. (1991) The social science PhD: a literature review, *Studies in Higher Education,* 16(3): 319–32.

Hockey, J. (1997) A complex craft: United Kingdom PhD supervision in the social sciences, *Research in Post-compulsory Education,* 2(1): 45–66.

Johnston, S. (1997) Examining the examiners: an analysis of examiners' reports on doctoral theses, *Studies in Higher Education,* 22(3): 333–47.

Ramazanoglu, C. (1987) Sex and violence in academic life or you can keep a good woman down, in J. Hamner and M. Maynard (eds) *Women, Violence and Social Control.* London: Macmillan.

Spender, D. (1981) The gatekeepers: a feminist critique of academic publishing, in H..Roberts (ed.) *Doing Feminist Research.* London: Routledge & Kegan Paul.

Tinkler, P. and Jackson, C. (2000) Examining the doctorate: institutional policy and the PhD examination process in Britain, *Studies in Higher Education,* 25(2): 167–80.

Weiner, G. (1996) Both ends of the research process: funding, publications and power. Paper presented to the Annual Conference of the British Educational Research Association, Lancaster, September.

5

Becoming an Educator: Communities of Practice in Higher Education

Janice Malcolm and Miriam Zukas

Old masters

> There he moistened thirsty hearts with divers streams of teaching and
> varied dews of study; busily giving to some the arts of the science of
> grammar (grammaticae rationis artes), pouring into others the streams
> of the tongues of the orators; these he polished on the whetstone of
> law, those he taught to sing in Aeonian chant, making others play on
> the flute of Castaly, and run with the lyre over the hills of Parnassus.
> But others, the said master made to know the harmony of heaven and
> the sun, the labours of the moon, the five belts of the sky, the seven
> planets, the laws of the fixed stars, their rising and setting, the move-
> ments of the air and the sun, the earth's quake, the nature of men,
> cattle, birds, and beasts, the different kinds of number and various
> (geometrical) figures; and he gave sure return to the festival of Easter;
> above all, revealing the mysteries of holy writ, for he opened the abysses
> of the old and rude law.
>
> Alcuin, master of the school at York Minster, speaking of his pre-
> decessor Albert, c. 750 AD.
>
> (Leach 1915: 58–9)

Albert was a member of an early, and very small, educational community.
To the modern reader it appears that he had 'mastery' of an astonishing
range of subjects, but managed to retain a clear consciousness of his broader
(religious, and thus social) responsibilities. His conception of *disciplina* –
teaching – was very different from ours, whilst his role as master within a
community of scholarly masters and novices was perhaps more explicit, and
more clearly understood, than that of his distant successors. What constitutes educational knowledge, how it is produced, and the location and
identity of teachers and taught have changed almost, but not quite, beyond

recognition in the intervening centuries. However, we can still recognize the educational character of his work, as he would recognize our work as a distant descendant of his own, despite Finnegan's claim that such a comparison involves the 'unthinking invocation of a myth' (1994: 181).

The reason for bringing this ancient pedagogue into our account of 'becoming an educator' is that it may help us to illuminate what has happened to the 'communities' of higher education. An essential element of Albert's understanding of educational work would have been its holism: all of the 'subjects' which he taught would have been understood by him, and by his students, as interconnected aspects of an integral and universal reality. This reality was attributed to the will and actions of a deity, and thus the content of educational knowledge was subsumed within a grandly theological narrative. At the time this was still a fairly radical narrative: Albert was consciously teaching to change the world, long before educators such as Brookfield (1995) and others became involved. The essentially religious nature of the educator's role meant that its purposes and duties (and its ultimate rewards) were fairly clear. Our fragmented and overspecialized reality offers no such comforting certainties; the process of becoming and being an educator is no longer straightforward in a world where we belong to multiple communities.

The current policy context of higher education, which simultaneously changes the teaching role (through massification, modularization, and so on) whilst subjecting it to ever-increasing scrutiny, problematizes both the educator's role and the nature of community in HE. Teaching as an aspect of knowledge production is impoverished and constrained by the rigidity and power of disciplinary structures, and by the false distinctions which continue to be promoted between knowledge and skills, and between research and teaching. The separate quality assurance regimes established for these two latter aspects of academic activity provide an example of this distinction; paradoxically, so does the newly established Institute of Learning and Teaching, which presents itself as a body concerned to raise the status of teaching relative to research but which has little interest in academic research activity except that which is directly concerned with teaching. Divisions between disciplines or fields of study, between academic and vocational educational routes, and between teaching and research orientations in academic work, have implications both for the 'communities of practice' involved and for the process of knowledge production itself. Young's (1993) argument in favour of 'connective specialization' as a structural and curricular response to a socially, economically and technologically complex future could equally be applied to the need for a more integrated understanding of the role of teaching and research in the generation of knowledge. This chapter addresses the need in modern higher education for a connective approach which promotes a more holistic understanding of the nature of knowledge production, but which does not reduce any aspect of this production to 'generic' practices divorced from knowledge itself.

Communities of practice in higher education

In Britain, a peculiar fracture has developed between research-based and pedagogical communities of practice, complicating still further the existing divisions between disciplinary or 'epistemic' communities. Whilst the validity of disciplinary divisions is clearly problematic, and is explored further below, we use the term 'discipline' throughout this chapter as a vernacular and convenient shorthand for what people mean when they say 'I'm a sociologist/biologist/textile designer'. Researchers located within disciplines may conceive of themselves as community members at a number of different levels. At a departmental level they have an identity as part of a group working within one subject area; within the wider subject community at a national and international level, they are members of 'invisible colleges' (Crane 1972) who meet, correspond and communicate at regular intervals and among whom the identity and knowledge content of the discipline is contested and developed. Within their own specialism they may be members of a much smaller and geographically spread community, perhaps limited to linguistic or regional groupings, consisting of those few academics who focus on researching and teaching a small area within a discipline. Within the university, they have another identity as members of the local academic community, as distinct from the administrative staff, technical staff, or whatever, and this in turn contributes to their identity as part of the national and international 'higher education community'. These multiple forms of identity and community membership are common in higher education throughout the world. The peculiarity of the British situation is that university *teaching*, rather than being seen as an integral part of these multiple identities, is increasingly being divided from them.

The reasons for this division are complex, and attributable in part to the historical development and stratification of higher education in this country. One manifestation of the division is the evolution of 'staff and educational development' (henceforth SED for convenience) as a distinct area of British higher educational practice. Emerging from a training rather than an educational tradition (owing to recent policy orientations which extended far beyond higher education), staff development has promoted a set of understandings and language conventions which are used increasingly to describe and explain educational work. As Vygotsky (1978) would have been pleased to confirm, language functions as a tool for constructing social understandings and consciousness within a community, ultimately generating forms of practice. Thus the language of outcomes, objectives, assessment and reflection, rather than emerging from the practice of teaching, comes from outside it, shapes it to its own likeness and produces particular forms of educational practice. This has encouraged the idea that teaching is a separate and essentially different activity from research, and has, in many cases, promoted the dislocation of pedagogical thought and practice from disciplinary knowledge and development. The location of teacher education for higher education within disciplinary or educational academic departments is still rare in this country; in many universities the development of teaching staff is assigned to a distinct 'unit', often with a range of other responsibilities, and not necessarily containing any academic staff at all. In many other countries the situation is different; in Canada for example, 90 per cent of the membership of the Society for Teaching and Learning in Higher Education (STLHE, the Canadian equivalent of the Staff and Educational Development Association (SEDA)) consists of academics working within subject specialisms, rather than SED specialists.

The oddity of the notion that teaching is separate or essentially different from other forms of disciplinary activity can be illustrated by a look at an imaginary world where research is treated the same way. Thus universities might have generalist, non-academic 'research developers' who would educate academics in research methodology, methods of analysis, research ethics, writing and so on. These research developers could offer workshops on 'scientific method', 'hypothesis formulation', 'ethnographic analysis', or 'deconstruction'. They would claim no disciplinary expertise, of course, but could nevertheless offer academics '53 ways to improve your abstractive capacity'. They would not necessarily be researchers themselves, but could offer part-time courses, assessed by themselves, which would certify academics as qualified research practitioners. This imagined reality seems ludicrous to us, of course, because we understand research as an aspect of specialist knowledge production, not as a set of generalist techniques. (The new M.Res. degree, in the few places where it exists, is taught by academic researchers, and can only function as the preliminary stage of discipline-based research training.) It is currently impossible to conceive of any course of full research training which would simultaneously cater for linguists, physicists, historians and zoologists. The education of researchers is generally put into the hands of those who understand and have contributed to the production of knowledge within a specialist area – that is, academic staff offering research supervision. In this respect the training of researchers is firmly located within a situated learning tradition; apprentice or novice academics work under 'master' academics to attain their own mastery of disciplinary research (and the academic title is a clear historical indicator of this process).

This glimpse into the looking-glass world of research development should give us pause when we consider the current state of university teaching. Once the subject of largely tacit understandings and unexamined community practices, teaching has again become a focus of attention in higher education. This is to be welcomed in principle, but in practice much of the attention paid to teaching has been characterized by 'quick-fix' empiricism and technicist discourse – 'surface learning about teaching', as Rowland (1999) describes it – which does teaching no academic favours, and which may have the opposite effect to that intended. In many institutions, university teaching is the only subject which is not regularly taught within an academic department or located within a culture of academic research (apart, perhaps, from 'study skills' and 'learning support' provision, which also seems to have created a generic, non-academic place for itself in many universities, and thus in community thinking). This bifurcation of pedagogical thought and practice from the disciplines and research activity has serious implications for the status of teaching in higher education, the prospects for 'connective specialization', and the process of knowledge production itself.

Whilst there is a long tradition of attempts to analyse the epistemological and other characteristics of the disciplines themselves, and their impact on people and structures in higher education (see, for example, Lodahl and Gordon 1972; Biglan 1973a, b; Becher 1989), this type of analysis has rarely been applied directly to pedagogy. Conversely, within the pedagogical literature, there is a widespread reluctance to consider the implications of pedagogical research for the conceptual framework and content of disciplines. Increasingly, the disciplines are 'counted in', in the sense that the problems of teaching particular subjects are addressed, but the content, context and epistemology of the disciplines are rarely challenged, or even explored. 'Disciplinary expertise' often seems to be viewed as something above comment, beyond mere pedagogical comprehension, despite the fact that the very existence of disciplines is contested in the more conceptual and policy-oriented literature. Yet if we, as teachers, ask legitimate pedagogical questions, such as 'what kinds of questions can be asked and answered?'; 'how can this problem reasonably be analysed?'; 'how do we know if an answer is correct or appropriate?'; 'what are our students learning to be?', it is inevitable that we interrogate fundamental disciplinary assumptions and chafe against disciplinary boundaries – just as we do when undertaking 'disciplinary' research. That part of academic work which involves teaching, in other words, is just as much a part of knowledge production as research activity; pedagogical questions are in part questions about epistemology. It is paradoxical, given the justified complaints of those concerned with teaching and learning in higher education about the inferior status of teaching relative to research, that so much of the rhetoric surrounding educational development hives off the 'scholarship of teaching' from the forms, rigours and processes of other kinds of scholarship. This again appears to be linked with the 'training' orientation of much SED thought and practice, which often relies on a very limited field of research emerging from particular psychological traditions (Malcolm and Zukas 1999), and which seems to venerate, rather than problematize, the conceptual integrity of the disciplinary structure. The false separation of pedagogy from epistemology and practice, within and between disciplines, limits the possibility of promoting any 'sense of intellectual commonality' (Becher 1994: 64), which would give university teachers and students a more coherent identity as a community of intellectual practice.

Versions of pedagogy as situated practice

Our recent research[1] has focused on identifying pedagogical 'models' implicit in current writing on higher educational teaching, and on creating a bibliographical map of the literature. Our aim has been, not to use these models as reifications of educational practice, but rather to uncover the identities or 'masks' (Bailey 1977) attributed to educators within the literature, and to consider their implications. This process, and the tentative models which we have identified, have been described elsewhere (Zukas and Malcolm 1999). One of the original models, that of the educator as situated learner within a community of practice, seems, from our perspective, to offer considerable scope for analysing and understanding some of the issues covered here. Whilst the work of Lave and Wenger (1991), and more recently Wenger (1998), is often encountered in the discourse of higher educational pedagogy (and indeed some 'new' educational development practices, such as mentoring, do suggest a 'situated learning' orientation), it has not generally been explored in terms of its theoretical and practical implications for the education of university teachers. We feel that it has much to offer, in part because it enables us to situate university teaching clearly in a cultural, historical and social context, and to consider the possible forms of 'legitimate peripheral participation' in a community of critical scholar-educators. We therefore use it here as a conceptual tool for analysing pedagogical and disciplinary identity in other versions of 'the educator' which we have identified. Within each model, we consider the identity of masters and apprentices/novices, and the implications of particular forms of legitimate peripheral participation for the student and institution. Put more simply, we ask 'who educates the educators, to teach whom, and for what purpose?'

The educator as reflective practitioner

Deriving in general from the work of Schön (1987), the notion of reflective practice has become almost taken for granted in much of the writing on higher educational pedagogy. The meaning of the term is only infrequently considered (although in other educational sectors it has long been a matter of dispute – see, for example, Bright 1996; Ecclestone 1996); discussion usually focuses instead on how reflective practice can be built into the curriculum, encouraged and assessed. Within this model the practitioner – the university teacher – appears to be identified principally as a pedagogical actor, although there may be some hint of a subsidiary identity as a disciplinary practitioner. This is much more apparent in the reflective practice literature of, for example, medical and nursing education, and it is arguable that the model only makes any 'situated' sense when students are being prepared specifically within a professional community of practice. This does not prevent reflective practice from being widely promoted as conventional good pedagogical practice, regardless of discipline. The focus on the *practice* rather than the content or purpose of teaching, and the implicit affinity with the other realms of professional practice as explored by Schön himself, tend to bring pedagogical identity to the fore. Consequently, it is difficult to discern the nature and structure of the community. Whilst teachers undergoing 'development' may have the status of masters in disciplinary terms, they are deemed to be novices in terms of reflective pedagogical practice; the masters in this community are, presumably, those who teach them how to 'do' reflective practice, and assess whether they have done it or not.

Where this leaves students is unclear; they are not themselves learning to be reflective *pedagogical* practitioners, unless they are on a course of teacher education. If the 'masters' in this scenario are not themselves disciplinary *and* pedagogical practitioners (as, for example, in those instances where the development of higher education teachers is carried out by academic educationalists), there is in effect no community of practice. In fact, the masters are often SED specialists who do not necessarily have a disciplinary identity, and who may not even have undertaken pedagogical practice of the kind demanded of their 'novices'. The popular focus on generic notions of 'student learning' tends to obscure this fact; instead of teaching teachers to teach, SED specialists may be characterized as teaching university teachers about student learning – an imported and decontextualized specialism which apparently has little to do with the knowledge-content of the discipline, and which in effect leaves students without any real identity other than that of 'learners'. Reflective practice has the potential to offer useful insights to teachers in their community relations with their students, but without any epistemological context this potential is extremely limited.

The educator as critical practitioner

This model of the educator, deriving as it does from adult education and sociological approaches to educational practice and epistemology, inevitably casts teachers as members of a broader community than the pedagogical. The tradition of adult education (particularly in universities), with its focus on social and political purpose, demands interrogation of educational content as much as, if not more than, educational methods. The cultural, historical and social identity of *students* is of prime importance within this tradition, and this turns learner focus inside out by asking, not 'how can we help this person to learn?', but 'how can we, as students and teachers together, transform ourselves, our disciplines and our worlds?' The tradition has admittedly been under siege for some time, partly as a consequence of policy changes promoted in the name of quality assurance, but also because of the instrumental approaches to teaching and learning now being promoted in higher education.

Criticality as promoted within adult education thus involves not only a critical approach to how teaching and learning occur, but also to the content of what is taught, and what counts as educational knowledge within a discipline. Educators have to consider why their disciplines are as they are, and struggle to change oppressive or elitist structures and conceptualizations in order to make an education which *includes* their students, inevitably challenging traditional disciplinary boundaries in the process. This has given birth to curricular revisions in, for example, literature and social science, and to interdisciplinary approaches which challenge traditional disciplinary boundaries. It has also led to the emergence of whole new (inter-) disciplinary fields of scholarship, most obviously in cultural studies (Steele 1997), but also in areas such as women's studies and black studies. The critical practitioner is thus a member of a community within which disciplinary and pedagogical identity must co-exist, since they cannot be separated.

Within higher education, the tradition of research training in many disciplines displays the characteristics of the 'critical practitioner', and for many academics this model may also inform their personal approach to teaching. Barnett's (1997) advocacy of 'critical being' as a goal of higher education adopts the model in disciplinary and institutional terms. However, there is very little evidence of the 'critical practitioner' in much of the writing on higher educational pedagogy, despite the apparent popularity of Brookfield (1995) among staff developers. Webb (1996) is one of the few SED writers who considers educational purposes and the social and epistemological contexts within which educational work occurs. We would argue that the rarity of critical approaches is principally owing to the forced separation of pedagogy from discipline in the field; the 'critical practitioner' model demands that educators conceive of themselves as belonging to communities within which pedagogy, social context and disciplinary content are all inextricably linked, and equally open to critique. Even Barnett is seduced by the artificial distinctions promoted by the pedagogical literature; despite his attachment to 'critical being' as an educational aim, when turning his attention to pedagogy he falls back on the tired, and essentially *un*critical literature of 'deep' and 'surface' learning, which offers nothing to promote critical being (Barnett and Hallam 1999).

In terms of situated learning, the critical practitioner model involves educators developing critical consciousness within themselves and among their students and colleagues, actively creating a critical community. The essentially antidisciplinary and connective nature of critical practice, emerging as it does from the social reality of the student rather than from the structure of disciplines, ensures that the nature of the community itself is open to interrogation and transformation. The important point here is that this version of pedagogy is consciously holistic or antidisciplinary, rather than generic or non-disciplinary, in its understanding of the relationships between discipline and teaching. The prospects for developing this approach in the current higher educational context are not good, given the appropriation of pedagogy by the two models explored below, and it is certainly an unusual perspective in the current literature of SED. We argue that it is the only model of those described here which offers any prospect of building a connective community within higher education.

The educator as psycho-diagnostician and facilitator of learning

Within this ubiquitous model, the problem of pedagogy is seen as a largely technical problem of identifying certain student characteristics, such as learning styles or other psychological predispositions, and deploying certain pedagogical techniques, tools or approaches to ensure that 'learning' is facilitated. Particular psychological discourses – cognitive, humanistic and behavioural – are employed to 'explain' the teaching and learning process. This process is frequently conceptualized as interactional (rather than social) and involving only the teacher and the student or group of students. In this type of pedagogical writing, the content or purpose of teaching is often simply ignored; 'the aim of teaching is simple: it is to make student learning possible' (Ramsden 1992: 5).

For our present purposes, then, this model offers nothing to teachers in terms of an holistic identity within which disciplinary understandings can be incorporated. The discipline is viewed with ambivalence: on the one hand it is sacrosanct, and pedagogical thought can have nothing to say on the subject; on the other, disciplinary adherents are criticized for their failure to function as efficient psycho-diagnosticians and facilitators – in other words, as 'teachers'. Viewed through the lens of situated learning, this version of pedagogy, and the 'training' practices to which it gives rise, look distinctly incongruous in a university environment. Once more, SED specialists are educating university teachers, in this instance by providing a collection of questionable psychological constructs and presenting them as solid 'explanations' of learning and, by implication, of teaching. The SED 'masters' and the 'novice' university teachers might be seen as a pedagogical community were it not for the fact that the masters and novices do not, generally, do the same kind of work; in the many instances where teacher development is organized outside academic structures, the 'masters' are not actually involved in university teaching as such. The absence of discipline, and the characterization of students as collections of psychological characteristics, whose principal purpose is simply to learn, mean that students are not part of a disciplinary community of practice; the discipline itself remains unchallenged. The students are not themselves part of the situated learning continuum, but function, like the discipline, as material upon which the 'novices' will practise their trade.

The educator as assurer of organizational quality and service delivery person

Here, teaching is conceived largely as a contribution to organizational success, and much of the literature focuses on showing how this contribution can be both improved and demonstrated. It often utilizes elements of the previous model in its prescriptions for assuring teaching quality. Once again, it presents considerable problems when one tries to analyse it in terms of 'communities of practice'.

The relationship between research and teaching in the discipline is severed. Indeed, the discipline itself as a contested and dynamic entity with disputed boundaries and epistemologies is invisible. For teachers, mastery of the discipline itself is not as important as the external 'benchmarks' applicable across all taught versions of the discipline. Those setting the benchmarks, or reviewing the teaching of the subject through quality assurance processes such as subject review, are the masters. They 'know' what should be taught and prescribe what students should achieve. The novices are the university lecturers, inducted into the mysterious practices of setting objectives, enabling students to achieve benchmarks, and complex evaluative regimes such as peer review, which enable them to perform community rites to agreed standards.

If this analysis seems far-fetched, consider how important the role of subject reviewers is in enabling institutions to garner inside information on quality assurance processes; consider the eagerness with which overpressed university lecturers put themselves forward as subject reviewers. Indeed, the ease with which academics have been recruited as institutional auditors, when research and teaching time is so precious, indicates a frank institutional interest in 'insider trading'. Within universities, the 'masters' are those who have been or will be such reviewers and auditors who are required to work on mock audits, visits and so on, and to train 'novice' colleagues or clients in audit practices.

As above, students are not part of the situated learning continuum, although their characteristics and judgements may have considerable impact on quality measures. They are recipients of the discipline, who demonstrate whether or not benchmarks have been achieved.

Prospects for connective communities of pedagogical practice

It is apparent that something very odd has happened in the field of university teaching. Pedagogy, which was once an integral part of the university teacher's role, has been identified as a separate entity from disciplinary work, and a new community of pedagogical experts has sprung up to guide university teachers in carrying out their 'new' role. Although universities have a long history of engagement in educational research and in the education of educators, that is in pedagogical knowledge production, in many universities this is not the place where the new community has its home. Indeed, there appears to be an active reluctance among some of the community to be connected in any way with academic pedagogical expertise.[2] Nor does it spring from well established disciplinary communities, where one might expect pedagogical knowledge to exist, albeit in a tacit form. Even in those instances where discipline-based pedagogical networks or journals do exist, they often focus on the application of imported generic SED techniques and ideas to the disciplinary context, rather than to the integration and development of pedagogy within disciplinary understandings. The current inclusion of pedagogical research into discipline-based units of assessment for the Research Assessment Exercise will perhaps bring this problem more clearly into focus. At present, pedagogy is not usually seen as a branch of the existing *academic* community at all. The SED community is something of an epistemological anomaly, in that it does not simply reject existing pedagogical knowledge within universities, but often acts as if it did not exist, characterizing itself as functioning within an entirely new field of knowledge. It is difficult to imagine this happening, still less succeeding, in any other field of academic knowledge.

We thus have a situation in many universities where academic staff no longer determine, or even apparently claim expertise in, the pedagogical element of knowledge production; it has been marked out as someone else's domain. This contrasts with the situation prevailing in, for example, the education of school teachers, or of medical educators. In these fields, pedagogical 'masters' have generally progressed through the stages of novice in the (disciplinary) community of practice, and working practitioner (in the disciplinary *and* professional communities of practice) before proceeding to the stage of 'mastery' where they can educate novices themselves. Until recently, those who educate school teachers were required to maintain a record of 'recent and relevant' professional practice in schools; medical educators generally retain a commitment to their own medical specialism. One argument against this type of 'community of practice' is that it can be inherently conservative, reproducing exclusionary practices and promoting vested interests. These are obvious dangers, but they also arise in part from the disciplinary and professional divisions upon which these communities of practice are built, which we have argued should themselves be challenged. Equally dangerous is the current tendency within higher education to reduce pedagogical knowledge to generic techniques for 'supporting learning', thus disrupting the articulation between teaching and research in the production of knowledge. It must also be remembered that the SED specialism is just as vulnerable to accusations of conservatism, exclusion and the promotion of vested interests as any other community of practice; like other nascent professional groups, it needs to lay claim to a field of specialist knowledge and practice to ensure its long-term survival. This is achieved in many instances by clearly separating higher educational pedagogy from those other branches of pedagogical knowledge and practice which exist, for example, in university faculties of education. Thus an interesting account of a collaborative partnership between academic 'educationalists' and SED colleagues (Kelly 1995) is dismissed as 'idiosyncratic' by Smith and Brown (1995), and more informal discussions within the educational development community of practice suggest that academic accounts of pedagogy are held in low esteem.

From the point of view of legitimate peripheral participation within a community of practice, a true academic novitiate or apprenticeship would encompass *all* aspects of knowledge production, and would thus give full recognition to teaching. This would also mean that those charged with preparing situated learners, or 'novices', in academic work would themselves have to be situated teachers, just as, at present, situated researchers are required to supervise the work of academics who are not yet masters. A rigorous exploration during the novitiate of the nature of disciplinary knowledge production, and of the academic's active contribution to this process through research and teaching, would both raise the status of teaching in relation to research, and (one hopes) improve the often lamentable quality of pedagogical research. Situated teachers, conscious of their role within the community of practice, might be expected to act as situated teacher educators, without the intervention of generic external 'specialists'. This would not preclude the cross-disciplinary interchange which is one of the strengths of a more generic approach to teacher education, and which could be incorporated into the practices of the novitiate. The ownership of pedagogical identity and learning by the academic community of practice would, we suggest, both increase this interchange and promote connectivity between disciplinary areas, as academics themselves identified intellectual commonalities through pedagogical explorations. The loss of pedagogy as a specious specialism, and the cultivation of situated teaching, would force academics to reconsider seriously the nature of disciplinary boundaries.

We are arguing here, not for the destruction of educational development as an area of thought and practice, but for the return of pedagogical practice to the site of knowledge production: educational development should be part of the role of practising academics as situated teachers and researchers, not a bolt-on option available from outside. It is perhaps difficult to envisage how this might be implemented, particularly given the rather fatalistic conviction of many SED specialists that academics are not interested in teaching. One might speculate that they are not interested in the non-disciplinary pedagogical models on offer from SED units, and that alternative approaches need to be found. The long-term route would be to introduce teaching as a specific element in the current academic novitiate, the PhD. The development of researchers as graduate teaching assistants is already quite common in North America, where the vocational purpose of the PhD is perhaps more explicitly recognized – and where academic educationalists frequently take on this role. The development of academics as teachers can thus be seen as an integral part of their vocational preparation. Pedagogical research, and teaching itself, could be elevated to their proper status in academic communities by being consciously integrated into disciplinary work, rather than being placed on the level of skills development. This would help us to reconceptualize research and teaching as elements of connective academic practice, within a community of scholar-educators committed to critical endeavour. Knowledge production, Albert, but not as we know it.

Notes

1. ESRC research project no. R000222794.
2. See, for example, the discussion on the 'Improving Student Learning' mailbase list, on how to offer academic qualifications in education without involving university education departments. Accessed January 2000 at http://www.mailbase.ac.uk/lists/isl/2000-01/subject.html

References

Bailey, F.G. (1977) *Morality and Expediency: The Folklore of Academic Politics.* Oxford: Basil Blackwell.

Barnett, R. (1997) *Higher Education: A Critical Business.* Buckingham: SRHE and Open University Press.

Barnett, R. and Hallam, S. (1999) Teaching for supercomplexity: a pedagogy for higher education, in P. Mortimore (ed.) *Understanding Pedagogy and its Impact on Learning.* London: Paul Chapman.

Becher, T. (1989) *Academic Tribes and Territories: Intellectual Enquiry and the Culture of Disciplines.* Milton Keynes: SRHE and Open University Press.

Becher, T. (1994) Interdisciplinarity and community, in R. Barnett (ed.) *Academic Community: Discourse or Discord?* London: Jessica Kingsley.

Biglan, A. (1973a) The characteristics of subject matter in different academic areas, *Journal of Applied Psychology,* 57(3): 195–203.

Biglan, A. (1973b) Relationships between subject matter characteristics and the structure and output of university departments, *Journal of Applied Psychology,* 57(3): 204–13.

Bright, B. (1996) Reflecting on 'reflective practice', *Studies in the Education of Adults,* 28(2): 162–84.

Brookfield, S.D. (1995) *Becoming a Critically Reflective Teacher.* San Francisco: Jossey Bass.

Crane, D. (1972) *Invisible Colleges: Diffusion of Knowledge in Scientific Communities.* Chicago: University of Chicago Press.

Ecclestone, K. (1996) 'The reflective practitioner': mantra or a model for emancipation?, *Studies in the Education of Adults,* 28(2): 146–61.

Finnegan, R. (1994) Recovering 'academic community': what do we mean?, in R. Barnett (ed.) *Academic Community: Discourse or Discord?* London: Jessica Kingsley.

Kelly, T. (1995) The relationship between staff and educational development, in B. Smith and S. Brown (eds) *Research, Teaching and Learning in Higher Education.* London: SEDA/Kogan Page.

Lave, J. and Wenger, E. (1991) *Situated Learning: Legitimate Peripheral Participation.* Cambridge: Cambridge University Press.

Leach, A.F. (1915) *The Schools of Medieval England.* London: Methuen.

Lodahl, J.B. and Gordon, G. (1972) The structure of scientific fields and the functioning of university graduate departments, *American Sociological Review,* 37 (February): 57–72.

Malcolm, J. and Zukas, M. (1999) Models of the educator in higher education: problems and perspectives. Paper presented to the Society for Teaching and

Learning in Higher Education, Collaborative Learning for the 21st Century, University of Calgary, 16–19 June.

Ramsden, P. (1992) *Learning to Teach in Higher Education.* London: Routledge.

Rowland, S. (1999) Surface learning about teaching in higher education: the need for more critical conversations. Paper presented to British Educational Research Association Annual Conference, University of Sussex, 2–5 September.

Schön, D. (1987) *Educating the Reflective Practitioner.* San Francisco: Jossey Bass.

Smith, B. and Brown, S. (eds) (1995) *Research Teaching and Learning in Higher Education.* London: SEDA/Kogan Page.

Steele, T. (1997) *The Emergence of Cultural Studies: Adult Education, Cultural Politics and the English Question.* London: Lawrence & Wishart.

Vygotsky, L.S. (1978) *Mind in Society: The Development of Higher Psychological Processes.* London: Harvard University Press.

Webb, G. (1996) *Understanding Staff Development.* Buckingham: SRHE and Open University Press.

Wenger, E. (1998) *Communities of Practice: Learning, Meaning and Identity.* Cambridge: Cambridge University Press.

Young, M. (1993) A curriculum for the 21st century? Towards a new basis for overcoming academic/vocational divisions, *British Journal of Educational Studies,* 41(3): 203–22.

Zukas, M. and Malcolm, J. (1999) Models of the educator in higher education. Paper presented to British Educational Research Association Annual Conference, University of Sussex, 2–5 September.

6

Managerialism and University Managers: Building New Academic Communities or Disrupting Old Ones?

Rosemary Deem and Rachel Johnson

Traditional views about UK universities often included a perception of them as communities of scholars (Pratt 1990; Warren 1994). However, there is often a sense of romanticism about such descriptions and undoubtedly there have long been excluded as well as included groups in the politics of universities (Becher 1988). Universities, like most other organizations, do not have a single culture but several (Alvesson 1993). Although there is cultural traffic between them, this does not necessarily weaken the cultural, social and political boundaries with which those cultures surround themselves. Subject disciplines and status differentials are the bases of longstanding staff divisions in higher education, as are those between students and staff, and between academic staff and support staff. Academics do different kinds of work from support staff and also have quite distinctive professional and other identities (Henkel 2000). Academic identities tend to include, as Henkel and others note, a strong element of individualism, which may not lend itself to institutional consensus or cultural coherence, even for those, such as many scientists, who typically work in research teams.

The individualism of academics and its effects on universities as organizations is also compounded by institutional variation and difference. There was a diversity of types of university in the UK well before the polytechnics became incorporated universities in 1992 (Pratt 1997, 1999). Thus a 1960s greenfield campus university is very different from a city-based or federal establishment and also not at all like a former college of advanced technology. Universities are highly complex organizations with a multiplicity of cultures and communities. Their community character is not explained simply in terms of whether they possess a charter (the pre-1992 universities) or are incorporated institutions (the post-1992 universities).

This chapter uses preliminary analyses of interview and focus group data with manager-academics and professional administrators,[1] taken from a current Economic and Social Research Council funded project on new managerialism and the management of UK universities, to explore three dimensions of universities as managed and highly complex organizations and communities. These dimensions are chosen because they represent potential or actual major divisions in universities, which are, or may be, further mediated through the exercise of management roles. The first of these dimensions relates to the extent to which professional administrators/managers and manager-academics[2] see themselves as part of a management cadre, with shared values, technologies, narratives and practices, separate from, though responsible for, the staff, students, teaching, research, administration and financial health of their institutions.[3] The second dimension focuses on the extent to which subject disciplines may affect manager-academics' understandings of, and identification with, their institutions and smaller subunits. The final dimension relates to whether gender relations and processes divide manager-academics and professional administrators from each other or are irrelevant to management. These three dimensions refer to very different forms of social solidarity and cultural communities but together they provide some interesting insights into the layered complexities that comprise contemporary universities in the UK.

The greater size and complexity of universities, as well as the growth of an audit culture for teaching and research, and acute funding pressures, have led to other, more internal changes, such as a greater emphasis on the explicit management of core and support activities (Trow 1993; Deem 1998; Exworthy and Halford 1998; Shattock 1999). Some researchers have referred to this phenomenon in public services in general as 'new managerialism' (Ferlie *et al.* 1996; Clarke and Newman 1997), implying both a fresh departure for publicly funded institutions (using performance measurement, resource delegation, efficiency measures, greater team-based working and more use of centrally derived strategic direction), and a borrowing of cultures, values and practices from the private business sector. The enhanced activities of managerial groups and cadres in higher education have the potential to further disrupt traditional notions of academic communities, which have long been divided by disciplines (Becher 1989). Disciplines tend to encourage social relationships and cultures only within narrow confines, both inside and across institutions. Managing those confines clearly involves territorial action; however, it is not yet evident whether disciplinary loyalty is superseded when management roles extend beyond academic enclaves based on one or a small number of disciplines or subject areas. Gender can also form the basis for considerable cultural, social and economic divisions in higher education as elsewhere, and its effects may have become more acute as more women staff are recruited to higher education (Deem and Ozga 2000). The Bett Report noted the big gender gap in salary between women and men in the same category of academic post (*Independent Review of Higher Education, Pay and Conditions* 1999). Other research has suggested that gender processes can divide women and men academics and manager-academics from each other, whether in terms of practices or in relation to attitudes and values (Morley and Walsh 1995; Brooks 1997; Eggins 1997;

Morley 1999; Deem 1999). It is to an analysis of the extent to which these three dimensions of universities as managed, divided communities, are disruptive of institutional coherence, that we now turn.

Managerial communities of practice?

This section draws partly on the notion of communities of practice (Lave and Wenger 1991) to explore the extent to which manager-academics and professional administrators view themselves as a group with common practices and world-views as well as suggesting that the idea of a management cadre may be one worth exploring. The notion of a distinctive senior management cadre goes beyond suggesting that manager-academics and professional administrators may be united by the similarities of their practices. It suggests that there are also similarities in values, beliefs and interests. Concepts of communities of practice emphasize the learning aspect of those communities; and given the very limited extent to which most manager-academics in the UK appear (from our data) to be trained for their roles, learning to be a manager-academic is often informal but relies heavily both on what is done and said by people already established in those fields and on colleague expectations of manager-academics. Preliminary analysis of our interview data does not reveal a sense of shared solidarity and values across all the manager-academics interviewed but does suggest a common concern to try to get academics to do things in an environment where there are few incentives or sanctions. There are undoubtedly communities of practice amongst manager-academics, though these tend to depend on the level of management being practised, so heads of department (HoDs) do not necessarily have practices similar to those of pro-vice chancellors (PVCs). At very senior levels (PVCs and above), manager-academics may have more in common with senior professional administrators such as finance directors or human resource directors than they do with other academics.

How far has the importance of management permeated UK universities and what effects has it had? Our focus group data overwhelmingly confirmed a view of UK universities as permeated by managerial discourses and technologies:

> it's a sea change in culture from the collegiate to the corporate. It's not just the vocabulary, it's been forced through the whole thing.
>
> (Humanities learned society)

> one of the changes that's come, that's been implemented across the public sector . . . is the idea of the internal market . . . devolved budgeting has actually changed enormously the culture of the universities.
>
> (Social science learned society)

However, the responses also indicate that these changes are not always seen as relying on techniques derived from business, although such elements are perceived to be present. A number of our respondents suggested that those changes which stemmed from developments in the higher education sector as a whole (for example quality assessments) were equally significant:

> there are national constraints now which didn't exist, say ten years ago, to such a great extent. I mean we seem to go from RAE [Research Assessment Exercise] to TQA [Teacher Quality Assessment] to various internal reviews and so on . . . the strategy decisions are different from what they were ten years ago.
>
> (Science learned society)

In our interview data, those manager-academics who most strongly held notions of universities as communities with some common interests transcending small academic and other enclaves were those in senior management posts, typically vice-chancellors and pro-vice chancellors but also professional administrators (and yet they were often also the group most distanced from the rest of their institution). Although decision-making structures and roles within universities are changing, these managers attempt to mediate the process and impact of change on their institutions. Their approaches to change indicate efforts to accommodate, and to demonstrate sensitivity to, how they perceive the character of professional academics and the conditions that foster academic work. However, the gradual redefinition of academics' roles and the structures of decision-making in universities is also producing changed relationships, and new group identities and loyalties. This implies that the concept of universities as communities is being redefined at the same time as the conditions on which such communities are built and accepted are undergoing a process of transformation:

> Money is extremely important. If you can determine the flow of money, you can determine as much as you need to. The other thing is knowledge of what's going on nationally, because you've got the power of persuasion.
>
> (VC, post-92 university)

> universities are becoming more and more – they never will be businesses in the absolute sense of the definition of a business, but they're . . . becoming business-like in terms of generating non-HEFCE income. We have to be more business-like in terms of managing our costs and employing sub-contractors.
>
> (VC, pre-92 university)

The vice-chancellors (VCs) interviewed clearly identified themselves as leaders and managers of complex corporate enterprises. Whilst some VCs considered that they were dealing with intransigent, territorial and inwardly focused academics, others recognized that even if this is the case, academics are nevertheless key players in the university:

> The university, as an institution, has to be much more robust and self-perpetuating than any individual in it, but individuals can make a huge

difference . . . universities are collegiate organizations. I cannot make
any academic member of staff do research that they don't want to do.
I can't do that. I've tried it. When I was a head of department I tried.
It does not work.

(VC, pre-1992 university)

A number of VCs we talked to had begun to devolve budgets downwards,
whilst simultaneously introducing sharply defined institutional strategies,
and enhanced levels and techniques of central monitoring. Several of those
relatively recently in post also spoke of their attempts at de-layering their
institutions in order to facilitate decision-making and communications: 'I
wanted a really radical thing, I wanted to de-layer and get rid of faculties'
(VC, pre-1992 university).

Furthermore, almost all our VC respondents emphasized the necessity
for concentrated areas of academic excellence (in teaching and research),
the concept of institutional strategy, and the idea of 'academic integrity'.
There were frequent descriptions of the tensions that exist in attempting to
balance institutional coherence with the need to sustain levels of academic
autonomy and freedom of action. Some VCs saw themselves continuously
trying to bring about sensible compromises or reminding the more recal-
citrant academics of the highly constrained financial context for higher
education, *and* internal performance objectives. Many acknowledged that
they attempted to achieve change by wielding greater influence over new
appointments and stressing new and tighter conditions of performance for
existing staff. Similar views were expressed by some PVCs:

> The university is going to get a lot tougher about performance . . . But
> I would have to say those people have not performed . . . in a tougher
> world they might well have been dismissed for not fulfilling a contract
> or whatever else.
> (PVC, pre-1992 university talking about strategic early retirements)

PVCs we interviewed had considerable variation in their responsibilities
and portfolios. Many found themselves charged with the responsibility for
the implementation of change consequent on university strategy. Some
were previously highly successful researchers, others had been excellent
teachers, and a handful had industrial experience. As a group, they frequently observed that a solid academic reputation was necessary in order
to be able to achieve credibility with academics; only one or two saw this
as irrelevant: 'In the job I've got at the moment which is mainly resources,
I don't need the academic credibility' (Deputy VC, post-92 university).

Those who accepted the need for academic legitimacy did not, however,
always warm to their academic colleagues: more than a few saw the wider
academic community as a source of resistance, obstruction and frustration:

> I think what frustrates me a lot about universities is that they are very
> bureaucratic organizations at times . . . I think I see Senate as the abso-
> lutely worst of that, you have people who will discuss endlessly fine

subtle differences in the meaning of the particular word or a particular phrase . . . if it were my university I would not have a bloody Senate at all.

(Deputy VC, pre-1992 university)

Others recognized that their preferred way of working was not that of some of their colleagues:

I suppose one of the changes for me is this institution is much more unionized and I've learned to handle that . . . when you can't necessarily treat someone as a peer, not because you don't want to but because they don't want to . . . it then needs a different type of relationship negotiating.

(PVC, post-92 university)

The professional administrators whom we interviewed typically had a much clearer and more defined remit, whether finance, human resources, or planning, than many of the PVCs. Nevertheless, some, especially those from a background in private industry, found working in a university frustrating, often precisely because it seemed to function as a more democratic community than the organizations they were used to dealing with:

Well one of the things is, I have great difficulty at the moment in understanding . . . what powers I do have . . . I can recommend things to go to committees and lay people along with other members of the Schools who are on that committee will actually approve it. Where in industry I would have sat round the Board, we would have agreed what to do and we would have done it. Now the timescale involved is just horrendous as far as I'm concerned.

(Director of Finance, pre-1992 university)

Such anxieties and concerns were not universal since the arrangements for decision-making vary so much, particularly between the former polytechnics and the chartered universities. Undoubtedly, the significance of the former binary divide is continuing to blur. Nevertheless there are still some differences in decision-making structures, attitudes and staff contracts:

change happens easily here largely because it really only takes the will of the vice-chancellor for something to happen . . . in institutions with rather more formal decision-making structures that are laid down in its Charter and Statutes . . . quite a lot of time the vice-chancellor may have a great deal of influence but doesn't have the power ultimately to make the decision unless it's taken through Senate.

(University Secretary, post-92 university)

the relationships that you need to develop with the departments and the heads of departments are . . . quite complex in that you need to have some, you need to gain their trust, they need to be able to trust and want your advice. But in lots of ways, you actually have, I have no authority whatsoever. But I need to be able to influence what they do without actually telling them what to do.

(Head of Planning, pre-1992 university)

These differences do not appear to be as polarized as we might have anticipated at the beginning of the research. Indeed, as the pre-1992 universities are urged to adopt the teaching and quality management procedures of the former polytechnics, and as the post-1992 universities begin to differentiate themselves from one another and to take on some elements of the chartered universities (for example, support for research, encouragement of elected deans and PVCs, or appointing leading academics to management roles), the diversity of the system may be growing in some respects, as well as declining in others.

A number of administrators in both sectors declared themselves frustrated by what they described as old cultures of academe which refused to disappear. Although this reply is not typical of the responses from professional administrators, it certainly echoes similar views from a number of respondents:

> we're looking at contractual change . . . there is a lot of work to be done still to . . . get into a situation of obtaining a culture I think, where change is recognized and accepted . . . Local authority culture is still embedded in a lot of the support staff area and you know the support staff trade unions are public sector trade unions . . . there is still a reluctance if you like to disengage from those sort of practices and policies.

(Head of Human Resources, post-92 university)

Such pressures to change culture are not only consistent with ideas about new managerialism derived from the private sector (Ferlie *et al.* 1996; Clarke and Newman 1997; Exworthy and Halford 1998) but they also tend to mean that senior administrators identify with other senior administrators and senior management teams in a kind of 'us and them' scenario, which in effect means that the community of practice with which they identify is not one which includes the university staff as a whole.

Preliminary analyses of our data on senior manager-academics and professional managers or administrators suggest that there are differences in outlook partly consequent on the different backgrounds of VCs and PVCs, who have normally come via an academic career sometimes combined with periods in industry, as compared with professional managers. But the data also indicate that these groups, despite different views on how to achieve changes, have a shared community of practices and shared values and beliefs which are not comparable with those found in academic areas at faculty, school or department level. Despite frequent assertions from our manager-academic respondents (if not always our administrative interviewees), that they were concerned to keep a degree of consensus and inclusion, the greater specialization of management and the growing size and complexity of what is managed militate against the extent to which senior managers and those they are responsible for hold common values and want to achieve common goals. Even if it can be argued that all academics today manage something (a course, a research team, admissions or whatever), there remains a big difference between those who do this at a local level in their own discipline and those who have institution-wide portfolios. The latter do indeed seem to be moving, though not in every institution we studied, towards the formation of management cadres separate from the rest of the institution. This process may be exacerbated by the payment to senior manager-academics of very high salaries in comparison with those of academics in general.

Manager-academics: from discipline to disciplining?

The importance of academic disciplines to an understanding of the social relations and processes of academe has been well described and explained (Becher 1989). So too have the different processes by which academics inculcate research students into the field and habitus of academic disciplines (Parry *et al.* 1994; Delamont *et al.* 1997). Although we have been examining management *per se* rather than teaching or research, we have nevertheless been trying to ascertain how far disciplinary differences in manager-academics' backgrounds may have affected those managers' approaches to management and their values.

Recent analysis of the changing background of UK vice-chancellors has indicated that whilst science, Oxbridge, and public school backgrounds remained dominant in the 1990s (Farnham and Jones 1998), a number of social scientists, with a significant number of sociologists in particular (Brown 1999), were appointed to such positions in the final decade of the twentieth century. In addition, Farnham and Jones's evidence suggests that the dominance of Oxbridge and the public schools has been slightly lessened, though mostly in the 1960s universities, the one-time colleges of advanced technology and the former polytechnic sector. So the changing disciplinary base of higher education may well be significant for the nature of its very senior academic management (although this was not what Farnham and Jones were researching). We have not discerned much evidence in our interviews with vice-chancellors that this is so, except in so far as it may have an impact on ideas about institutional curricular profiles, subject priorities and financial allocations across different subjects.

There are many ways in which subject disciplines might affect how universities are run and managed, a point made by researchers looking at changes in the funding, conditions and work of academic scientists (Slaughter and Leslie 1997; McAuley *et al.* 2000). One of the basic differences between most science disciplines (except perhaps theoretical physics or pure maths) and the majority of non-science disciplines, is that scientists are more used to working in teams, whereas in other areas, academics are accustomed to working alone:

> It's a 'me' culture and that permeates a lot of activities; and that's a caricature because I've got some fantastic colleagues who are not 'me' people, but the culture in progression in higher education is a 'me' culture.
>
> (HoD, Business School, post-92 university)

So the basis for the subject community within an institution is likely to be different in different disciplines, although as several of our focus group discussions noted, teamwork is increasingly necessary in all disciplines if good teaching and research assessment scores are to be achieved:

> Almost all the goals I've got are, you know, get a 5, double the number of PhD students, double the grant income and those I think, all the important . . . all the targets our institution really *cares* about are ones I think you can only achieve collegially.
>
> (Social science learned society)

> There has to be much more *team* spirit now than there would have been ten years ago, because ten years ago you could get person X, who could be essentially a 'loose cannon'; now that person maybe does his lectures badly or turns up late or he doesn't do so well in the labs or even says, 'I don't believe in questionnaires, I don't believe in giving tutorials' . . . If you have such a person *now* on your team for Quality Assurance Agency purposes . . . you are looking at potential disaster.
>
> (Science learned society)

Some of those in very senior academic management positions thought that their discipline background had led them more easily into management than had their colleagues'. This might be, for example, because they had run a large research group or had industrial experience. Whilst these aspects of their biographies could lead them to favour some disciplines over others, we did not collect any data in the interview stage of our study which supported this interpretation. Whilst some academics at very senior levels have to some extent left their disciplinary identities behind, those who are deans and heads of department are more deeply immersed in them.

At the dean level, typically several disciplines have to be represented. Deanship appointments tend to be time-limited in both the new and the old universities. So these collective loyalties may themselves only be temporary and they may be difficult to 'manage':

> a dean of a planning unit is in a very different position to a head of department who has to fight his/her own corner to get the best deal for their group – I have to take a much wider and strategic view.
>
> (Dean of Science, pre-1992 university)

Nevertheless, there may be a perception amongst other academics in a faculty, that deans tend to favour their own subject department:

> within the Faculty, although it's business and management, it's quite diverse . . . because you've got your own tribe so to speak and there's always . . . people from other tribes think, oh well he favours his own tribe . . . probably I give my own tribe a harder time . . . But I mean anybody sees resources going there, so you're actually defensive.
>
> (Dean of Business, pre-92 university)

The reception of the faculty in the wider institution is also important because it affects whether the academic unit and its head are seen as a part of the wider institution:

> since I've been here it's my experience that we're regarded as an acceptable membership. Now, in two of the universities where I worked and they were old universities I have to say, it wasn't the case. Nursing was excluded from an awful lot, not really seen as a respectable profession, what's it doing in a university, 'why are you paying all these people such high salaries when they don't belong here?' and they weren't very well accepted.
>
> (Dean of Nursing, post-92 university)

There is also awareness even amongst some of those who feel their discipline is currently accepted, that the position is vulnerable to change in the future. This seems especially so not only for health-related subjects but also for arts and humanities, where the kind of entrepreneurialism being encouraged in universities is not as accepted or as easily achieved (Slaughter and Leslie 1997; Clark 1998; Pan 1998):

> what if Armageddon happened and X (present vice-chancellor) left and then some monster of a vice-chancellor arrived and said 'right I think we're gonna put engineering in the music building and we're gonna move you out'?
>
> (Dean of Music, post-92 university)

While deans may need to defend a range of subjects, for heads of department (HoDs), close disciplinary identification is essential and they must defend their subject in every situation where it is threatened, as well as promoting it whenever possible. Furthermore, there are other differences between HoDs and deans. Most deans are in their jobs because they want to be there. This is not necessarily so for HoDs. Indeed, we found a great many 'reluctant managers' as HoDs, especially in the pre-1992 universities, often working in a system where middle management roles are allocated on a temporary, rotating basis. Reluctant managers are not very likely to identify with senior management or professional administrators, especially if they arrived in their position by accident or default.

Some research on women headteachers in schools argues that their careers are often serendipitous and accidental and implies that men are more likely to have planned careers (Evetts 1990, 1994). In our interviews, we have found relatively few women *or* men who had planned a career in academic management. This was particularly so for HoDs. Although reluctant managers still tend to identify closely with their disciplines and their close colleagues, their role does not always make it easy for them to maintain a sense of community even within their department:

> I thought I might feel quite isolated in the department and I do, and I don't like that very much. It changes your relationship with everybody in quite difficult ways.
>
> (HoD, arts/humanities, pre-92 university)

But a high degree of disciplinary identification and cohesion is perceived as crucial, both for units and for the maintenance of their image in the wider university:

> It is important that Chemistry is perceived as well managed and with positive people. Whingeing doesn't work – some departments do it all the time, blaming others for their problems – it gives a wrong perception to the university.
>
> (Head of School of Science, pre-1992 university)

In the post-92 universities, there are also some different concerns. Some HoDs are in permanent posts, have much reduced teaching duties (even compared with their pre-1992 peers) and are also little involved in research, whereas we found only one HoD in a pre-1992 university who was not involved in research. Nevertheless, there were HoD respondents in post-1992 universities for whom research was important:

> I was appointed as an academic not as a manager. Here I was appointed to a department which had a lot of development to come, which we've duly completed I think . . . I'm pleased to say when the Research Assessment Exercise thing came around in 1992 most of the staff in this department were . . . [counted].
>
> (HoD, arts/humanities, post-92 university)

The physical location of a department also affects the sense its members and head have of belonging to a wider community. For example, in response to a question about collegiality:

> Art and Design has been so, has been satellited outside the university it's very difficult to answer that question really.
>
> (HoD, arts/humanities, post-92 university)

The struggle for resources in general brings in disciplinary loyalties as hard-pressed HoDs battle for a fair share:

> Why should we get less and have less opportunity, and students have an inferior learning experience than others in other departments, some of whom are over-resourced? Obviously because we're underdogs . . .

the problem I guess is that why I'm not getting the money is because there isn't the money, it's spent somewhere else on an over-resourced department . . . it's people and buildings and machines over in Engineering or something like that.

(HoD, Business School, post-92 university)

Engaging in this struggle also involves external subject and professional bodies that the rest of the university may have no dealings with:

Externally I suppose the role of the head of department is to represent the interests of the school . . . it's up to me to know that the relationships are working well with the Law Society and that our provision is on a par with law provision in other universities and that I'm up to date with what's going on and keeping the name of the Law School at the forefront where it needs to be.

(HoD, law, post-92 university)

Our data on disciplinary differences suggest that at HoD level in all the universities studied, the maintenance of tribe identities and subject boundaries is a crucial part of the role, even if the sense of community is flawed by the isolation of some HoDs from their colleagues. At more senior levels, disciplinary identity is less evidently a part of the academic management brief, and although disciplinary allegiances may remain a source of values and inform strategic planning (even if covertly or unconsciously), the discipline of regulation and control of colleagues, strategic direction of activities, people and budgets tends to displace subject disciplines. Even those keen to remain part of their discipline find it difficult to do so. Disciplines are, of course, one of the traditional divisions in universities; so far we have not found that they have a further crucial impact on senior management roles.

Engendering divided communities?

A further theme of our project has concerned itself with the extent to which gender processes have an impact on manager-academics and other colleagues. If these processes are significant, they must surely disrupt notions of communities of managers and other academics, in terms of both experiences and expectations. Studies of women managers in publicly funded institutions have suggested that women managers in general in this sector may have different approaches to management from men in similar posts (Yeatman 1990; Davies 1992, 1995; Marshall 1994; Tanton 1994; Itzin and Newman 1995). However, research comparing women and men managers in similar jobs in the private sector has indicated that women and men tend to do similar jobs in similar ways (Wajcman 1998). Nevertheless, Wajcman's study suggests that women and men managers do have quite different experiences of organizations: a point also made by a recent study of gender and careers in public and private organizations (banking, nursing, local government), which talks about the importance of studying embodiment at work

(Halford *et al.* 1997). Wajcman also argues that the management activities and performances of women managers are judged by different standards from those applied to male managers. If this is so in public sector organizations too, then it has important implications for the kinds of communities formed or divided by gender processes.

Bensimon (1995) has argued that collegiality between academics, when understood as a set of equal social relations between academic colleagues doing similar work without the need for explicit management and regulation, has always excluded and still excludes some individuals, such as temporary staff, women and black academics. Collegiality is a concept often regarded not only as a symbol of the sense of inclusiveness and solidarity that academics feel towards each other, but also as something fast disappearing in contemporary universities (McNay 1995; Dearlove 1997). Yet Bensimon's view of collegiality as an exclusive rather than inclusive form of academic solidarity is supported by other research. Acker's work on women teacher trainers in Canadian universities claims that these women often regard themselves as doing the good citizenship work (pastoral care, extra teaching, low-level administration) of university departments, whilst men get on with their research careers (Acker 1996, 1997).

In our own study, the extent to which gender processes inform management strategies, practices and values has been an important theme, drawing on previous research about women managers with feminist and pro-equity views in post-compulsory education (Deem and Ozga 1997, 2000; Deem 1999) and on studies involving a broader cross-section of male and female managers in further education (Prichard 1996; Whitehead 1996, 1998; Prichard and Deem 1999). In our focus groups, a few participants expressed views that declared gender to be irrelevant to the management of universities, or so complex that it cannot be untangled. A minority of men participants thought that women had an advantage in being positively discriminated in favour of when applying for a job:

> There's quite possibly positive discrimination . . . People are very encouraging to females but when it comes to working with one, I personally think that I would prefer to work in a department run by a man because I wouldn't want to be managed by a woman.
>
> (Science/technology learned society)

Others felt that male cultures were still pervasive:

> I think the old universities at any rate . . . have a very male culture about them and I think it's actually quite hard for women to . . . succeed within that culture . . . I think it's getting better, but desperately slowly.
>
> (Generic learned society)

In the focus groups, women, and especially mothers, were thought, by both men and women respondents, to struggle harder to become managers, to have more difficulty combining their career with care of children, more likely to have a grasp of the minutiae of managing a department (for example, spreadsheets, personnel practices) and less likely to take risks in their management roles.

In the interview phase of the project, we adopted a theoretical sampling strategy which allowed us to match women and men in the same jobs (though in different institutions), thus facilitating the kinds of comparison that Wajcman (1998) undertook in the private sector. Here again we encountered a variety of views. There were those who declared that gender was of no relevance to academic management:

> I don't think academic women are necessarily more civilized than men.
> (Male dean, social sciences, pre-1992 university)

> you need to be eloquent, you need to have presence . . . you need to be bright because you're dealing with very bright people and you need to be quick-witted in that sense. I mean there's nothing different between male and female in any of those I've mentioned.
> (Male deputy-VC, post-92 university)

A few men declared that gender was of no significance to academe in general:

> I did ask, a couple of years ago, I asked a member of staff . . . if she would actually go round the department and speak to all female members of staff to see if there were any issues regarding gender that they felt were becoming uncomfortable in the department or something like that, but I didn't get anything back, so perhaps that led me to be complacent about it, but I'm not aware of anything.
> (Male HoD, science, post-92 university)

Some other men took the view that if women had an aptitude for management roles, there was nothing to stop them:

> *Interviewer:* As far as I can see, your pro-vice chancellor group is entirely men . . . Is that an issue do you think?
> *VC:* I don't think so . . . I mean, if there had been a woman who was eligible they would be there. The key registrar essentially is a woman, the key head of planning is a . . . woman. No, I don't think it's an issue at all, I think it's just purely a question of who can do the job best.
> (Male VC, pre-92 university)

There were also men who thought that gender had relevance for mothers but not parents in general (despite most being fathers themselves) because of the long hours involved in management. Sometimes this was extended to all women:

> *Interviewer:* Presumably that caseload and workload would be difficult for you to be a woman in this job I suppose?
> *PVC:* Impossible. Although a woman of my age probably wouldn't have young children but it can be extremely gruelling . . . in the last year while I've been doing essentially three jobs.
> (Male PVC, pre-1992 university)

This is a 50 week a year job with long hours, in a lab-based subject working a lot with postgraduates in a heavily research-oriented environment; also it's a dangerous subject and there's a big role in relation to safety. So a woman with a family could not do the job and bring up children in the traditional way . . . you would have to do it in the modern way, leaving them at a nursery from three days old.

(Head of School of Science, pre-92 university)

Finally, there were a number of men who were very supportive of equal opportunities initiatives and argued that there needed to be more women in senior posts:

we are working towards equal opportunities but we've got some work to do yet and you know, there is not an equal gender split if you like at senior level.

(Male professional administrator, post-92 university)

Women interviewees included a small minority who thought gender made no difference at all, at any stage or phase of career:

Interviewer: Do you think that you had to approach your job differently or did you have different sorts of experiences because you were a woman head of department?
HoD: No, no.
Interviewer: Do people react to you differently do you think?
HoD: No, I don't think so.

(Head of Humanities, pre-92 university)

There was a much larger group who thought gender did make a difference, though many of them qualified it to say that it was mothers who struggled the hardest, an important theme in other research on women and academe (Leonard and Malina 1994; Leonard 1998):

In the career as a whole there is no doubt that in the university sector at the moment it is very difficult to combine family responsibilities and the level of hard work that is needed to get you to the stage which will give you the status you need to enable you to go into a senior position . . . [women] are more conscientious than men and I think women basically are less prepared to be ruthless.

(Female dean, humanities, pre-92 university)

Some women had tried explicitly to learn from their own experiences of gender discrimination in order to help other women, so that those women's experiences would be more positive. This was something also found in earlier research on women manager-academics with feminist and pro-equity values (Deem and Ozga 1997, 2000; Deem 1999):

I don't think that in this school for anyone it is a problem [now] . . . My personal experience was that for quite a period in my career I felt that someone somewhere had me down as a married woman with children for whom it wasn't important to have a career. Not because they knew but because I was in that sort of box and because I'm not the sort of person who is personally ambitious in the sense of wanting to sound my own trumpet and say how great I am all the time. I was taken for granted in a way that a man wouldn't have been.

(Female HoD, humanities, pre-92 university)

A few women said they had initially found it a struggle being a woman and a manager but that it had become easier:

I was the only woman senior manager . . . And it took quite a while for the chaps, and they admit it now and we laugh about it, to, they didn't like to deal with me . . . they freely admitted that . . . I wasn't part of the job 'cause I didn't got to the toilet with them and things like that, but that's where all the real discussions go on, you know, in the loos, before the meetings of course . . . Well, initially it took a while . . . now they are fine.

(Female HoD, Business School, post-92 university)

Other women suggested more complex experiences, both positive and negative, in their own careers and those of others; again this is not inconsistent with some analyses of women academics and women manager-academics in existing literature (Brooks 1997; Eggins 1997; Morley 1999):

well, I've mostly found that there has been an advantage in being a woman, because you stood out. If you were working in a man's world and you were good, that you stood out, but . . . I do also believe in the adage that you have to be not only as good, you do have to be better and I have had some unfortunate experiences along the way, as I've been promoted to senior lecturer and latterly to head of department, where I had extremely unpleasant reactions from men whom I actually beat for the job . . . I mean reactions that went on for six months and longer. You know, very, very uncomfortable and actually, on two occasions, physically threatening.

(Female HoD, Business School, post-92 university)

The picture that is presented in our focus group and interview data about the perceived impact of gender processes is complicated and does not lend itself to simplistic or binary explanations about women's and men's careers as manager-academics. However, as far as allegiances and alliances, community spirit and shared solidarity are concerned, there is quite a body of evidence that suggests that women may find it more difficult to enter academic management and harder to permeate male cultures once they are in such posts. The data on whether they do the job differently have not yet been analysed sufficiently for us to draw any conclusions. Overall, at this stage of the project it looks as though gender processes do work both to include and to exclude within universities. Hence Bensimon's (1995) argument that women have been excluded by notions like collegiality does begin to look a little convincing. Communities of practice in universities are also often, we tentatively suggest, communities of gender too.

Conclusion

This chapter has examined a number of threats to the notion of universities as cohesive communities of scholars. Just as the student base of UK universities has changed massively since the 1980s, so too have the social composition of their academic staffing, the internal and external constraints and audit requirements. We have concentrated here on three threats to communities of academic staff: the supposed increase in the management function of higher education institutions, the longstanding impact of subject disciplines on manager-academics, and the possible effects of gender differences and processes. First, the greater emphasis on explicit management of academic and support staff by a cadre (or community of practice) of senior manager-academics and administrators, who are often quite separated from the core activities of teaching and research which they are supposed to be managing, does seem to have the potential to divide notions of universities as communities of like-minded academics with coherent though varying purposes. Although we have not found evidence that manager-academics at the head of department level are part of this cadre, they often face isolation from colleagues as a result of having to interpret and implement demands from above.

The second threat, that of subject disciplines, is one that is relevant to universities not only as academic communities in an holistic sense (albeit a longstanding one) but also as a potential divide in the management cadre. Above the level of dean, this was not evident. The concern for control, discipline and regulation of the workforce appeared more important than subject discipline at senior management level, but below that, new conditions of work, resource allocation models and competition for students seem to have made manager-academics from different disciplines see themselves as potential rivals rather than as complementary to each other.

Finally, we examined whether gender and gender processes might also give rise to threats to the unity of academic and manager-academic communities. The data on this are complex and do not facilitate straightforward explanations, but they do suggest that gender solidarities (for both men and women) are present amongst manager-academics in UK universities and provide a basis for exclusion as well as inclusion. The contemporary UK university does indeed, from our preliminary data analysis, seem to encompass both of these processes.

Acknowledgements

Many thanks to focus group participants from a number of UK learned societies and our interviewees in universities across the UK. We are grateful to the rest of our project team: Heidi Edmundson (project administrator), Oliver Fulton, Sam Hillyard, Mike Reed and Stephen Watson, and to Cheryl Scott for her tape transcriptions. Thanks also to Peter Scott for his helpful comments when the paper was first presented at Manchester. The views presented here are not necessarily those of the project team as a whole. The project is funded by ESRC grant no. R00237761.

Notes

1. The focus group discussions were held in late 1998 and early 1999 with manager-academics and administrators belonging to a range of UK learned societies. The discussions concentrated on participants' perceptions of what is currently happening to the management of universities. The interviews used were conducted with professional administrators and manager-academics from six pre-1992 and five post-1992 UK universities during 1999. The focus of these interviews was on the careers, backgrounds and biographies of the respondents, and also explored their management practices, personal values and identities.
2. The term 'manager-academic' is used to refer to academic staff who have taken on management roles, whether temporarily or permanently. This avoids the confusion created by the term 'academic manager', which might refer to academics in management roles or to professional administrators who literally 'manage academics'.
3. The data used here are from the first two stages of the project, namely 12 focus groups with learned societies and interviews with manager academics and professional administrators from 11 universities. We have also completed, but not yet analysed, interviews from a further 5 universities. The final stage of the project will use a small number of case studies to look in more detail at how management is embedded in universities.

References

Acker, S. (1996) Doing good and feeling bad: the work of women university teachers, *Cambridge Journal of Education*, 26(3): 401–22.

Acker, S. (1997) Becoming a teacher educator: voices of women academics in Canadian faculties of education, *Teaching and Teacher Education*, 13(1): 65–74.

Alvesson, M. (1993) *Cultural Perspectives on Organizations*. Cambridge: Cambridge University Press.

Becher, T. (1988) Principles and politics: an interpretative framework for university management, in A. Westoby (ed.) *Culture and Power in Educational Organizations*. Milton Keynes: Open University Press.

Becher, T. (1989) *Academic Tribes and Territories*. Milton Keynes: SRHE and Open University Press.

Bensimon, E.M. (1995) Total quality management in the academy: a rebellious reading, *Harvard Educational Review*, 4 (Winter): 593–611.

Brooks, A. (1997) *Academic Women*. Buckingham: SRHE and Open University Press.

Brown, M. (1999) Time to take us seriously, *Guardian Higher*, pp. ii–iii.

Clark, B. (1998) *Creating Entrepreneurial Universities: Organizational Pathways of Transformation*. New York: Elsevier.

Clarke, J. and Newman, J. (1997) *The Managerial State: Power, Politics and Ideology in the Remaking of Social Welfare*. London: Sage.

Davies, C. (1992) Gender, history and management style in nursing; towards a theoretical synthesis, in M. Savage and A. Witz (eds) *Gender and Bureaucracy*. Oxford: Blackwell.

Davies, C. (1995) *Gender and the Professional Predicament in Nursing*. Buckingham: Open University Press.

Dearlove, J. (1997) The academic labour process: from collegiality and professionalism to managerialism and proleterianisation? *Higher Education Review*, 30(1): 56–75.

Deem, R. (1998) New managerialism in higher education: the management of performances and cultures in universities, *International Studies in the Sociology of Education*, 8(1): 47–70.

Deem, R. (1999) Power and resistance in the academy: the case of women academic managers, in S. Whitehead and R. Moodley (eds) *Transforming Managers: Engendering Change in the Public Sector*, pp. 68–83. London, Falmer Press.

Deem, R. and Ozga, J. (1997) Women managing for diversity in a post-modern world, in C. Marshal (ed.) *Feminist Critical Policy Analysis: a perspective from post-secondary education*, pp. 25–40. London and New York, Falmer.

Deem, R. and Ozga, J. (2000) Transforming post compulsory education? Femocrats at work in the academy, *Women's Studies International Forum*, 13(2): 153–66.

Delamont, S., Parry, O. and Atkinson, P. (1997) Critical mass and pedagogic continuity: studies in academic habitus, *British Journal of Sociology of Education*, 18(4): 533–49.

Eggins, H. (ed.) (1997) *Women as Leaders and Managers in Higher Education*. Buckingham: SRHE and Open University Press.

Evetts, J. (1990) *Women in Primary Teaching*. London: Unwin Hyman.

Evetts, J. (1994) *Becoming a Secondary Headteacher*. London: Cassell.

Exworthy, M. and Halford, S. (eds) (1998) *Professionals and the New Managerialism in the Public Sector*. Buckingham: Open University Press.

Farnham, D. and Jones, J. (1998) Who are the vice-chancellors? An analysis of their professional and social backgrounds 1990–1997, *Higher Education Review*, 30(3): 42–58.

Ferlie, E., Ashburner, L., Fitzgerald, L. and Pettigrew, A. (1996) *The New Public Management in Action*. Oxford: Oxford University Press.

Halford, S., Savage, M. and Witz, A. (1997) *Gender, Careers and Organisation*. London: Macmillan.

Henkel, M. (2000) *Academic Identities and Policy Change in Higher Education*. London: Jessica Kingsley.

Independent Review of Higher Education, Pay and Conditions (1999) The Bett Report. London: HMSO.

Itzin, C. and Newman, J. (eds) (1995) *Gender, Culture and Organisational Change*. London: Routledge.

Lave, J. and Wenger, E. (1991) *Situated Learning: Legitimate Peripheral Participation*. New York: Cambridge University Press.

Leonard, P. (1998) Gendering change? Management, masculinity and the dynamics of incorporation, *Gender and Education*, 10(1): 71–84.

Leonard, P. and Malina, D. (1994) Caught between two worlds – mothers as academics, in S. Davies, C. Lubelska and J. Quinn (eds) *Changing the Subject: Women in Higher Education*, pp. 29–41. London: Taylor & Francis.

Marshall, C. (1994) Politics of denial: gender and race issues in administration, in C. Marshall (ed.) *The New Politics of Race and Gender*, pp. 168–74. London: Falmer Press.

McAuley, J., Duberly, J. and Cohen, L. (1999) The meaning professionals give to management and strategy, *Human Relations*, 53(1): 87–116.

McNay, I. (1995) From the collegial academy to corporate enterprise: the changing cultures of universities, in T. Schuller (ed.) *The Changing University*, pp. 105–15. Buckingham: SRHE and Open University Press.

Morley, L. (1999) *Organising Feminisms: The Micropolitics of the Academy,*. London: Macmillan.

Morley, L. and Walsh, V. (eds) (1995) *Feminist Academics: Creative Agents for Change.* London: Taylor & Francis.

Pan, D. (1998) The crisis of the humanities and the end of the university, *Telos*, 111 (Spring): 69–106.

Parry, O., Atkinson, P. and Delamont, S. (1994) Disciplinary identities and doctoral work, in R.G. Burgess (ed.) *Postgraduate Education and Training in the Social Sciences*, pp.34–52. London: Jessica Kingsley.

Pratt, J. (1990) Corporatism, competition and collegiality, *Reflections*, 2(2): 33–7.

Pratt, J. (1997) *The Polytechnic Experiment 1965–1992.* Buckingham: SRHE and Open University Press.

Pratt, J. (1999) Policy and policymaking in the unification of higher education, *Journal of Education Policy*, 14(3): 257–69.

Prichard, C. (1996) University management: is it men's work?, in D. Collinson and J. Hearn (eds) *Men as Managers; Managers as Men: Critical Perspectives on Men, Masculinities and Managements.* London: Sage.

Prichard, C. and Deem, R. (1999) Wo-managing further education: gender and the construction of the manager in the corporate colleges of England, *Gender and Education*, 11(3): 323–42.

Shattock, M. (1999) Governance and management in universities: the way we live now, *Journal of Education Policy*, 14(3): 271–82.

Slaughter, S. and Leslie, G. (1997) *Academic Capitalism.* Baltimore: Johns Hopkins University Press.

Tanton, M. (ed.) (1994) *Women in Management: A Developing Presence.* London: Routledge.

Trow, M. (1993) *Managerialism and the Academic Profession: The Case of England.* Stockholm: Council for Studies of Higher Education.

Wajcman, J. (1998) *Managing Like a Man.* Cambridge: Polity Press.

Warren, R.C. (1994) The collegiate ideal and the organization of the new universities, *Reflections*, 6(2): 39–55.

Whitehead, S. (1996) Men/managers and the shifting discourses of post-compulsory education, *Research in Post-Compulsory Education*, 1(2): 151–68.

Whitehead, S. (1998) Disrupted selves: resistance and identity work in the managerial area, *Gender and Education*, 10(2): 199–216.

Yeatman, A. (1990) *Bureaucrats, Technocrats, Femocrats.* Sydney: Allen & Unwin.

7

Territorial Disputes: The Impact of Quality Assurance on Relationships between Academic and Institutional Values

John Brennan and Tarla Shah

Disciplinary defined communities in higher education institutions are coming under pressure from a variety of forces: expansion, modularity, managerialism and so on. The classic 'loosely coupled' forms of academic organization are giving way to more 'tightly linked' forms, at least in some places. Institutional mission statements compete with disciplinary values to direct academic work.

In this chapter we explore the role of systems of external quality assurance in altering the relationship between basic units and their parent institutions. We draw upon the results of a number of studies of the impact of quality assurance which we have undertaken over the past few years.

Writing on entrepreneurial universities, Burton Clark explored some of the tensions which can exist between what he terms 'enterprise' (whole institution) values and 'disciplinary' (departmental/faculty) values (Clark 1998). Many authors have emphasized the importance in academic organization of basic units and academic disciplines (see, for example, Becher 1989; Becher and Kogan 1992; Biglan 1973). The high degrees of autonomy enjoyed by basic units, the loyalties of their members to values shared with extra-institutional groups comprising the membership of similar basic units elsewhere, nationally and internationally, have been defining features of academic life. Even when the boundaries of basic units are not defined by traditional academic disciplines, their claims on the loyalties of their members nevertheless remain strong, for example derived from an area of professional practice or an interdisciplinary theme rather than from institutional 'mission'.

In his earlier influential work on the higher education system, Clark noted that 'how an academic system distributes and legitimises power may well be its most important aspect' (Clark 1983: 108). Legitimized power constitutes authority and, as Clark and many others have noted, authority in higher education has been predominantly discipline-based, albeit taking a variety of forms (for example collegial, professional). As Becher and Kogan note: 'basic units are especially important in the determination of professional values and in the maintenance and development of particular areas of academic expertise' (1992: 87). Although other forms of authority have existed, for example in institutional senates and ministries of higher education, their capacity to influence the daily activities of academic life have been relatively limited. To be sure, there have been differences in this respect between countries and between institutions within countries, but the general patterns have been clear: the loyalties of academic staff have been principally towards norms and values derived from disciplinary and professional communities outside of the particular institution in which they work.

Changes in recent years have threatened the autonomy of basic units. In particular, institution-wide policies have come to invade their 'territories'. The source of many of these policies has been increased competition between institutions, coupled with a rise in consumerism. Through mission statements, institutions have sought to consolidate or increase their market share. Modularization of the curriculum has shifted power over questions of who learns what and when decisively away from academic staff to students. In the process, academic departments have had to fit their teaching into standardized curriculum frameworks imposed by the institution. Many departments do not even have their 'own' students any more, becoming 'providers' of courses and teachers to institutionally owned programmes and students. New organizational units – the 'modular office', the 'educational development unit' – take over functions previously exercised at departmental level. In addition, managerial imperatives to increase institutional efficiency – with reduced levels of funding – and to achieve greater accountability have opened up academic departments to much greater scrutiny than had been common hitherto (Scott 1995).

External quality assurance

National arrangements for the assurance of quality in higher education have been introduced in most European countries during the 1990s (Vroeijenstijn 1995; Brennan *et al.* 1997a; Brennan and Shah 2000). To what extent does the work of national quality assurance agencies constitute a further attack on the autonomy and values of higher education's basic units? Or are there circumstances under which they might provide a form of defence of disciplinary academic values against institutional and external pressures?

On the face of it, there is a certain amount of support for the latter position. After all, peer review lies at the heart of the quality assurance methodologies of most new national agencies. Several authors (for example, Finch 1997) have claimed that the use of academic peers in quality assurance processes has been the crucial element in ensuring the authority and legitimacy of these processes. We have argued elsewhere, however, that this is not necessarily so, distinguishing between the 'moral' authority possessed by the peer group assessors by virtue of their shared membership and values of disciplinary communities and the 'bureaucratic' authority derived from the powers of the sponsoring quality agency (Brennan *et al.* 1994). The more the agency seeks to impose its norms and values through checklists, guidelines and training, the more it is likely that moral authority will be replaced by bureaucratic authority. In cases where quality assurance focuses upon the 'audit' of institutional quality procedures rather than upon the direct 'assessment' of the work of subjects and departments, external quality assurance appears even more likely to help to promote institutional over basic unit values.

Quality assurance and its impact upon the life of higher education institutions

The values of quality assurance

In our study of the effects of quality assurance systems in OECD member countries (Brennan and Shah 2000), we identified four value systems underpinning the work of different quality assurance agencies. These are summarized in Table 7.1.

Table 7.1 Values of quality

Type	Characteristics
Type One 'academic'	Subject focus – knowledge and curricula Professorial authority Quality values vary across institution
Type Two 'managerial'	Institutional focus – policies and procedures Managerial authority Quality values invariant across institution
Type Three 'pedagogical'	People focus – skills and competences Staff developers/educationalist influence Quality values invariant across institution
Type Four 'employment focus'	Output focus – graduate standards/learning outcomes Employment/professional authority Quality values both variant and invariant across institution

Type One is based on traditional academic values. Its focus is upon the subject field and its criteria of quality stem from the characteristics of the subject. It is normally associated with strong professorial authority and control and on academic hierarchy based on quite rigid socialization and induction processes into the subject community. Conceptions of quality are based on subject affiliation and vary across the institution which has limited scope to define and assess quality. In external assessment systems, the 'invisible college' of subject peers may by-pass the authority of the institution and speak directly to its members. Type One academic values remain significant ones in quality assessment although they are under challenge.

Type Two values we term 'managerial'. These are associated with an institutional focus of assessment, with a concern about procedures and structures, with an assumption that quality can be produced by 'good management'. Quality characteristics are thus regarded as invariant across the whole institution. Total quality management (TQM) provides an underlying ideological justification for this approach. Potentially it is an approach that can apply equally to all the functions and activities of a higher education institution, not just the academic. Indeed, there may be relatively little direct focus on academic matters in this approach.

Type Three quality values we have described as 'pedagogical'. The focus here is on people, on their teaching skills and classroom practice. It is strongly associated with training and staff development. Like Type Two, quality characteristics are regarded as invariant across the institution. There is little emphasis on the content of education but a lot of emphasis on its delivery.

Type Four values are employment-focused. Emphasis is placed on graduate output characteristics, on standards and learning outcomes. It is an approach which takes account of 'customer' requirements where the customers are frequently regarded as the employers of graduates. It tends to take into account both subject-specific and core characteristics of high-quality education. Thus, quality comprises some features which are invariant across the institution and some which vary according to subject.

In practice, conceptions of quality in particular countries and institutions can entail several types of values. But the balance among the types differs. Where new arrangements for quality assessment challenge existing values, they are more likely to be resisted. Whether resistance is likely to be successful will depend on questions of power.

If we consider the recent history of quality assurance in the UK, we can trace a movement away from a reliance upon Type One values (with Type Four values important in certain fields) to a system designed to embrace all four value systems, but with an enormous strengthening of Types Two and Three. Thus, external examining and the CNAA course-based validation process, focused on the basic unit level, were concerned with knowledge and curricula primarily in disciplinary groupings and tended to strengthen the authority of such groupings against institutional intrusions. Accreditation by a professional body embraced a somewhat different set of values, but these were also derived externally from the institution and potentially (and often in reality) constituted a source of resistance to the imposition of institutional values.

The twin processes of institutional audit and subject-based teaching quality assessment in the UK embraced managerial and pedagogical values respectively. Although the focus of the latter was at basic unit level, its use of classroom observation and concern about pedagogical skills embraced values that could be applied across the whole institution. Thus, in our own study of the effects of teaching quality assessment upon higher education institutions in England, several respondents referred to an 'HEFCE conception of quality'[1] which was frequently seen as being in opposition to the discipline-based approaches and distinctiveness of the subject department (Brennan *et al.* 1997b). The process of academic (later quality) audit was concerned almost exclusively with institutional procedures of quality management and placed great emphasis on institutional-level responsibilities and how they were discharged. Although neither of these quality assurance procedures prevented variations in practice at basic unit level, they certainly opened up basic units to institutional scrutiny against values and criteria which were not discipline-based.

The latest system of quality assurance to be introduced in the UK appears to be an attempt to support all four value systems (something for everyone?). Subject benchmarking, although largely consumerist in content, appears likely to reinforce Type One 'academic' values. The continuation of audit and teaching quality assessment (albeit under different names) marks a maintenance of 'managerial' (Type Two) and 'pedagogical' (Type Three) values. The former seem likely to be strengthened by provision for a variation to external quality assurance arrangements according to the degree of confidence that could be placed upon the *institution's own* quality arrangements. The latter seem likely to be strengthened immeasurably by the introduction of a system of higher education teacher accreditation through the new Institute of Learning and Teaching. Finally, Type Four 'employment' values will be strengthened by the attention to be given to graduate standards and learning outcomes.

Although the new British arrangements seem to be designed to strengthen accountability requirements for quality across the board and in terms of all possible dimensions, it should be remembered that three out of the four value systems described above are *not* derived from disciplinary cultures, so that the net effect seems likely to be a strengthening of institutional-level authority.

The methods of quality assurance

We have already touched upon the methods used in quality assurance. Here we attempt to summarize the main variations to be found and consider

Table 7.2   Methods of quality assurance

Focus of assessment	Authority for the assessment	
	External	Internal
Institution	A	C
Basic unit	B	D

their likely consequences for the balance between institutional and disciplinary values.

Quality assurance methods can be regarded as differing along two dimensions:

• whether the focus is upon a whole institution or one of its basic units
• whether the assessment is carried out on behalf of an external or an internal authority.

The two dimensions are summarized in Table 7.2.

As we have already noted, the external assessment of whole institutions (quadrant A) generally constitutes an examination of institutional quality procedures (however defined) and the effectiveness of their operation. There are exceptions – the French Comité National d'Evaluation evaluates institutions in terms of the quality of the work of their constituent departments – but the overall effect is likely to be a strengthening of institutional at the expense of disciplinary values.

In principle, the opposite should be true of quadrant B. Peer review of the work of basic units is invariably a subject-based affair but, as we have already noted, the extent to which the focus of such assessment is defined in subject terms or agency terms varies considerably. In the case of many continental European quality systems, the former seems to be true with subject committees of leading scholars in the discipline undertaking nationwide reviews on behalf of the agency. The same was largely true of the old CNAA system in the UK. More recent manifestations of quadrant B assessment in the UK appear to have been driven by agency-set criteria which take little account of disciplinary contexts and cultures. Assessors are trained and follow guidelines which reflect agency thinking rather than particularistic disciplinary concerns.

Quality assurance methods in quadrants C and D inevitably reflect institutional agendas and concerns, frequently based upon and reinforced by the requirements of the national quality agency.[2] However, disciplinary concerns can still be an important part of such methods. Institutions may deliberately seek to strengthen disciplinary norms and values by bringing in external experts to participate in internal review. Self-evaluation at basic unit level is likely to reflect largely internalistic disciplinary values if left alone by the institution. The collective nature of self-evaluation activities can indeed lead to a strengthening of these values.

We must conclude, therefore, that, in principle, quality assurance is largely neutral in its effects on the balance between disciplinary and institutional values. It depends on how it is done and the values of those in charge of the assessment process.

The impact of quality assurance

In our previous work (Brennan and Shah 2000), we have discussed three mechanisms of impact of quality assurance on institutions: through rewards and incentives, through changing institutional structures and processes, through changing institutional cultures. The relationship between these mechanisms of impact and various methods of quality assurance is summarized in Table 7.3.

We argue that the impacts of quality assurance mark a potential shift towards institutional values ('enterprise' in Clark's terms (Clark 1998)) away from academic disciplinary values, but a shift which remains contested within basic units.

The rewards and incentives that arise from quality assurance – rewards of reputation and influence probably being more important than funding – can operate at all institutional levels, depending on the quality assurance methodology. Most commonly, they affect basic units and in so doing expose their inner lives to external and institutional scrutiny. Basic units are rarely able to set the terms and criteria of external assessments and must frequently 'translate' their work into a new vocabulary of assessment. As we have already noted, even though peer review is generally the key element of the assessment process, criteria of quality are rarely derived from disciplinary norms and values. Moreover, where rewards are involved, institutional leaderships take greater interest in the assessment process and are likely to

Table 7.3   How quality assurance (QA) makes an impact on institutions

	Method	*Timescale*	*Actor*
Rewards	External QA reports	Financial – immediate Reputational – long-term	External groups Institutional management
Structures/policies	Institutional QA External reports	Dependent on institutional decision-making	Institutional management
Cultures	Self-evaluation Institutional QA	Long-term	Basic units Individual staff

impose their own additional requirements – procedures to be followed, information to be obtained, criteria to be used – upon basic units. Self-evaluations will need to be 'approved' by the institution before being sent off to the external agency. The existence of 'rewards' in the assessment process produces a competitive relationship between basic units on grounds not of their own choosing. Too important to ignore, basic units must pursue excellence in terms of the values of the assessment process, not in terms of the values of the discipline itself.

Both our own and other studies of the impact of external quality assessment indicate the growth of institution-wide policies and procedures for the assurance of quality (Brennan *et al.* 1997b; Brennan and Shah 2000). Institutional codes of practice are *imposed* over the activities of basic units. Many institutions set up their own internal review procedures, both as a dress rehearsal for external assessment and as a useful management tool within the institution. The work of cross-institutional groupings – educational development units, administrative support units – is enhanced. Above all, internal systems of accountability are set up to mirror and to satisfy the procedures and climate of external accountability. As Trow has remarked, these relationships of accountability stand in place of traditional relationships based on trust (Trow 1994).

As far as changing culture is concerned, the picture is more confused. Despite some talk in the literature about the growth of a quality or evaluation culture (Neave 1988), our own and other studies (see, for example, Bauer and Henkel 1998) suggest some considerable resistance at basic unit level to institutional and agency conceptions of quality. Certainly some individual academics are energized by new emphases on pedagogy and by their own involvement in peer review assessment processes (see, for example, McDowell and Colling 1997). But disciplinary loyalties run deep, remain the basis of research reputations (sometimes, as in the UK, buttressed substantially by external assessment of research), and remain the defining characteristic of most basic unit 'territories'. What, however, may be changing are the relationships within basic units. More appraisal, more accountability reduce the freedoms of individual academic staff members and enhance the powers of academic leaders and managers. Personal objectives and research plans linked to unit objectives and institutional mission are the norm in many institutions, even if reality frequently fails to match up to the statements so made. In other words, quality assurance and associated management processes are taking more time and are imposing new demands on staff without displacing disciplinary values as the prime defining and motivating factor within basic units.

Employing the group/grid model for analysing culture developed by Douglas and applied to higher education by Maassen (Douglas 1982; Maassen 1996), we can conclude that the group dimension (defining the territorial boundaries) remains quite strong but the grid dimension (of relationships within the group) is being significantly altered by quality assurance processes linked to new forms of management within higher education. In so far as the group dimension is being threatened, this is being driven by changes in forms of knowledge and research (Gibbons *et al.* 1994) as well as by developments of interdisciplinary teaching and modular forms of curriculum organization (Scott 1995; Watson 1997). It does not appear to be a direct consequence of quality assurance.

Conclusion

We conclude that, at the basic unit level, disciplinary norms and values prevail despite the increasing requirements being made on units for accountability through quality assurance measures from both outside and within the institutions. Units comply with the requirements from both internal and external quality assurance procedures but their allegiances remain with their subject/disciplinary grouping. Whilst resistant to many elements of the new quality assurance procedures, certain things may be included and adopted. Thus a positive outcome of quality assurance that is welcomed by staff in many institutions is the increased focus of attention to teaching/pedagogy (Brennan *et al.* 1997b). Basic units select what they want out of quality assurance and 'comply' with the rest. As yet, there appears to be little sign that basic units are yielding their 'territories' to the values and imperatives of either institutional or external requirements.

Notes

1. Teaching quality assessment was carried out by the Higher Education Funding Council for England (HEFCE).
2. The Quality Assurance Agency for Higher Education in the UK issues national codes of practice which individual institutions are expected to follow in their own internal arrangements.

References

Bauer, M. and Henkel, M. (1998) Academic responses to quality reforms in higher education, in M. Henkel and B. Little (eds) *Changing Relationships between Higher Education and the State*. London: Jessica Kingsley.

Becher, T. (1989) *Academic Tribes and Territories: Intellectual Enquiry and the Cultures of Disciplines*. Milton Keynes: SRHE and Open University Press.

Becher, T. and Kogan, M. (1992) *Process and Structure in Higher Education*, 2nd edn. London: Routledge.

Biglan, A. (1973) The characteristics of subject matter in different academic areas and relationships between subject matter characteristics and the structure and output of university departments, *Journal of Applied Psychology*, 57(3): 195–213.

Brennan, J., El-Khawas, E. and Shah, T. (1994) *Peer Review and the Assessment of Higher Education Quality: An International Perspective*. London: QSC/OU.

Brennan, J., deVries, P. and Williams, R. (eds) (1997a) *Standards and Quality in Higher Education.* London: Jessica Kingsley.

Brennan, J., Frederiks, M. and Shah, T. (1997b) *Improving the Quality of Education: The Impact of Quality Assessment on Institutions.* London: HEFCE/QSC.

Brennan, J. and Shah, T. (2000) *Managing Quality in Higher Education: An International Perspective on Institutional Assessment and Change.* Buckingham: SRHE and Open University Press.

Clark, B.R. (1983) *The Higher Education System: Academic Organization in Cross-national Perspective.* Berkeley: University of California Press.

Clark, B.R. (1998) *Creating Entrepreneurial Universities: Organizational Pathways of Transformation.* Oxford: Pergamon.

Douglas, M. (1982) *In the Active Voice.* London: Routledge & Kegan Paul.

Finch, J. (1997) Power, legitimacy and academic standards, in J. Brennan, P. de Vries and R. Williams (eds) *Standards and Quality in Higher Education.* London: Jessica Kingsley.

Gibbons, M., Limoges, C., Nowotny, H., Schwartzman, S., Scott, P. and Trow, M. (1994) *The New Production of Knowledge.* London: Sage.

Maassen, P. (1996) *Governmental Steering and the Academic Culture: The Intangibility of the Human Factor in Dutch and German Universities.* Maarsen: De Tijdstroom.

McDowell, L. and Colling, C. (1997) *Improving the Quality of Education: The Impacts of Subject Specialist Assessor Experience.* Bristol: HEFCE/University of Northumbria at Newcastle.

Neave, G. (1988) On the cultivation of quality, efficiency and enterprise: an overview of recent trends in higher education in western Europe, 1986–88, *European Journal of Education,* 23(1/2): 7–23.

Scott, P. (1995) *The Meanings of Mass Higher Education.* Buckingham: SRHE and Open University Press.

Trow, M. (1994) *Academic Reviews and the Culture of Excellence.* Stockholm: Council for Studies of Higher Education.

Vroeijenstijn, A.I. (1995) *Improvement and Accountability: Navigating between Scylla and Charybdis.* London: Jessica Kingsley.

Watson, D. (1997) Quality, standards and institutional reciprocity, in J. Brennan, P. de Vries and R. Williams (eds), *Standards and Quality in Higher Education.* London: Jessica Kingsley.

8

From Ivory Tower to Knowledge Factory? The Impact of Industry Links on Academics in a Chinese University and a British University

Su-Ann Oh

Confidentiality and citizenship in the academic community

Confidentiality in research and consultancy has become a significant part of university/industry research. Two forms of confidentiality have been identified: contractual confidentiality and secrecy. For contractual confidentiality, more often than not the power of veto lies with industrial partners, as most academics understand companies' need for confidentiality agreements and are wary of breaching them. However, the control that industrial partners have over academics does not always hold; academics who have 'marketable' and unique research interests are less likely to accept confidentiality agreements.

In this chapter, secrecy refers to academics withholding information from other academics regarding their consulting activities. Some British academics have objected to this on the grounds of the ideological nature of research, proposing that there should be transparency. Academics seem to object more to secrecy than to confidentiality agreements.

British and Chinese academics seem to have different concerns. Chinese academics are more concerned with the proportion of basic and applied research than with secrecy. Their ideological concerns differ from those of their British counterparts. However, both sets of academics are concerned with the structure and hierarchy of the academic profession, in which certain members are more able to benefit from confidential agreements because they are in a position which allows them the luxury of forgoing opportunities for publishing and promotion.

Background to the study

The focus of this chapter is academics' views of confidentiality in links with industry. This approach was chosen because research on university collaboration with industry has tended to be on structural issues such as link formation and management (Reed 1991; Ding 1994) and models of collaboration (Li *et al.* 1990; McKinsey and Co. 1991). These studies have tended to point to the differences in orientation of academics and industrial partners and the need for further co-operation and 're-orientation' of attitudes. It is hoped that an approach based on the actors' perspective will put these issues into the context of the academics' world, with reference, where relevant, to students, postdoctoral researchers and other groups in the university.

The data used here are part of a study on how academics view and address issues such as teaching and research, ethical conflicts and power struggles while collaborating with industry. This is drawn from interviews with about forty academics and administrators in a Chinese university (1998), and another forty at a British university (1999), supplemented by observational studies and document reviews. The questions in the interviews were directed mainly at understanding the attitudes and ideas of respondents regarding collaboration with industry. Academics from science (chemistry, biology, mathematics), engineering (mechanical, chemical) and management departments were interviewed. The names of respondents have been replaced by codes (P1 etc.). These have been placed in parentheses after quotes and views attributed to them. The Chinese university is referred to as C University and the British one as B University.

Using Becker's concept of perspectives (Becker *et al.* 1961), the viewpoints of academics involved in industry links, as well as those who are not, are presented and interpreted in this chapter. 'Perspectives' describe:

> a co-ordinated set of ideas and actions a person uses in dealing with some problematic situation . . . a person's ordinary way of thinking and feeling about and acting in such a situation. These thoughts and actions are co-ordinated in the sense that the actions flow reasonably, from the actor's perspective, from the ideas contained in the perspective. Similarly, the ideas can be seen by an observer to be one of the possible sets of ideas which might come from the underlying rationale for the person's actions and are seen by the actor as providing a justification for acting as he does.
>
> (Becker *et al.* 1961: 34)

In this sense, it is important to take into account a certain type of group 'perspective' or 'culture':

> we understand that we must see the process of socialization as at least potentially a collective experience, undergone by a group acting in and

interpreting their world together, rather than as individuals; and we realize that we cannot ignore the influence of extraorganizational social groups.

(Becker 1995: 77)

This concept is a theoretical tool which we can use to understand and gain insights into the community of academics working in the two universities studied. This will enable us to explore their views on links with industry, not as a phenomenon on its own, but in relation to their work as academics.

Universities' links with industry

B and C Universities were chosen because of similarities in their subject base. Both universities have had a considerable number of links with industry in the past and have set up administrative divisions to deal with such work.

There are, of course, differences in the culture of universities in China and Britain, which pertain to the political, economic and social contexts of each country. In China, there is a parallel party structure in the administration of universities; and issues such as academic freedom and autonomy are subject to strong political control (Lo 1991; Agelasto 1995). The absolute funding figures of both institutions are vastly different. In 1997, C University received Rmb 176,944,000 (£11,796,266) in funding from the state, and Rmb 500,931,000 (£33,395,400) from other sources (research, services, and so on). B University received £60,719,000 from the Higher Education Funding Council and £149,293,000 from other sources in the year 1996/97. B University is registered as a charity, and this limits the nature of its entrepreneurial activities – it is unable to charge profits on research activities. C University does not have this status but is unable to charge overheads or profits because companies would then be less likely to pay for research. Its workshops and university-owned enterprises are exempt from tax.

The differences in context are relevant here because they serve to highlight contrasts between the two institutions, and bring into relief issues which might have been overlooked in only one setting. Nevertheless, the data show a considerable similarity between the two institutions. Thus when the organizations are stripped down to a certain structural level, the incentive and power systems cause individuals to respond in consistent and similar ways. This is another reason to compare universities in China and Britain. As Clifford Geertz wrote, we 'need to look for systematic relationships among diverse phenomena, not for substantive identities among similar ones' (1973: 44).

For the purpose of clarity, a loose definition of industrial links in both universities is set out here, although it has been observed that academics have different definitions of this. External organizations includes 'society enterprises' (*shehui qiye* = private enterprises) and state-owned enterprises (*guoyin qiye*), foreign companies (Ford Motor Company) and provinces in China. In Britain, this kind of work is also called 'work for outside bodies' and includes charities. There are also 'in-house' enterprises. At C University, this is a unique feature: the university has both spin-off companies and companies of a non-academic nature, such as factories, workshops and photocopying companies run by departments. At B University, in-house enterprises consist solely of spin-off (or spinout) companies. Both institutions have established science parks, or a science area in the case of C University (Ding 1994) although this is much more established at B University. Consultancy work refers to one-off, short-term projects, such as testing and evaluation. Contract research on the other hand, refers to investigation of phenomena done on a contractual basis.

Confidentiality

In his research, Bridgstock (1996) found that in general the ethos of public safety did not seem to be compromised by possible industrial interests. However, in two areas some traditional academic values appeared to be undermined by industrial considerations. University scientists were presented with possible situations on cards and asked to say what they would do when confronted with the dilemma and why. In the areas concerning whether to disseminate research findings to other researchers conducting similar research or to students and in lectures, many said they would not. 'The adoption of a commercial approach indicated that, once they had fulfilled their contractual obligation, there was nothing further for them to do' (p. 280). Bridgstock concludes that the 'destruction of traditional university research and teaching is one possible consequence of increasing contact with industry. The traditional involvement of academics with issues of public interest is another such' (p. 283).

Bridgstock's study gives us an idea of what academics say they would do when presented with such situations. However, it would be more interesting to know why they would behave thus. Similarly, Ding (1994) looked at university and industry collaboration in several universities in England and China and found that confidentiality agreements were accepted but tolerated only grudgingly. It is believed that academics are having to deal with both ideological and organizational factors which influence their decisions regarding confidential industrial work; this is explored below.

Two forms of confidentiality have been identified. The first refers to confidentiality clauses required by companies sponsoring university research (commercial confidentiality). These are often contractual and involve intellectual property rights and patents. The other form pertains to the secrecy surrounding academics' consulting activities. Both types require confidentiality, but there is more secrecy involved in the latter.

Commercial confidentiality

Commercial firms want to protect their interests by keeping research confidential. Not all firms have this requirement, and some organizations are non-profit-making ones. The agreements can range from vetting of papers before publishing to absolute secrecy. In Britain, projects funded by the research councils, funded jointly by research councils and industry, and basic research projects do not normally require confidentiality agreements. Confidentiality is usually required only when companies want to keep specific technology from rivals. The level of confidentiality required usually increases with the specificity and application of the research. Examples include pharmaceutical drugs, and research sponsored by the Ministry of Defence.

In China, confidentiality agreements are also required by sponsoring companies. Since most of these companies are small and medium-sized enterprises, they often sponsor specific applied research. Thus, they are more likely than their larger British counterparts to require confidentiality and full rights to the intellectual property.

B University's policy on confidentiality agreements is to try to keep them to a minimum. However, it has a flexible arrangement where the company can have full confidentiality and intellectual property rights if it pays high overheads. Many academics understood that companies would want confidentiality since they were paying for the research. However, they did seem to have thought about the consequences if they breached the agreement. One group of academics believed that this could be resolved at the beginning as long as everyone knew what they were participating in. In an interview with a senior academic, the researcher noted:

> He says industry and academics can compromise regarding confidentiality, as long as it's all set out before. Lots of confidentiality for defence as well as biomedical school. They have a lot of contracts with industry, gave example of genetically modified foods. Industry could actually shut down project if the results are unfavourable and no one must know what they're doing.
>
> (Lecturer in biology, P8, 61: 106)

Another group seemed quite philosophical about it, and rather resigned to the difficulties of breaching confidentiality agreements. This academic seemed cautious about not offending the company involved and not being sued:

> *Interviewer:* But what would happen if you had some results which would affect in a big way, public . . . public health, and you weren't allowed to publish? What would you do?
>
> *R:* Well, um, I guess it's part of the agreement, you couldn't. Very very cautious . . . probably try to persuade these people in power that, the idea about keeping confidential was not a good one. At the end of

the day, if you have an agreement, and you break it, you end up being sued for no end of damages. Um, fortunately, I haven't actually been in that situation . . . relatively mild, didn't really affect public interest at all. It only affected people doing actual research. You would hope not to get involved with a situation where you were having to work for somebody you knew . . . public interest. You try not to get yourself into that situation.

(Lecturer in biology, P10, 445: 494)

At the Chinese university, academics took it as given that the work would involve confidentiality. It is possible that this stems from the fact that more of C University's work is applied research than is the case at B University. Although there are no figures to support this, the collaborative research that academics described seemed more developmental than at B University.

Many of the respondents at B University were quite wary of upsetting companies.

But certainly, if you found, if you were working on something, and you discovered something that you found was actually not mainstream to what the company was doing, then it would belong to . . . even if the company will . . . But I suppose if that discovery was actually potentially detrimental to the company, then it would be ours to do what we want with it. I wouldn't go around upsetting companies deliberately. . . .

(Lecturer in biochemistry, P12, 446: 459)

This academic feels somehow that the balance of power over the dissemination of his research is weighted towards the side of the sponsoring company. Why? First, many industrial projects are funded by a core number of companies only. Second, for many research council projects, there is a requirement that companies are involved, as in the LINK and CASE programmes. In order to obtain industrial research funding, they need to maintain good relations. Third, industrial research has become a significant part of research in science and especially engineering, so that upsetting a company could affect one's funding. Finally, academics and company researchers make up a whole community of people who attend the same conferences and read similar technical literature.

Academics who are not involved in confidential research may also be bound indirectly by the agreement. This academic was very adamant about not talking about the confidential project being undertaken by the professor of his group:

that would be a misuse of trust that I've been given. So I am not doing it because I don't want to. I haven't signed any agreement that I am . . . bound to.

(Lecturer in chemistry P19, 90: 161)

On the other hand, some academics are totally against confidentiality arrangements. This academic was particularly vehement:

Oh, . . . companies wanted exclusivity for their money, and . . . finally they don't get it. Because you see, I strictly refuse a few things. I strictly refuse that a student or a postdoc signs a confidentiality agreement. If they have to sign a confidentiality agreement, then they should hire that person inside their organization. If the student is here, then he should not sign a confidentiality agreement, he should be able to talk to whoever comes into the lab. He should be able to talk to his fellow students, you know. And a confidentiality agreement would stop students from talking together . . . And the other thing, I would refuse money if there is no chance to publish results, because as I mentioned, my first goal is to educate people and publication is part of the education, and the second goal is to do . . . research, and that . . . again needs publication. So that's why I cannot take any collaboration if they wanted confidentiality, and if they wanted no publications at all. And some companies want exclusivity and so forth for not much money, and I mean, they can go elsewhere. They may find it, maybe other universities, maybe in other countries, fine, I cannot help it.

(Professor of chemistry, P20, 625: 696)

It would seem that the difference in opinion between this academic and the ones before stems from two factors. This academic has substantial industrial funding and runs a centre which is unique in Britain. Thus, industrial companies' demand for the expertise in the centre is great. However, the other academics do not have this edge over the companies who might be interested in their work. Their specialities are not unique. Therefore, they are more likely to feel that they have less power over whether to refuse confidential agreements.

Secrecy surrounding consultancy work

The other type of confidentiality refers to the secrecy engendered by staff members' consultancy work. This work is sometimes kept secret because it is not totally approved of within the department, although it is officially sanctioned in both universities. (Academics at B University are permitted a certain number of days to undertake such work.)

At B University, two members of staff in engineering departments A and B showed their displeasure at the way certain professors used their research groups to conduct consultancy work. They felt that professors exploit their industrial contacts for personal benefit, either in the form of income or through the acquisition of other resources within the department. As one academic explained:

And I think that it is the governing and dominant problem in engin-eering departments at the moment, is that the professors can make very large amounts of money, there are certainly a few millionaires in this department based on that. But in doing so, they corrupt the atmosphere of the department because there is so much secrecy in that they know they are bending the rules too far, so they prevent anybody telling the rest of the department what they're doing or what their research is about. There's a nice description of university research that it should be like watching fish swimming in a goldfish bowl in the sense that it should be possible for anybody to come here and peer in and see what's going on. One of our difficulties with that kind of behaviour is that it becomes the opposite, we become highly secretive.

(Lecturer in engineering, P57)

There are several issues embedded in this quote, one of which is the perception of how an academic department should be run, as well as how academic research should be carried out. The ideological basis of this comment is that the activities of an academic department should be open to scrutiny, and that this is being threatened by these professors' activities.

At C University, the points that were emphasized had less to do with the ideological basis of academic research than with the unfairness arising from differing abilities of academics to set up consultancy links. First, the notion that academics were secretly working on consulting projects was not raised. It is possible that this is due to the different work habits of Chinese academics. Many Chinese academics do not have their own office at their department; it is normal that they work from home. In this sense, it is less likely that their colleagues know what they are doing concerning consultancy work. Second, there might be more of an acceptance that academics keep their activities undisclosed, based on historical and political reasons. Following from this, it is likely that the notion of academic transparency is not as prevalent or held in as great esteem as it is in the West.

The above shows how historical and political contexts have had an influence on the perspectives of academics regarding the ideological basis of academic work. However, the internal reward structures of both C and B Universities have produced similar conflicts regarding links with industry.

As the lecturer in engineering department A explained, he felt that the professors are able to pursue what is considered unethical behaviour because there is no other way of controlling them.

The only control they [professors] have over me is my promotion. So that's the only mechanism which is used to force me to behave in the right way. And that's why the professors are such a problem, that there is no further control over them but they are the people with decision-making authority.

(Lecturer in engineering, P57)

When two professors within the same department were asked about their consulting activities, they did not mention these ethical dilemmas. One professor was quick to point out that the money from consultancy work carried out by his group went into a 'slush' fund and not into his personal income. This fund is used for travel expenses and buying equipment, and occasionally used to fund 'speculative' work (P56). He confirmed that the income from consultancy is large enough to do this. Another professor said that this extra income is used occasionally to fund the first year of doctoral students, and he tries to obtain funding from other sources for the subsequent years (P60).

There seems to be a difference in opinion between the lecturers and the professors. The former group believes that the professors are affecting the nature of university research ideologically as well as manipulating the formal power structure for their own purposes. Professors, on the other hand, believe that they are indirectly contributing to basic research through their consultancy activities. It is possible to account for this difference when the group structure of the department is taken into account. Professors do help with equipment acquisition and basic research, but this help is restricted to those in their group. It is believed that they have a vested interest in making their research group successful. Their loyalty is to their group because they work closely with the group members, and have invested time and effort to build them up (P56, P60). Those who are not in these groups are therefore unable to benefit from this extra income.

In the Chinese case, ranking as well as subject speciality create a formal and informal power structure enabling some academics to benefit more from consultancy links than others. In an informal chat with a colleague working at the university, it was noted that:

> There are under-the-table deals, but usually only with older academics. Those in the highest levels. Professors, because they have more to gain financially and less promotion-wise. Younger academics don't usually do this because such research contracts can work against their promotion prospects.
>
> (Personal communication, June 1998)

In the case of subject speciality, those academics involved in specialized subjects have more time to go on work-related trips to set up links for consulancy work. Also, those who are involved only in research are able to do this. In a group interview of three academics in the teaching division:

> [F] said that they needed to change the structure and blamed it on the USSR model that was adopted – the separation of teaching and research. She believes that teaching should not just be in the teaching/research groups [*jiaoyanzu*], but in the whole department. They should change the system and all agreed that the faster this occurred, the better. All nodded heads in agreement and emphasized this.
>
> (Notes from group interview, engineering, P61)

Organizational structure and ideology

The issues that have been raised stem mainly from the organizational structure and academic ideology of these universities. First, the hierarchy of academics and the nature of career progression are considerable factors in conflicts regarding confidentiality and secrecy. In both universities, younger academics are unable to take on the substantial financial contracts that professors can because this would affect their ability to publish academic papers. Academics with less 'marketable' specialisms are in a weaker position with regard to accepting confidentiality agreements.

Second, other groups within the university are also affected by confidentiality agreements. As one academic put it, 'most confidential work is done by postdoctoral researchers, who accept that their work will not be published' (Professor of engineering, P8, 61: 106). Doctoral students are also affected if they sign confidentiality agreements (group interview). This academic at B University describes his experience:

> *R:* You mean during my PhD studies . . . Well, I could not publish anything that was directly related to the objectives of the company.
> *Interviewer:* And after the PhD?
> *R:* After the PhD, the project was basically patented and after it's patented then, you can publish . . .
> *Interviewer:* How long . . . ?
> *R:* Um, . . . after my PhD around 2 years. Writing . . .
> *Interviewer:* I assume it is quite important for you to publish. (Oh yeah, of course, of course.) Does that affect you in any way?
> *R:* Well, it didn't affect my particular case, I don't know about other . . . but, of course it is a bit worrying at the beginning because if you want publication, on the other hand, references are as important.
> *Interviewer:* References from whom?
> *R:* From whoever you have worked with, . . . write your references . . . But of course most people appreciate that if you have been working on a confidential project, that you are not immediately allowed to publish. And most people will appreciate that fact, so, well, that's my experience anyway. So, no, it hasn't really affected me much or my progress.
> (Lecturer in chemistry, P19, 193: 241)

Furthermore, academics who are not directly involved in confidential research are also bound by loyalty not to speak about the research.

While academics have considered the consequences of confidentiality agreements and secrecy, it seems that they are more concerned with the nature of research being affected by secrecy. Moreover, secrecy in B University seems to generate a tighter-knit group structure based on research interests, but possibly to the detriment of a wider community ethos at departmental level.

'Ivory tower' or 'knowledge factory'?

The idea of research being open to all is inconsistent with confidentiality agreements. From the interviews, it seems that academics at B University do believe that transparency is a crucial part of the institution of academic research. However, this ideal is not compatible with the nature of industrial research funding. As a result, many academics have had to act in ways which are inconsistent with their beliefs. The nature of career incentives and rewards has also incorporated indirect aspects of success in links with industry.

In this sense, the nature of the academic profession in science and engineering has started to incorporate links with industry, indirectly. In Britain, this has manifested itself in the increasing need to show industrial collaboration before one can obtain research council projects in programmes such as LINK and CASE. In China, academics believe that it is easier to obtain research funding through companies than through government funding for which there is intense competition. More academics are turning to industry even though this might affect their ability to publish. The income from the collaboration might compensate them more than being promoted.

Are these two universities 'ivory towers' or 'knowledge factories'? It seems that the core debate revolving around research and knowledge being accessible to all is considered important in Britain. In China, the debate is centred around the belief that the university should be a centre of new and novel research. With regard to collaborative work with industry, these two notions do sometimes conflict with the way in which academics can become successful in their career. While academics do have beliefs regarding the transparent nature of university research, the reward structures they face are slowly being influenced by external forces, which are beyond their control. In turn, they can affect the principles of openness and collegiality that are key factors in the traditional academic community, and the challenge of exposure to colleagues that helps to ensure standards in that community. Is freedom of information more important than privacy for the citizens in this community?

References

Agelasto, M. (1995) Politics in charge: politically correct higher education in the People's Republic of China, *Education Journal*, 23(2): 51–69.

Becker, H.S. (1995) The self and adult socialization, reprinted in R.B. Burgess (ed.) *Howard Becker on Education*. Buckingham: Open University Press (first published 1968).

Becker, H.S., Geer, B., Strauss, A.L. and Hughes, E.C. (1961) *Boys in White: Student Culture in Medical School*. Chicago: University of Chicago Press.

Bridgstock, M. (1996) Ethics at the interface: academic scientists' views of ethical and unethical behaviour involving industrial links, *Industry and Higher Education*, 10(5): 275–84.

Ding, D. (1994) Higher education and external links: a comparative study of Britain and China. Unpublished PhD thesis, University of Lancaster.

Geertz, C. (1973) *The Interpretation of Cultures: Selected Essays*. London: Hutchinson.

Li, Z., Sun, Y. and Wu, Y. (1990) Points regarding the strengthening of the colleges' and universities' horizontal networking with the economic and scientific–technological circles: inspirations and lessons learned from the Investigative survey of the horizontal networking recently launched by Qinghua University, *Chinese Education: A Journal of Translations*, 23(4): 39–51.

Lo, L.N. (1991) State patronage of intellectuals in Chinese higher education, *Comparative Education Review*, 35(4): 691–720.

McKinsey and Co. (1991) An interactive model of business/academia, *Industry and Higher Education*, 5(4): 223–7.

Reed, J.V. (1991) Exploitation of research in UK universities, *Industry and Higher Education*, 5(4): 229–32.

Part 2

The Hinterland Community

9

The Role of Higher Education for Adults in their Communities: Nurturing Social Capital

Julia Preece

This chapter presents action research findings on two contemporary issues: the concern to create an accessible and relevant higher education for adults and considerations of the wider benefits of learning amongst people who do not contribute directly to the nation's wealth creation through waged work. It argues that for some adult learners, their contribution to global arenas must stem from individuals having a strong sense of self. This means education must recognize different and multiple identities, communities and cultures and contribute to strengthening of social wealth from the grass roots. The distinctive qualities of higher education have an essential role in regenerating communities. Participation is dependent in part on how minorities and their identities are allowed space in the new globalization discourses for integration and convergence. A future kind of higher education must be flexible and accommodating if it is to be accessible to the many.

The research focused on how higher education might nurture a sense of self in communities – contributing to social regeneration but at the same time making the HE experience 'higher'. The contents are selective and derive from a project which aimed to deinstitutionalize higher education for a number of minority social groups. The focus of discussion here is on the interface between mass higher education and today's emerging society, which is 'global in its reach, market driven, socially and culturally fragmented, individualistic in its moral commitments and powered by the technology of an information revolution' (Williamson 1998: 116). The context is higher education's increasing need to diversify in order to survive and therefore to be seen to be more valuable to a wider public than hitherto. The first part briefly discusses this context in relation to recent debates on globalization and social capital, particularly where they impinge on current debates on the purpose of higher education. The second part introduces the framework of the research project's widening participation programme and discusses one participant group of women learners in relation to the theory.

Globalization and local communities

There is insufficient space here to explore all the complexities of globalization, but some significant features impact directly on how higher education positions itself in the future, as well as how local communities interface with the process of globalization. In summary this process reflects the constriction of time and space brought about by the rise of the 'network society' (Castells 1996). The effects of globalization include the recasting of national communication boundaries, increasing mobility, transnational companies operating independently of national policy, and the formation of new kinds of compressed time/space boundaries, relationships and hierarchies. These impact on countries, regions and communities (Robertson 1992; Waters 1995; Held *et al.* 1999). Waters (1995: 35) conceptualizes the idea of a global village, where distant events can have their effect on different locations across the world. In other words there is 'an intensified consciousness of the world as a whole' (Robertson 1992: 8). There is a sense that people are moving from a sense of *Gemeinschaft* (community) to one of *Gesellschaft* (society) (Robertson 1992: 11).

However, as globalization increases, people and their communities may refragment to retain their distinctiveness (Friedman 1994; Bauman 1998). In other words, people want to shape what they consume in order to fit their own identity and needs. Higher education is geographically positioned within local communities but also interfaces, through a ripple effect, with its region and the wider world. It needs to be sensitive to the economic and political consequences of attending to all these. It is also an investment resource, now competing with other players, for the development of society's future human capital (the skills and knowledge required for wealth creation).

Although a connection is not overtly made in public policy, interest is now also growing in the potential link between continuous learning and people's involvement in local activities – of a citizenship or social nature. This coincides with the globalization theorists' perceptions of people's inclinations to regroup in the face of global reordering of society. There is therefore a renewed focus, in the UK at least, on the 'local'. UK policies are now seeking the 'non-economic benefits' of learning, particularly in local communities (Department for Education and Employment 1999). This might be measured in terms of increased citizenship activity or some kind of reduction of demands on welfare agencies as a result of increasing participation in learning. The broad umbrella term for these accumulated reserves and their potential to generate such activity is 'social capital'.

Social capital

It is not at all clear that a future capitalist society will consist of full, paid employment for all. Giddens (1998) and Beck (1998) suggest that this uncertainty needs to be accommodated in the way we view employment.

They argue for a discourse which recognizes active participation in voluntary organizations as an alternative to employment: 'Those who commit
themselves to voluntary organisations are no longer available for the labour
market and in this sense are no longer "unemployed". They are active
citizens' (Beck 1998: 63). By giving grass roots social action a credible
visibility, such activity gains 'economic organisational and political weight'
(Beck: 63–4). Giddens makes the economic connection with this kind of
activity by calling it 'social capital':

> Conventional poverty programmes need to be replaced with commun-
> ity focused programmes which permit more democratic participation
> as well as being more effective. Community building emphasises sup-
> port networks, self-help and the cultivation of social capital as a means
> to generate economic renewal in low income neighbourhoods.
>
> (Giddens 1998: 110)

Both claim that there is a need to recognize the reality of the non-waged
employed as a sector of society. Giddens calls this the 'beyond the work
society' (p. 105).

Wann (1995) suggests that social capital is a form of social wealth which
provides what the market cannot. In this sense, then, social capital has economic value. It is a non-market-driven means of exchanging 'knowledge
skills and power' (p. 103). It is a means of creating the ability to manage
unpredictability by relying on spontaneous responses to local situations
generated through an ethos of self-help. There is a danger, however, that
normative definitions of citizenship and social capital will themselves exclude recognition of certain activities, particularly the less public activities
of women (see, for example, Lister (1997) and Ackers (1998) on women
and citizenship). Brah (1996) points out that the fragmentation of communities and simple assertions of difference do not guarantee a place for
the minority voice since difference also represents a vehicle for legitimation
of dominance (p. 90). Marginalized differences may need a helping hand
to redress the imbalance of power.

Educational achievement and participation amongst some groups is therefore a complex business, made more complex by the issue of personal and
social identity.

Identity

Woodward (1997) points to the paradoxically increased tensions for identity, brought about by a transient and converging world. Nation states and
communities are breaking up and re-forming, and economic and cultural
life is becoming increasingly transnationalized. This has resulted in changing consumption and production patterns with a convergence of consumer
identities and new identity positions or resistances to convergence. This,
and resultant migration, has impacted on the pluralization of identities and

also helped to create contested identities (p. 16). For those migrants whose ethnic and cultural selves are significantly different from the host society, the word 'diaspora' has been coined. Diaspora represents the experience of identities which are not located in one home and cannot be traced back to one source. Hall (1990: 235) describes diaspora identities as 'those which are constantly producing and reproducing themselves anew, through transformation and difference'. Individuals from diasporic communities find their identities are shaped and located in and by different places. For some there is a tendency to regroup and reassert the identity of the country of origin. Multiple identities constitute our 'subjectivities' – our sense of self in relation to how we perceive that others see us in a particular social context. The conceptualization of these selves is constrained by the discourses available to us at any period in time. The sense of self, however, is a critical influence on individual decisions to participate in education (West 1997; Preece 1999).

As yet, the role of higher education in the wider base of community learning is not part of the government's agenda. For instance, UK higher education is encouraged to widen participation on an institutional 'access' basis (Higher Education Funding Council for England 1999) where input and output of more diverse university students can be measured as a result of direct intervention to recruit certain social groups. There is evidence to suggest, however, that higher education in the community can also contribute to the 'capacity building' of those communities at a local level (McNair 1999). Whilst such arguments have long been documented (Fordham *et al.* 1979; Ward and Taylor 1986), the McNair report and other literature (for example, Trotman and Pudner 1998) place such activity in its modern context: of endemic unemployment, pluralism, demand for qualifications and increasingly stark divisions between the well-off and poor. The community project described here undertook a learning model which engaged with both human and social capital goals. It has openly provided an off-campus service but in doing so has appropriated current discourses for an adult and a distinctively 'higher' education.

The purposes of higher education

It is important for the higher education sector as a whole to be able to identify its distinctiveness in an increasingly competitive market. Barnett identifies some 'essential conditions' which make higher education 'higher' than other forms of learning. He claims that education:

> Only becomes higher when the student is able to form an independent evaluation of what he or she has learned . . . to put it into some kind of perspective . . . see its strengths but also its limitations.
>
> (Barnett 1990: 165)

In other words, the university student is encouraged to make independent judgements about knowledge, based on informed understanding from several perspectives. To place this experience in the higher domain of learning, Barnett identifies some of the essential conditions which achieve that goal as a 'deep' understanding and 'radical critique' of knowledge claims. These include the ability to conduct some form of independent inquiry and present that critique in open dialogue, alongside critical self-reflection (p. 203). The essence of learning at this level is the application of a 'critical spirit'. Other writers support the notion that universities have historically been about the creation, testing and transmission of knowledge (McNair 1997a, b) and that graduate skills include the ability to analyse, synthesize, reason critically and think creatively (Knapper and Cropley 1995).

Most of these visions precede recently generalized conceptions of a 'learning age' but are in the wake of a drive for the now common catchphrase of 'lifelong learning' (National Committee of Inquiry into Higher Education 1997; Department for Education and Employment 1998). Both these terms suffer from a fuzziness of definition, though an economically grounded discourse for lifelong learning is beginning to be shared by politicians. At the more liberal end, Knapper and Cropley (1995) suggest that lifelong learning is about bridging the gap between education and the outside world, linking education with everyday life needs. Higher education's new role, they suggest, is to 'equip people with lifelong learning skills' (p. 45). They define these as the ability to set personal objectives, apply knowledge, evaluate personal learning, skills of information retrieval and interpretation of materials from different subject areas.

Alongside these images of higher learning run two related debates. The new university must be seen within a perspective of continuous learning throughout the adult lifespan, which will have to deal with a more heterogeneous student body than previously. Some argue that universities need a stronger regional role and accountability to the public (Williamson and Coffield 1997).

A new higher education

There is no shortage of suggestions about how this broader purpose of higher education might function, ranging from the conceptual to the organizational. Barnett's (1997a) vision is broadly conceptual. He suggests that if higher education's role is to problematize knowledge then the new institution should build an environment which emphasizes critical learning, rather than teaching. He states that we need a new concept of higher education, one 'which starts from the understanding that the world is unknowable in any serious sense' (p. 43). The new metabilities to be developed will combine the traditional academic domain of critical thinking with a greater exploration of the role of self (reflexivity) in dialogue, and application of practical understanding (praxis) – resulting in 'metacritique' (p. 42). He proposes a synthesis of critique between knowledge, the self and the world: 'Critical being means investing something of yourself' (Barnett 1997b: 172).

Watson and Taylor (1998) identify some key organizational features which they see as inevitable for the higher education system. The new system is envisaged to be inclined to a stronger focus on work experience, to have a wider, more interdisciplinary curriculum base, probably devised more collaboratively and in closer interaction with the wider community, and to be part of a credit-rated system with flexible teaching which leans more towards facilitation of learning rather than a traditionally top-down imposed teaching style. To this, Williamson and Coffield (1997) add that universities will need more emphasis on collaboration with outside agencies in devising and accrediting learning.

McNair (1997b, 1998) more specifically focuses on the relationship between the student experience and knowledge – which links back to Barnett's notion of critical being. McNair suggests that adult learners will bring their own experience and understanding to the traditional curriculum. This will mean a stronger student engagement in knowledge creation, challenging its traditional monopoly over the validity of knowledge (McNair 1997b). The result will be a curriculum which inevitably relates more closely to the outside world and meets many needs, with outcomes which are achievement-led, rather than leading to the traditional three-year degree programme. In elaboration of a NIACE (1993) policy vision for adult students, McNair also, more openly than most, suggests that 'higher' education may not necessarily happen solely within the university. It will be a kind of education which is made explicit by its style rather than content or place of learning. He cites three key features which will underpin the new higher education system. First, a skills-based core curriculum would consist of analysis, critical thinking, problem-solving and communication. Second, there would also be a strong learner support and guidance system. A learner-, rather than subject-centred curriculum would require tutoring and guidance as its central function, rather than to act as bolt-on services. Third, a credit framework which enables maximum flexibility and mobility of students would be modular and have clearly defined learning goals.

From these proposals it is possible to conceive of some form of generic approach for a new kind of higher education. There will be an emphasis on the learner experience, combining theory, reflection and practice and a closer dialogue with the outside world, including the public at large. Higher education, if it is to survive, has not only to become more relevant to the paymasters, but also to identify and make transparent its distinctive contribution to knowledge creation. What is missing from these visions is a reality perspective of how the macro will translate into the micro. How can higher education enter into a dialogue with its community at its most local level? How do we engage with a credit system which focuses on achievement and works with open entry from a disenfranchised adult public? How can 'higher' translate into 'mass', so that it includes the most excluded? How do we develop a lifelong learning curriculum for those who are already outside the labour market? How does higher education begin to deconstruct its traditional knowledge bases to engage with experiential knowledge? What is the interface between these experiences and social capital? The research project as a whole offered one way of addressing these questions. The focus here is on the interface between a higher education experience and social capital. To contextualize that focus it is necessary to give a brief overview of the programme as a whole.

The programme context

The project was funded largely through a Higher Education Funding Council widening participation grant between 1995 and 1999. Its function was to provide short courses in community locations. Its model of practice was typical of many community development initiatives. A core of academic staff liaised with community organizations, sometimes meditated through local leaders who had a social, cultural or other identification with their local communities. The range of participants included:

- women from minority ethnic communities
- members of self-help and statutory disability groups
- young people working with the youth service
- older adults attending their local Age Concern centre
- 'women returners'
- people who were long-term unemployed.

Courses were developed at all times of the year, using a university approved Access level 'skills' credit framework which consisted of four modules under the headings of 'personal awareness', 'study', 'enterprise' and 'investigation' (research). Content was negotiated with the community organization and its syllabus constructed to fit one of the skills frameworks. The syllabus topic was designed and decided largely by the community organization itself and based on that community's interests or needs for the (usually) preordained student group. Each tailor-made course was then quality assured through one of the credit frameworks. As the frameworks had already been validated by the university system, each course could be approved on its merit through a departmental committee set up specifically for the programme's ongoing course development process. The consultation and approval procedures were thereby equally divided between community groups and leaders (the community stakeholders) and academic staff (the university stakeholders).

The provision thus addressed many aspects of the organizational proposals outlined by McNair and by Watson and Taylor. As such, they were accessible, relevant and delivered at a time, pace and place to suit the learners, supplemented by additional learner support where necessary (such as crèche, transport, sign language, guidance and interpreters). Quality assurance included attention to negotiation procedures, study support, content relevance to the social or cultural perspectives of the learners and their community affiliations as well as subject coherence and ability to meet academic criteria such as critical analysis. A further distinctive quality assurance feature of the courses was the attention paid to tutor background and their sociocultural affinity to the learners.

In almost all cases the learners were on low income or claiming benefit. They had left school at the earliest opportunity with no or very few qualifications. They would be considered by some, including themselves, as least likely to benefit from higher education.

Briefly, the research methodology for investigating the impact of this project was an action research approach supplemented by case study analysis of three learner cohorts. The findings explore how individual experiences interfaced with their higher education learning, demonstrated through themes of social capital and identity. To protect anonymity all places and names are fictitious. It is the stories of one group which are discussed in the remainder of this chapter.

The case study

Of the ten female students interviewed in this example, two were white and English, one was a Kenyan Muslim Asian and the remaining seven were all Muslims who were born in Pakistan but came to England at varying stages during their childhoods. All spent their final school years in England but few had qualifications beyond 'O' level or GCSE. Their ages ranged from 25 to 50 in 1997. All had children. Most attended a series of study skills courses on various topics relating to Islam.

Although coming from different backgrounds, the women shared two constraints: a general sense that education was not 'pushed' at home, for them at least, and a more recent struggle of ongoing commitments towards young children throughout their participation in the courses. The Asian women's stories of when they arrived in England and all the women's stories of their school experience and family relationships contributed to how people saw themselves. These self-images were mediated by their particular interchange with surrounding discourses about education and women as well as how they responded to those discourses.

The women's learning choices, for example, might appear to the outsider as incoherent in terms of career development, but the women interpreted learning value in the context of their multiple roles within the family and community. So Shaheen's course consisted of crèche, computer and sewing courses plus an Islamic focus within the studies skills module:

> The crèche course, . . . I wanted it for career value, but also to understand my children's needs and what they needed at certain times of their life. 'Cause I think even though motherhood might come to you naturally you don't always know what they need at which stage. The Islam course, to gain further knowledge about different areas of Islam. Studies skills course because at school they never teach you how to

do essays, you know, it doesn't come naturally. Now I feel that I can do essays better. And my sewing course because I can sew but I've forgotten everything about sewing . . . My computer course because computers is something that you need today.

Learning value for Shaheen intersected with her unwaged role as a mother, as a bearer of cultural values (Yuval Davis 1992), as a resource for future ambitions and a recognition of the modern technological world in which she lived. The concept of employability was multifaceted, with an eye on many fronts. Shaheen's own efforts to reskill herself with human capital were already interfacing with her multiple relationships with globalization and social capital.

In other ways the global concept of Islam became a focus for broadening local perspectives and raising awareness about wider global debates which affected local issues. Arifa, after attending the Islamic studies courses, was keen to draw on this knowledge for the benefit of other women: 'I want to write on the plight of women. I don't know, something Islamically and yet also in society today for women.' In this way she was capitalizing on old, but global, knowledge to maximize its value in the modern, local context. Giddens (1991) calls this making sense of the past in the present.

Many of the women were trapped in a set of discourses which produced a gendered social status which might at first appear passive. In spite of this they often showed signs of an active mutuality which gave them an opportunity to trust each other and to reciprocate as well as validate their activities separately from the men. If higher education was to play a role in nurturing critical reflexivity it would have to do so from within those boundaries, both geographically and socially. The community higher education activities would therefore 'mingle' with whatever else was on offer.

Social capital

The focal point for almost everything that the women belonged to was the community centre where the playgroup, higher education and other adult classes were held. Here they formed friendships, exchanged information, tried out new activities and built up support networks for themselves. Amy, for instance, said: 'Through the toddler group, I met Angie [playgroup leader] and then found out about the classes.' If the women did not obtain their information direct from attending the community centre then they would do so from links via people who did. Such people usually held some known position of authority for the women: 'I used to see sister Shameen [college and community centre outreach worker] going to school and she's a governor at school, so I used to talk to her and she gave me some information about the courses' (Aisha).

The mutuality of needs would spill over and intersect with all the centre's activities, as Arifa commented when discussing one of the higher education courses: 'And we might have sorted a few problems out, you know each others' problems by just talking, 'cause you've got different views.' Social capital is understood as an arena for generating trust, establishing expectations, and in creating and enforcing norms (Coleman 1994). For the Muslim women this meant interfacing with their wider family and community, building on their own sense of agency derived from the shared social experiences of being a Muslim: 'It has affected my life, I've changed myself and I'm now applying it [Islam] to myself . . . my children . . . my husband, to the family members . . . so everything is just changing' (Arifa).

In this sense their experiences of the higher education courses reinforced Wann's (1995) claim that social capital is also a form of social wealth which would help the women to manage the unpredictability of their changing identities and circumstances. The courses tapped into existing social capital but the courses themselves extended that capital so that it could be used as social wealth.

Whilst the women's social capital was a well developed and sophisticated web of networks that were founded on mutuality, their economic value was constrained by the dominant discourses which gave no status to women's networks or activities and which set boundaries on the women's spaces, both geographical and social. In the end these women were constrained by racial and gender relationships which created tensions in different ways for all of them as they struggled to make sense of their own identities in a world of conflicting discourses and meanings. To judge the women's participation and the higher educational outcomes in terms of human capital alone, therefore, would be to deny the role of higher education for a whole community of adults. A connected factor linking the courses to the development of social capital was an issue of the women's personal identity.

Identity

Trust in others stems from the strength of one's subjectivity or sense of self (Giddens 1991). As Giddens points out, however, identity formulation is a reflexive process, mediated by ongoing experiences and changes around each individual and the constant internal aim of trying to make sense of the whole subject within whatever discourses are at their disposal. Brah (1996) talks about multiple axes on which identities are formed and re-formed. For diasporic women, even the notion of 'home' is a contested discourse. Although Surrya had lived in the UK for thirty years, for instance, she still talked of Pakistan as 'home'.

At least three of the women identified themselves as being mentally unwell, either nervous or depressed. The university courses had a significant impact on their psyche. Here was a new context with new discursive arguments which could radically shift how they felt about themselves. Arifa, for instance said: 'I've had bouts of depression before . . . because it was a university course I was really pleased with myself that I did well . . . think it brought something from inside, something that I had that I didn't realize that I had it.'

Aisha is a single parent but nevertheless attended classes at the community centre almost every day, plus a counselling group, in defiance of family opposition, until she received her foundation credit for the course: 'When they heard that I'd passed . . . they were very happy and they kept telling everybody about it . . . they were proud of me.' This apparent contradiction of acceptances within the family was a common story for the women. It was as if their earlier identity had been constructed before they were born by discourses which had been formed without reference to their internal psyche. Once their personal agency was verified by a new authoritative entity (the university) then their position was accepted within that new framework. But each new piece of identity was often hard won, as it broke into the coherence of old, and safer, discourses. For these women, then, the convergence opportunities of a globalized world brought both tensions and resistances, resulting in plural and contested identities. The courses gave the women space to regroup and to build up their own sense of self.

Lessons for wider application

For these women the higher education courses had a multiple role. First and foremost the programme enabled them to broaden existing social capital and reconstruct the power relations which influenced their sense of self and ability to trust others. The women-only classes were a critical feature of this process. Furthermore, they had been able to regroup as women, reassert old Muslim identities but within the context of their diasporic world. The convergence of educational expectations brought about by changing dimensions of time and space meant that the women became more conscious of their denied place as citizens with rights. Participation in the courses helped them to start reshaping their lives. They did this by seeing their minority religious status in its global context and at the same time constructing a local citizenship where they were members of a local, political, social and cultural community.

The expansion of informal education into other forms of support groups or activities is a common feature of community courses (McGivney 1990; Jamieson *et al.* 1998). Education was used in this case almost as a general consumer item which could be shared and passed round friends and relatives – something of value, but not something which had to be claimed for individual gain. Higher education, however, was perhaps something which the women would use as a form of shared power. It was also something which had to be acquired when other forms of support were already in place. Furthermore, it depended on the strength and status of individual identities at any point in time.

These are only a few of the ways in which the women would make connections with the past and reconstruct themselves in the present. Whilst their stories were all different there were some common patterns. Their choices of subject matter and learning environment were connected to their sense of self in relation to their life experiences and the attitudes of those around them. The courses offered opportunity for interfacing with new discourses and new relationships. The university courses were both sources of power-knowledge (Foucault 1980) and a platform from which to look at themselves as critical beings.

Acknowledgements

Whilst the programme engaged with different communities, the first researcher for this group was Raana Bokhari. Her insights into the early stages of the research were invaluable. She left the programme before the research period was completed. I am grateful to the current community tutors and liaison staff Nalini Patel and Helen Ali for their feedback on the content of this paper.

References

Ackers, L. (1998) *Shifting Spaces: Women, Citizenship and Migration within the European Union.* Cambridge: Polity Press.
Barnett, R. (1990) *The Idea of Higher Education.* Buckingham: SRHE and Open University Press.
Barnett, R. (1997a) Beyond competence, in F. Coffield and B. Williamson (eds) *Repositioning Higher Education.* Buckingham: SRHE and Open University Press.
Barnett, R. (1997b) *Higher Education: A Critical Business.* Buckingham: SRHE and Open University Press.
Bauman, Z. (1998) *Globalization.* Cambridge: Polity Press.
Beck, U. (1998) *Democracy without Enemies.* Cambridge: Polity Press.
Brah, A. (1996) *Cartographies of Diaspora: Contesting Identities.* London: Routledge.
Castells, M. (1996) *The Rise of the Network Society.* Oxford: Blackwell.
Coleman, J.S. (1994) *Foundations of Social Theory.* Boston, MA: Harvard University Press.
Department for Education and Employment (1998) *The Learning Age: A Renaissance for a New Britain.* London: The Stationery Office.
Department for Education and Employment (1999) The wider benefits of learning. Invitation to tender for a research centre. London: DfEE.
Fordham, P., Poulton, G. and Randle, L. (1979) *Learning Networks in Adult Education: Non-formal Education on a Housing Estate.* London: Routledge.
Foucault, M. (1980) *Power-knowledge.* London: Harvester Wheatsheaf.
Friedman, J. (1994) *Cultural Identity and Global Process.* London: Sage.
Giddens, A. (1991) *Modernity and Self Identity: Self and Society in the Late Modern Age.* Cambridge: Polity Press.
Giddens, A. (1998) *The Third Way.* Cambridge: Polity Press.
Hall, S. (1990) Cultural identity and diaspora, in Rutherford, J. (ed.) *Identity, Community, Culture, Difference.* London: Lawrence & Wishart.
Higher Education Funding Council for England (1999) Widening participation in higher education: request for initial statements of plans. Invitation to bid for special funds: 1999/2000 to 2001/02, Bristol: HEFCE.

Held, D., McGrew, A., Goldblatt, D. and Perraton, J. (1999) *Global Transformations.* Cambridge: Polity Press.

Jamieson, A., Miller, A. and Stafford, J. (1998) Education in a life course perspective: continuities and discontinuities, *Education and Ageing*, 13(3): 213–28.

Knapper, C. and Cropley, J. (eds) (1995) *Lifelong Learning and Higher Education.* London: Kogan Page.

Lister, R. (1997) *Citizenship: Feminist Perspectives.* Basingstoke: Macmillan.

McGivney, V. (1990) *Education's for Other People.* Leicester: National Institute of Adult Continuing Education.

McNair, S. (1997a) Changing frameworks and qualifications, in F. Coffield and B. Williamson (eds) *Repositioning Higher Education.* Buckingham: SRHE and Open University Press.

McNair, S. (1997b) Is there a crisis? Does it matter? in R. Barnett and A. Griffin (eds) *The End of Knowledge in Higher Education.* London: Cassell.

McNair, S. (1998) The invisible majority: adult learners in English higher education, *Higher Education Quarterly*, 52(2): 167–78.

McNair, S. (1999) *Evaluation of the HEFCE funded non-award bearing continuing education projects 1994–1998.* Bristol: HEFCE.

National Committee of Inquiry into Higher Education (1997) *Higher Education in the Learning Society* (Dearing Report). London: NCIHE.

NIACE (1993) *An Adult Higher Education: A Vision.* Leicester: National Institute of Adult Continuing Education.

Preece, J. (1999) *Using Foucault and Feminist Theories to Explain Why Some Adults are Excluded from British University Adult Education.* Lampeter: Edwin Mellen Press.

Robertson, R. (1992) *Globalisation: Social Theory and Global Culture.* London: Sage.

Trotman, C. and Pudner, H. (1998) What's the point? Questions that matter in a community based curriculum partnership, in J. Preece (ed.) *Beyond the Boundaries: Exploring the Potential of Widening Participation in Higher Education.* Leicester: National Institute of Adult Continuing Education.

Wann, M. (1995) *Building Social Capital.* London: IPPR.

Ward, K. and Taylor, R. (1986) *Adult Education and the Working Class: Education for the Missing Millions.* London: Croom Helm.

Waters, M. (1995) *Globalisation.* London: Routledge.

Watson, D. and Taylor, R. (1998) *Lifelong Learning and the University: A Post Dearing Agenda,* London: Falmer Press.

West, L. (1997) *Beyond Fragments.* London: Taylor & Francis.

Williamson, B. (1998) *Lifeworlds and Learning.* Leicester: National Institute of Adult Continuing Education.

Williamson, B. and Coffield, F. (1997) Repositioning higher education, in F. Coffield and B. Williamson (eds) *Repositioning Higher Education.* Buckingham: SRHE and Open University Press.

Woodward, K. (ed.) (1997) *Identity and Difference.* London: Sage.

Yuval Davis, N. (1992) Fundamentalism, Multiculturalism and Women in Britain, in J. Donald and A. Rattansi (eds) *'Race' Culture and Difference.* London: Sage/ Oxford University Press.

10

Higher Education and Diversity: Regional Learning Infrastructures and Student Progression in the Post-Dearing Era

Judith Watson, David Yeomans, David Smith, Nick Nelson and Patrick Ainley

Diversity has become a watchword in UK higher education policy. It is exemplified in expectations that higher education engages with broad social agendas concerning inclusion, access and opportunity through widening participation, whilst simultaneously contributing to the growth of the knowledge economy through innovation, technology transfer and job creation. Since the creation of a unified higher education system in 1992, higher education policies have sought to encourage institutional diversity through the use of selective funding policies. Selectivity in research funding, for example, is intended to concentrate limited public funding in a smaller number of centres of research excellence. Meanwhile, policy-makers have taken the first steps towards recognizing and rewarding the differential costs of recruiting students from more diverse backgrounds and as an inducement to widen participation still further. The assumption is that the levers of increasingly selective funding policies will produce the desired degree of institutional diversity: the access-oriented universities catering for the social and vocational expectations of mass higher education and the research-led responding to scientific and technological advance, industrial competitiveness and the knowledge economy.

In practice these policies have been complicated by the overlay of market forces and deeper shifts in the relationship between the economy and the science system. Despite selective funding, involvement in research as an activity is spreading into a wider range of university and non-university institutions as the nature and relationship of research to innovation and the knowledge economy change (Gibbons *et al.* 1994). On the one hand, post-1992 institutions have developed important research functions, often in close collaboration with industrial and commercial sponsors, particularly of applied research, while on the other hand, research-led universities have shown no desire to abandon aspirations to be comprehensive institutions. Indeed, as a characteristic of the system, diversity is increasingly accommodated not just through interinstitutional differences in mission, but also through intra-institutional reorganization as universities separate out their scientific (research) and social (teaching) functions. Such responses are exemplified in the creation of semi-independent, often interdisciplinary, research centres (Clark 1995) as well as through engagement with a range of other activities dubbed in one recent analysis as academic capitalism (Slaughter and Leslie 1997).

These responses have to be interpreted in the light of other shifts in the policy environment. Of these the most important is the emergence of the region as a critical space for the engagement between universities and their communities. The context is the (disproportionate) devolution of political powers to Wales, Scotland, Northern Ireland and the English regions. These regions are set in competition with each other for government aid and for inward investment by UK and overseas firms. The idea of competitiveness prioritizes economic growth and requires higher education institutions (HEIs) to engage with regional, or at least subregional, economies in a drive to become 'learning' or 'high-skill' regions. Two forms of engagement are involved. The first involves the close interaction between research and innovation. Finegold (1999), for example, argues that the emergence of high-skill ecosystems – regions characterized by dense clusters of high-technology companies whose interactions generate self-sustaining knowledge creation and growth – depends on close relationships with nearby universities as sources of innovation and university/firm labour mobility.

The second form of engagement between higher education and its regional communities concerns student participation and progression. Although national in scope, policies designed to widen participation and promote lifelong learning depend on a range of regional, subregional and local relationships between higher education and other providers in the post-compulsory system of education and training. Far from being integrated as a tertiary sector, further and higher education remain institutionally separate, despite some some blurring of the boundaries. This distinction was confirmed in the government's White Paper *Learning to Succeed* (Department for Education and Employment 1999) which set out a vision for a new culture of learning spearheaded by the Learning and Skills Council for England (LSC) accompanied by local Learning and Skills Councils (LLSCs). Although the stated intention is 'to drive forwards improvements in standards and bring greater coherence and responsiveness', the reality is that higher education remains outside the framework of the LSC. The result is that further and higher education remain connected primarily through the progression of students making their way from one 'system' into the other. In practice, such progression is facilitated by a wide range of local or subregional collaborative arrangements, partnerships and other important, but ad hoc, arrangements between educational providers. These arrangements substitute for more far-reaching strategic and structural linkages and have become the principal means towards the goals of wider participation and increased achievement within 'lifelong learning'. They are, in effect, the primary means of mobilizing higher education's relationship with local and regional communities.

This chapter explores the nature of this relationship. It focuses on emerging patterns of participation and progression through further and into higher education in three contrasting subregions: the county of East Sussex, including the unitary authority of Brighton and Hove: the city of Leeds; and south east London, defined as the boroughs of Bexley, Greenwich and Lewisham. Evidence is drawn from an ESRC-funded pilot project (R000222781) designed to test the official policy intention of providing various pathways through the 'system' of post-compulsory education and training. It has examined a range of data sources, particularly the Further Education Funding Council's database of individual student records ('the ISR') as a means of testing patterns of participation in post-16 education and training. It has pioneered the 'tracking' of individual students from the ISR records into the higher education data. As well as tracing the movement of students from various backgrounds (not just school) through their learning in further education colleges (FECs), the project has introduced two important additional dimensions for understanding the interaction between further and higher education. First, it has identified students following higher education courses in FECs. Second, it has mapped students' progression from level to level, including from further education into higher education, within the designated subregional areas. With assistance of routines developed by the HEFCE, the project traced the records of individual students as they moved into and through further education, into higher education or out of the formal, publicly funded, education and training system.

The chapter is divided into three sections. The first problematizes higher education's regional role with respect to student participation and progression and sets developments within the concept of the regional learning infrastructure. The second maps the main patterns of participation and progression in the three sample subregions and analyses differences in the actual movement of participants through the learning infrastructures of each area. In the final section we review the evidence and highlight the key policy and structural dilemmas created by the emergence of regionalized expectations of higher education in a learning society

Problematizing the role of higher education in the 'learning' region

The Robbins Report on higher education (1963) and the Dearing Report *Higher Education in the Learning Society* (National Committee of Inquiry into Higher Education 1997) provide the two major landmarks of higher education in the second half of the twentieth century. Of the two, Robbins is still generally regarded as the 'great event' of the last half-century, noted as much for the scale and scope of its mapping of higher education as for its unity with the culture and spirit of its times. By its side, the Dearing Report was much more circumscribed, less bold and adventurous in its scope and its recommendations, but still a benchmark of sorts for late twentieth century higher education. Yet, for all the unfavourable comparisons of Dearing to Robbins, the two reports bear some remarkable similarities. Both took place in a curious atmosphere of fear mixed with unbridled confidence in the capacity of higher education to offer solutions to social and economic change.

For Robbins, 'the crisis immediately ahead', as the report termed it, was the emergency created by the postwar baby boom and the need to expand higher education to keep pace. Looming behind were deeper and more widely held fears about falling behind other nations – the Soviet Union and America in particular, Europe in general – in an age of 'space race' science and technology. Much of the focus of Robbins therefore was on higher education's twin role in ensuring 'the maintenance of our material position in the world' and providing the 'condition for the realisation in the modern age of the ideals of a free and democratic society' (Robbins 1963: 267). More than three decades on from Robbins, the Dearing inquiry was convened in a similar atmosphere of fear. This time it was not fear of nations specifically, but of global competition, skills deficit and unemployment, of lack of economic and technological innovation; of disaffected youth, social exclusion and a breakdown of the kind of civil society that postwar generations had known and (in the folk memory at least) enjoyed. The solutions offered by the two reports to their respective crises were inevitably different in detail and emphasis. However, both shared a common focus on the need to reconfigure the underlying relationship between higher education and society. And both set out packages of recommendations for what was required of higher education.

In Dearing's case these recommendations were spelt out in the form of a new compact between all the stakeholders of higher education. This compact made clear that higher education's future required formal commitments to lifelong learning, the creation of a learning society, social cohesion, research and technological innovation, public accountability and economic regeneration. Like Robbins, however, Dearing was critically short on the arrangements required if higher education was to engage effectively with the requirements of such diversity of mission. On the restructuring of the system, the organizational forms, policies and funding which might be required in order to deliver on diversity, there was little or no real guidance. Although it was assumed that institutions would need to collaborate more in the future, how this might be achieved was again left to the imagination. Nor was it clear which parts of the policy framework might need redesigning in order to facilitate higher education's contribution to the Dearing vision. While diversity has become entrenched (and celebrated) as a principle of both policy and practice, at the start of the new millennium the system is no nearer to understanding how it can or should reconfigure itself to deliver on the expectations of the Dearing compact.

Although Dearing was clear that the momentum of regional development was influencing the agenda of HEIs, making them increasingly alert 'to their local or regional impact and role' (National Committee of Inquiry into Higher Education 1997 Report 9: 154), an important policy gap has now emerged. While policy-makers continue to think in terms of separate higher and further education sectors, achievement of regional agendas for inclusion and learning require a conceptual leap from 'sectors' to something qualitatively different (Newby 1999). In order to reflect this conceptual shift we argue the need to replace sectors with the idea of 'regional learning infrastructures' (RLIs). These infrastructures comprise all the social institutions in a given region that facilitate learning, from pub quiz nights to research universities, and associations of small and medium-sized enterprises (Watson and Jones 1999). In this sense, everywhere has a learning infrastructure. As the 'regional agenda' progresses, it makes increasing sense to think of the whole infrastructure at a regional level. A major element of the RLI is the publicly funded education and training system. It is not the whole of the RLI, and the crucial questions are not just how it connects with other institutions that facilitate learning (for example, education and the workplace, education and the community) but how the still conceptually separate higher education 'sector' relates to the infrastructure.

Reconceptualizing thinking about further and higher education away from sectors towards regional (or at least subregional) learning infrastructures raises important questions about the ways in which participants experience, and navigate their way through, the system. Arguably, the core of the problem is to be found in the continued policy reliance on an increasingly flawed 'pathways' metaphor as a description of the ways in which students and system interrelate. As Dwyer and Wyn (1998) have argued in the Australian context, the 'pathways' metaphor assumes a model of 'linear transitions from school via further study and then into the world of work and an independent adult way of life' (p. 293). Post-Dearing, a similar imagery of linear pathways survives in the British policy model. But how realistic is it to think in these terms in a diverse and massified system which is increasingly shaped and constructed according to a complex range of local, subregional and regional influences? To shed light on this question we turn to evidence from our research into subregional patterns of participation and progression through and between the further and higher education systems.

Mapping patterns of participation and progression

Our analysis of progression starts from a database of individual student records (the ISR), supplied to us by the Further Education Funding Council

(FEFC), whose contribution we gratefully acknowledge. The ISR consists of four datasets for each student: the student dataset (personal information); the qualification aims dataset (information about study); the qualifications on entry dataset (a record of each qualification held before beginning study during that academic year); and the module dataset (supplementing the qualification aims dataset for each qualification that is modular). Our database contains all records for further education students aged under 25 in 1995/96 studying in colleges located in each of our case study areas in 1995/96 and/or 1996/97. It also has students in the same age group and for the same years who are resident in one of our three areas but studying at a college outside their home area. Apart from student names, we hold all fields supplied by colleges to the FEFC in the student dataset, qualification aims dataset, and qualifications on entry dataset. There are also some variables constructed by the FEFC, for example age constructed from date of birth. We do not have the module dataset, which contains little information not already in the qualification aims dataset.

To process these data we have developed a series of coding algorithms that facilitate description of a student's progression aims, in full detail as well as in broad categories. This is a significant innovation, since the ISR is not otherwise a record of the progress of a participant, despite its name. We worked with some main qualification types, corresponding as far as possible with the national qualifications framework, but with sufficient detail to allow us to address key research issues in post-compulsory education. The qualification types retained are based on the highest-level course taken by the student. For example, short courses in computer skills would be ignored if a student was also taking an 'A' level. They are as follows:

- Higher education level (coded 4, 5 or H in the national qualifications database)
- Higher education in conjunction with one or more 'A' levels
- 3 or more 'A' levels (or AS equivalent)
- Access to higher education
- 1 or 2 'A' levels (or AS equivalent) with a vocational course at Level 3 (NVQ equivalent)
- 1 or 2 'A' levels (or AS equivalent) with no vocational course at Level 3
- Vocational course at Level 3
- 4 or more GCSEs
- 1 to 3 GCSEs
- Vocational course at Level 2
- Course at Level 1
- Course without an official level equivalence.

We used ISR data for 1995/96 as our basis and traced through into the following year those students who re-enrolled in the same further education college. We were also assisted by the Higher Education Funding Council for England (HEFCE), who applied the routines that they have developed for tracking the movement of individuals from one HEI to another. HEFCE kindly enabled us to find the higher education record of each further education student who progressed into an HEI.

From these data we have been able to construct progression maps detailing the actual movement of participants through the learning infrastructures of our sample subregions. Three such maps are included here (Figures 10.1–10.3). They compare movement through the system in each of our three case study areas for students aged under 25 at the start of the academic year. We have also used the technique to compare the experiences of different gender and ethnic groups. However, the maps do not capture the whole of the learning infrastructures. Training funded by Training and Enterprise Councils, other public sources, employers and individuals is missing and so are sixth forms in secondary schools. Moreover, we have not yet tried to track movement through different levels of higher education. The method is designed to be capable of extension to the whole system, depending on the availability of data.

The purpose of the maps is to depict the dynamic nature of participation in post-compulsory education and training. The figures are scaled to capture participation at different learning levels and progression from those levels. Courses of study are arranged by the level in the national qualifications framework, from Level 4/5 at the top, down to courses at Level 1 or with no level equivalence. For each level, three arrows are shown, and it is the width of each arrow that indicates the numbers involved. The width of the upward arrow indicates the number passing and progressing to a higher learning level. The width of the turning arrow shows those 'recycled' to repeat the same or a lower level. Finally, the width of the horizontal arrow shows those not re-enrolling in the same college or in an HEI. Taking the three categories together, the total width of the three adjacent arrows is proportional to the number enrolled on and due to take a qualification at that level. Raw numbers of students are shown; while the total populations of the three areas are of roughly the same order, they are not identical. The 1991 total population figures were East Sussex 560,233, Leeds 680,772 and south east London 654,428.

The three maps show contrasting patterns. In East Sussex, we see the effects of both relative social affluence and of the fact that most schools do not have sixth forms. This means that there are many students at Level 3, especially taking full-time courses of three or more 'A' levels. Leeds also has many students taking courses at Level 3, although it is overtaken by the numbers at Level 2. Vocational routes are important at both these levels, and pass rates on them are relatively high. We can see here that there are fewer Leeds residents progressing from further education into higher-education-level study. However, the greatest contrast is within the affluent south. South east London residents in the age group are less likely to be further education students at any level. They are less likely to achieve a qualification and less likely to go on to higher-education-level study either in an FEC or an HEI.

Participation in some kinds of provision is associated with the extent of social deprivation in the student's ward of residence (measured by the 1991

Figure 10.1 Progression map: further education students resident in East Sussex

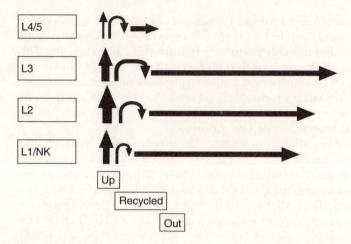

L4/5

L3

L2

L1/NK

Up

Recycled

Out

Figure 10.2 Progression map: further education students resident in Leeds

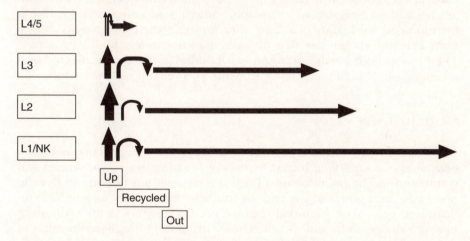

L4/5

L3

L2

L1/NK

Up

Recycled

Out

Figure 10.3 Progression map: further education students resident in south east London

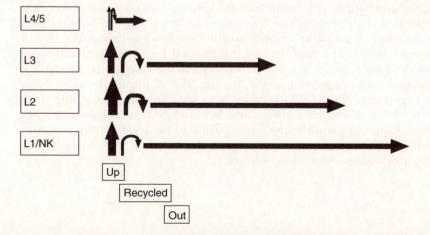

L4/5

L3

L2

L1/NK

Up

Recycled

Out

Department of Employment index). This is particularly true of access to higher education courses, while HE-in-FE and even Level 3 vocational study have a negative association. This point is very important for widening participation. Deprived wards are found in all three of our areas, but with the greatest average levels in south east London. Members of ethnic minorities are heavily concentrated in the most deprived area. Participation and achievement at Level 3 (university entrance) are affected by gender, with men less likely to qualify at this level in each of our areas.

We also used the idea that students are 'on time' in their study if they achieve qualification levels at the usual earliest occasion. By this criterion they should have reached Level 1 at the end of Key Stage 3 (age 13 at the start of academic year), pass a range of good GCSEs in Year 11 (age 15 at the start of the academic year). Then they would be ready to take 'A' level or equivalent at 17 and a sub-degree higher education course like an HND at 19. Few of the students in our sample are 'on time' by these criteria, but nearly twice as many are so in East Sussex as in south east London. Disability is particularly strongly associated with delay in achieving qualifications; so too are sex and race. There are many more students in East Sussex qualifying for university-level study two years after finishing their compulsory education. This reflects the fact that the area does not have school sixth forms. The FECs in both Leeds and south east London are evidently affected by a creaming off of higher-achieving students who remain in their schools.

Conclusions

Our focus in this chapter has been on the relationship between higher education and emerging infrastructures of learning in specific subregional communities. The policy context for this relationship is important. Devolution of political power to the regions coincides with a growing emphasis on 'learning regions' or 'high-skill regions' as critical spaces in the creation of new knowledge, skills and wealth. The contribution of higher education to the agenda was given explicit recognition in the Dearing Report. However, the response of the sector is complicated by a combination of historical and structural obstacles and by a continuing problem at the interface between the higher and further education sectors. Although blurred in terms of how participants actually experience the system of learning, this boundary remains substantially intact in terms of institutions, funding and policy (Smith and Bocock 1999). The problem is compounded by the government's (reflecting Dearing?) lack of insight into the ways in which regional patterns of participation and progression really operate. For example, the main logic of the *Learning to Succeed* White Paper is to separate 16–19 learning from 'adult' learning. At the same time, there is a traditional emphasis in higher education's attempts at widening participation to focus on mature students. Meanwhile, most recent policy announcements focus on expanding higher education in further education colleges.

Our data demonstrate some of the flaws in this thinking. They emphasize that the key to unlocking the policy potential of widening participation in higher education is to be found in understanding patterns of participation and progression in further education. Further education is a site not just of 16–19 education but of mass participation across a wide range of ages, literally from 8 to 80. For many of the students the motivation for participation and achievement is the promise of progression. However, the progression data for our sample subregions reveal two particularly important policy implications.

The first concerns the aim of expanding higher education in further education. From the progression maps we can see that students aiming for higher-education-equivalent qualifications are not a large proportion of the total, only 4.3 per cent. There also seem to be regional differences in the offer. At first sight, Leeds and East Sussex both have relatively well developed HE-in-FE, while south east London lags behind. However, this higher education provision is not all of the expected kind. The institution with the greatest higher education offer is not one of the specialist colleges, nor one of the large general further education colleges, but a sixth form college in East Sussex that entered students for Open College Network units at Levels 4 and 5 alongside full-time 'A' level courses. Take this out of the picture and it is in fact Leeds that has by far the most developed HE-in-FE as it would normally be understood. Leeds has specialist institutions that cross over the FE/HE divide: Leeds College of Music, Leeds College of Art and Design, and Leeds College of Building. However, Park Lane College (a general further education college) has more higher-education-level students than these three specialist institutions put together. The attempt to base expansion of higher education within the further education colleges must recognize that HE-in-FE is developing from a relatively small base, one which depends on patterns of provision developed over decades, and in which the interface with HEIs remains crucial.

The second policy implication concerns movement through the further education system. Our data reveal evidence of a problem of progression to Level 3 and beyond. The problem is not associated primarily with young students attempting 'A' level or its equivalents immediately after school. Nor do we believe that the situation of mature returners is mainly at issue. (Our quantitative analysis did not include the over 25s.) There appear to be particular difficulties for the 19–24 age group, whose learning experiences are already protracted. This accords with recent FEFC findings that this age group is problematical in terms of retention and achievement (Stronach 1999). This age group in further education does not fit neatly into either a 'youth' or an 'adult' model of learning. They are continuing their initial pre-university or pre-work education at an age when most of their contemporaries are either at university or in the labour market. Already behind in their education, they are enrolled in FECs in relatively large numbers, but are less likely to be studying at Level 3 than are their younger fellow-students. Both access to Level 3 and achievement at Level 3 are also associated with locality of residence, gender and ethnicity. We would suggest that the goal of 'widening participation' is insufficient without attention to the progress of participants in disadvantaged groups.

At the heart of these detailed issues in progression lies a deeper concern, however. Dearing was not forthcoming on how the system might develop in structural terms to deal with the relationship between higher education and its learning communities. Practice at the moment is dominated by a plethora of collaborative arrangements put together under the mantra of partnership, yet in the absence of any great strategic vision of how higher education can really be integrated within the learning region. The concerns expressed by the Dearing Report about the quality implications of franchised courses were one manifestation of the bottom-up approach to developing various forms of regional partnerships. Indeed, it is only recently that the HEFCE, after commissioning research and carrying out consultation exercises, issued its own code of practice on indirectly funded higher education in further education colleges (Higher Education Funding Council of England 1999).

This is not to deny the existence of some individual collaborative beacons of light, some of them organized on an explicitly regional basis. However, it would be hard to argue with the view that the policy goals of widening participation and lifelong learning have yet to produce the scale and scope of structural realignment necessary if many learning aims are to become reality. It is difficult to escape the conclusion that the structure of UK higher education and its relationship with further education remain inadequate to the achievement of key elements of the emerging regional learning agenda.

References

Clark, B.R. (1995) *Place of Inquiry: Research and Advanced Education in Modern Universities.* Berkeley, CA: University of California Press.

Department for Education and Employment (1999) *Learning to Succeed: A New Framework for Post-16 Learning.* Nottingham: DfEE.

Dwyer, P. and Wyn, J. (1998) Post-compulsory education policy in Australia and its impact on participant pathways and outcomes in the 1990s, *Journal of Education Policy,* 13(13): 285–300.

Finegold, D. (1999) Creating self-sustaining high-skill ecosystems, *Oxford Review of Economic Policy,* 15(1): 60–81.

Gibbons, M., Limoges, C., Nowotny, H., Schwartzman, S., Scott, P. and Trow, M. (1994) *The New Production of Knowledge: The Dynamics of Science and Research in Contemporary Societies.* London: Sage.

Higher Education Funding Council of England (1999) *Higher Education in Further Education Colleges: Code of Practice on Indirectly Funded Partnerships.* London: HEFCE.

National Committee of Inquiry into Higher Education (1997) *Higher Education in the Learning Society* (Dearing Report). London: NCIHE.

Newby, H. (1999) Higher education in the twenty-first century – some possible futures, *Perspectives: Policy and Practice in Higher Education,* 3(4): 106–13.

Robbins, Lord (1963) *Higher Education: Report of the Committee appointed by the Prime Minister under the Chairmanship of Lord Robbins 1961–63*, Cmnd 2154. London: HMSO.

Slaughter, S. and Leslie, L.L. (1997) *Academic Capitalism: Politics, Policies and the Entrepreneurial University*. Baltimore: Johns Hopkins University Press.

Smith, D. and Bocock, J. (1999) Participation and progression in mass higher education: Policy and the FHE interface, *Journal of Education Policy*, 14(3): 283–99.

Stronach, C. (1999) FEFC's work on widening participation. Paper presented to the Third Annual Further Education Development Agency Conference on Research in Further Education, Cambridge, December.

Watson, J. and Jones, L. (1999) A case study in the Thames gateway. Paper presented to seminar 'Further and Higher Education in Local Economic Development', LEPU, South Bank University, London, 28 April.

11

The European Community: A Case Study of Higher Education Policy Making

Anne Corbett

The European Community's best known initiative for higher education co-operation, the Erasmus programme, is widely taken as a demonstration of the best of the *communautaire*. It is supported by almost every university within a wider Europe. 'It works at every level, symbolically, practically and politically ... It has a huge impact on the young. It costs little to Community funds ... a model for policy areas which aim to reach the public' (Mény 1999).

This chapter explores the question of why the European Community has a policy of higher education within a treaty structure which, until 1992 and the Treaty of Maastricht, made no explicit provision for education/higher education or citizenship.[1] This sounds like a simple question. But the higher education literature on the EU and higher education has produced a variety of answers. The core literature suggests links between European policies and globalization (Field 1998; Beukel 1994), and sees the EU as part of internationalization (Green 1997; van der Wende 1997; Scott 1998), or to compare national systems (Neave 1984; Gellert 1993, 1999; Teichler 1993). The literature which focusses on political explanations of higher education policy-making at Community level suggests an incremental process: that a long experience of co-operation on higher education and/or education in the 1970s overcame the fears of member state governments that any Community co-operation might lead to harmonization and binding common policy; a push from Community jurisprudence was in essence a way of strengthening an existing political preference (de Witte 1989, 1993; van Craeyenest 1989; MacMahon 1995; Bousquet 1999).

My aim in this chapter is to show that explanations of a community higher education policy which suggest that the political process was incremental, are unconvincing. Drawing on a literature that explains policy change over time by focusing on factors that shape the choices of decision makers – such as policy agents, issue or problem definition and the flow of policy ideas (Kingdon 1984; Barzelay 2000) – I examine policy formation in higher education in the Community in the period from 1971 up to the decision stage of the Erasmus programme in 1987. The empirical data are drawn from Community institution sources, notably the collected *European Educational Policy Statements* published by the Council of the European Communities (1988), the monthly *Bulletin of the European Communities* published by the Commission, and the *Official Journal* of the European Communities, amplified by interviews with participants in the higher education policy formation process in various stages and in various institutions.

My strategy has been to adopt an explanatory framework, familiar in institutionalist studies, based on John Kingdon's *Agendas, Alternatives and Public Policies* (Kingdon 1984) and to adapt it to European Community institutions. Kingdon's model of policy-making in the pre-decision stage has been widely recognized as appropriate for analysing policy change. Moreover this 'processual' approach provides a conceptualization with which policy players themselves can identify (Barzelay 2000).

The theoretical explanation underlying this approach is that public policy decisions are determined not only by votes, or by initiatives and/or vetoes by heads of state or government, but also by the fact that some subjects and proposals emerge in the first place and others are never seriously considered.

The first part of the chapter demonstrates the difficulty of deducing the political process from the landmark decisions in Community higher education policy in the period 1971 to 1987. The second section analyses the Kingdon model as giving us a handle on the process. The third and fourth sections identify key moments of the policy process in Kingdon terms. Section three focuses on the development of policy ideas, and section four on the nature of the political opportunity the Commission had in 1985 to draft the Erasmus Decision.

Landmark decisions in Community higher education, 1971 to 1987

The Council of Ministers General Secretariat (Council of the European Communities 1988) records ten policy statements directly related to higher education in the period which produced the Erasmus Decision, 1971 to 1987 (Table 11.1). These decisions tell us about outcomes of a political process.

What we learn from these documents can be summarized as follows. On 16 November 1971, the ministers of education of the member states established a venue in which to co-operate. They were not prepared to use the 'hard law' of the Community such as regulations and directives and at this meeting they did not even use the 'soft law' (Wellens and Borschardt 1989) of Community resolutions. Their chosen process was political co-operation between sovereign states as in foreign affairs or intergovernmentalism, as prevails at the Council of Europe and the OECD. The significance of the meeting was that ministers agreed that the time had come to supplement

Table 11.1   Council statements relevant to policy formation in higher education

Year	Statement	Official Journal
1963	Council Decision of 2 April 1963 laying down general principles for implementing a common vocational training policy	OJ 63 20 April 1963
1968	Regulation (EEC) no. 1612/68 of the Council of 15 October 1968 on freedom of movement for workers within the Community (extracts)	OJ L 257 19 October 1968
1971	Resolution of the Ministers for Education meeting within the Council of 16 November 1971 concerning co-operation in the field of education	n/a
1974	Council Resolution of 6 June 1974 on the mutual recognition of diplomas, certificates and other evidence of formal qualifications	OJ C 98 20 August 1974
1974	Resolution of the Council and of the Ministers for Education meeting within the Council of 6 June 1974 concerning co-operation in the field of education	OJ C 98 20 August 1974
1976	Resolution of the Council and of the Ministers for Education meeting within the Council of 9 February 1976 comprising an action programme in the field of education	OJ C 038 19 February 1976
1980	General Report of the Education Committee agreed in substance by the Council and the Ministers for Education meeting within the Council at their session of 27 June 1980	n/a
1983	Conclusions of the Council and Ministers of Education meeting within the Council of 2 June 1983 concerning the promotion of mobility in higher education	n/a
1983	Solemn Declaration on European Union signed by the ten heads of state or government in Stuttgart on 19 June 1983 [extracts]	n/a
1985	Report of the Committee on a People's Europe, approved by the European Council in Milan on 28 and 29 June 1985	n/a
1986	Council Decision of 24 July 1986 adopting the programme on co-operation between universities and enterprises regarding training in the field of technology (Comett) (86/365/EEC)	OJ L 222 8 August 1986
1987	Council Decision of 15 June 1987 adopting the European Community action scheme for the mobility of university students (Erasmus) (87/327/87)	OJ L 166 25 June 1987

n/a not applicable
Source: Council of the European Communities (1988)

the Treaty of Rome 1957, which made no provision for Community competence for education 'as such' (Neave 1984; MacMahon 1995). Before 1971,
higher education had figured on the Community agenda only as 'spillover'
from Community activity in policy domains which were part of the Community's competence under the founding Treaty of Rome. Ministers were
accustomed to legislating in Treaty areas, such as freedom of establishment and freedom of movement (Lenearts 1994). Such activity had led to
a policy interest in such questions as modes of recognition of diplomas, and
the need for vocational training to contain a general education component
(Neave 1984). The review process was to be carried forward by a committee
('a working party') with which the Commission would be associated, to
consider two possible ways forward.

It took two and half years for ministers of education to agree, on 6 June
1974 by a non-binding Community resolution, to rules for co-operation (OJ
C 98 of 20 August 1974). They wanted development by 'progressive stages'.
Harmonization was ruled out. It was the *bête noire* of the British and the
Danish in particular when interpreted as meaning binding directives or
regulations and not wanted by the Commission formed in 1973. The management of policy development was placed in the hands of an education
committee, consisting of representatives of the member states and the
Commission, charged with reporting back to the Council within a year.
Commentators consider the resolution a delicate balancing act between
acceptance of the Community framework ('educational cooperation could
not act as a barrier to the exercise of powers conferred on the Community
institutions' (de Witte 1989: 15)) and national sovereignty (MacMahon 1995).
However, education and training policy was never a reserved and unim-
peachable domain of member state competence (Shaw 1999: 557). As ministers recognized (OJ C 98), 'this cooperation must not hinder the exercise
of the powers conferred in the institutions by the European communities',
as related to treaty processes such as the freedom of movement. On 6 June
1974, following the agreement to the resolution on co-operation, the ministers sat as the Council of Ministers to resolve (OJ C 98 of 20 August 1974)
that procedures for the mutual recognition of diplomas (a Treaty matter)
would be guided by the desire for a flexible and qualitative approach.

After their 1974 resolutions, it took the ministers almost two years to
confirm that they had a proactive stance on education and higher education, indeed a vision, with a 22-point Action Programme in education, 8
points of which were dedicated to higher education. The resolution also
suggested a jurisdictional advance. The process was that of the Council and
ministers of education (OJ C 038 of 19 February 1976) indicating that the
ministers of education had agreed to a formula which henceforward enabled them to deal with Community and intergovernmental business on the
same agenda. Moreover, ministers agreed that the lion's share of the action
should go to Community institutions, meaning, in effect, the Commission.
Working with the Council's Education Committee, the Commission would
set up pilot projects on university co-operation and academic mobility and

Table 11.2   Treaty of Rome, Articles 128 and 235

128   The Council shall, acting on a proposal from the Commission, and
after consulting the Economic and Social Committee, lay down general
principles for implementing a common vocational training policy, capable
of contributing to the harmonious development both of national economies
and the common market

voting procedure: simple majority

235   If action by the Community should prove necessary to attain, in the
course of the operation of the common market, one of the objectives of
the Community and the Treaty has not provided the necessary powers, the
Council shall, acting unanimously, on a proposal from the Commission, and
after consulting the European Parliament, take the appropriate measures

voting procedure: unanimity

discuss and report on aspects of national systems of higher education which
made co-operation and mobility difficult.

Yet, as we see from the policy statements, education and higher education issues then dropped off the ministers' decision agenda for a full ten
years. For four years there was no action by the designated decision-makers,
the Council, on education or higher education issues. For five years the
political action swung between the Education Committee, which, on 27
June 1980, submitted a general report to Council and ministers of education meeting within the Council, ministers acting intergovernmentally
(the 2 June 1983 Conclusions on promoting mobility in higher education)
and the European Council (the statements of Stuttgart 1983, and Milan, the
'People's Europe' report on 19 June 1985). At Stuttgart the Community's
leaders hoped that academic exchanges would develop. In Milan, the leaders backed the 'hope' of the ad hoc Committee on a People's Europe that
there would be a 'comprehensive' European interuniversity programme of
exchanges.

The return to Community processes occurred suddenly in 1986 and,
surprisingly, in the form of full Treaty processes. On 24 July 1986, the
Council of Ministers adopted the Comett programme, designed to promote
co-operation between universities and enterprises on training in technology
(86/365/EEC) (OJ L 222 of 8 August 1986). The Decision was made under
Articles 128 and 235 of the Treaty (see Table 11.2) related to vocational
training policy and the Council of Ministers' (limited) right to extend the
Treaty. Almost a year on, 15 June 1987, the Council of Ministers adopted
the best known programme of them all: the European Community action
scheme for the mobility of university students – Erasmus (87/327/87) (OJ
L of 26 June 1987). The Treaty terms were the same as for the Comett
Decision Articles 128 and 235, drawing additionally on the precedents of
the Council Decision of 1963 on vocational training and a regulation of
1968 on the education of children of migrant workers were used.

This overview of the programme tells us the outcome of a non-incremental process. Yet what we do not know from this account is likely to be the most interesting part of the story for policy-makers. Where did Erasmus come from? Where were the initiatives being taken and by whom? What were the factors that transformed structured university co-operation and academic mobility from bright idea to Community law?

Disaggregating problems, policies and politics

It is helpful to see how Kingdon (1984) conceptualizes the policy process in order to understand why higher education had characteristics which allowed it to get onto the Community agenda and reach the decision stage. In Kingdon's frame there are three separate 'constructs'. The first consists of disaggregating the agenda into three functionally different phases. The least developed agenda is *systemic*, when an idea floats around the policy community or the public at large. The next stage of development is *governmental*, being the list of subjects which focus the attention of officials and those around them. The most developed agenda is *decisional*, being the list of subjects up for an active decision by government (Kingdon 1995: 3–4).

The second construct in the Kingdon model is the conceptualization of the policy process in terms of three separate streams, each with its own dynamic: problems, policies and politics. *Problems* become problems in the Kingdon sense only when people in and around government institutions can (Wildavsky 1979) or want to (Kingdon 1984) do something about them. Before that they are conditions. A condition is transformed into a problem by a focusing event such as a crisis, a change of administration, major legislation, or when a change of trend in key indicators places an issue in the problem stream (Kingdon 1995). *Policies* emerge: floating, combining and recombining or fading from sight. An idea may be pushed by experts; it may also be developed within the governmental agenda. The factors which enable some policy ideas to survive in the policy stream are multiple, apart from such issues as technical feasibility linked to opportunities in the problem or political stream. The dynamics of the *political* stream include such factors as the national mood, organized political forces, governmental processes in the political stream and consensus-building in the political stream.

The third Kingdon construct provides a key for analysing the process which brings the streams of problems, policies and politics together and as a result forces an issue onto and up the governmental or decision agenda. Kingdon defines two functional requirements. One is the focusing event. The other is the policy entrepreneur or policy advocate looking for 'problems' to which to attach 'their' solution, and for political developments that can be used to the advantage of themselves or their office. Kingdon's model, derived from empirical data within the stable American institutional system, makes the policy entrepreneur seem the energetic and persistent individual whom colleagues readily identify as responsible for policy advance or change.

The opportunity for action or a given initiative is a 'window' for the policy entrepreneur. A 'problem window' is opened when decision-makers, convinced that a problem is pressing, reach into the policy stream for a solution. A 'political window' opens, typically pre-election, when politicians, casting around for proposals to solve their problem or election/re-election, reach into the policy stream. The window is unlikely to be open for long. If a solution is not available, a problem is not sufficiently interesting or if political support is not forthcoming, the decision-makers turn their attention to other subjects. Kingdon's empirical research showed policy entrepreneurs behind the joining of streams in the vast majority of cases. But there may be 'spillover' from other policy areas, and there may be chance elements to the way 'streams' join: the unexpected or the random (Kingdon 1995: 165–95). In principle, each of the active participants can be involved in each of the important processes of problem recognition, policy generation and politics. Policy is not solely the province of analysts, nor politics solely the province of politicians.

I apply the Kingdon model to two cases: (i) the development of the idea of higher education co-operation structured around student exchange in 1971–87 and (ii) the window of opportunity that enabled the Commission to propose in January 1986 that the Council of Ministers agree the Erasmus programme under Treaty processes.

Policy ideas for Community higher education, 1971 to 1987

The policy stream for the period 1971 to 1987 shows a build-up of policy aspirations on higher education which gave the Commission a direct contact with universities through a policy of structured university co-operation, and a possible reach into national policies. The policy stream in this phase of the Community's higher education policy history was set in motion when the Commissioner for Industry and Research, Altiero Spinelli, seized the opportunity of the 1971 ministerial resolution on co-operation in education, to produce a memorandum on key issues for a Community education policy. Working through a director with earlier experience of education at Community level, Félix-Paul Mercereau, Spinelli commissioned Professor Henri Janne, a well respected figure and a former minister of education for Belgium, to conduct discussions with an agreed list of education 'personalities' and to report back. This Janne did in 1973 (Commission of ECs 1973). Spinelli, Mercereau and Janne started with the idea of European higher education co-operation in which the base would be university institutions linked in some form of consortium within an eventual 'harmonized' European educational policy, which as I argue elsewhere (Corbett n.d.) was likely to mean convergence, not regulation. They wanted to structure co-operation around exchange schemes. They had an ambitious view of academic mobility as a universal experience, at least for postgraduates. The possibility of compulsory exchanges was raised.

The Janne ideas were, however, reassessed and defined more prudently in 1973 by all the main players in the Commission and the Council. The Community was enlarged in 1973 to include the UK, Ireland and Denmark. The key figures in this were the commissioner, Ralf Dahrendorf, a pragmatist in contrast with the federalist Spinelli, and a young Welshman, Hywel Ceri Jones, who had come from the British tradition as exemplified by the innovative University of Sussex. The Commission proposals were more modest than Spinelli and Mercereau or Janne in terms of instruments and policy substance. The resolution of the Council of Ministers (Education) on 4 June 1974 followed suit. Ideas of compulsory mobility and consortia had been dropped. Co-operation was defined as: (i) increased co-operation between higher education institutions – consortia were not mentioned; (ii) improved possibilities for academic recognition of diplomas and periods of study; and (iii) the encouragement of student and academic mobility.

However, the idea of organized co-operation reappeared among the eight higher education action points of the 1976 Action Programme. The officials, including Jones, in the new education directorate had got into their stride and set about developing policy issues. But the programme was seen as complementing the wider political aspirations of the Community institutions in the economic and social domains (Bousquet 1999: 13). As the Commission's education directorate developed issues, negotiations with the Education Committee were at times tough: there were 23 meetings of the Committee between 1974 and 1976. But the Commission was nevertheless recognized as the appropriate institution to undertake most of the initial work. One important job was to set up pilot projects, involving universities directly, to assess the feasibility of joint study programmes and short study visits for academics and administrators of the different systems of the member states. These programmes were a model of structured co-operation requiring academics to enter into partnerships on exchanging students and academic recognition.

But the Action Programme not only introduced experimental forms of co-operation with universities in member states, it also required the Commission to investigate barriers to mobility which were a consequence of every member state having a different higher education system. Draft resolutions presented to the Education Committee focused on the need for a 'common policy' on the admission of Community students, and on scholarships and academic recognition. The Danes called for a halt to the process on the grounds that the Community institutions had no competence on education. The French objected, not to the principle of such development, but to the process that did not make use of the Treaty Articles which recognized new development as being undertaken by sovereign states. The problem could not be resolved at diplomatic (COREPER) levels. The Council of Ministers (Education) meetings were cancelled in 1978 and 1979. Community policy development in areas which impinged directly on national educational processes became impossible. The issues known as 'Grey Area' issues, since although they were not Treaty issues they had got political backing, were taken off the governmental agenda.

Theorists might think that for the policy entrepreneurs of the education policy section of the Commission, the opportunity to concentrate on the co-operation area without close ministerial oversight was a golden opportunity to strengthen a policy monopoly (Baumgartner and Jones 1993). The actual experience of the pilot programmes of joint study programmes and short study visits developed significantly in the period under Jones's overall direction, and through a dynamic technical team led by Alan Smith. They built up a growing circle of university participants whose networking was developed through Commission conferences and newsletters. However, for those involved, this 'Grey Areas' dispute was a period of political failures. The Commission officials did, however, have allies in the European Parliament, and the Education Committee kept the existing processes moving. Thus, pilot programmes were renewed and funded despite the impossibility of getting Ministers to approve new developments under Community processes.

In 1983 Ministers tried to reopen co-operation processes under intergovernmental, rather than Community processes. Led by the French, with the argument that it was better to act pragmatically than get blocked on process, ministers of education produced a set of proposals for multi-national rather than Community co-operation on higher education which included the twinning of universities. But at the moment the intergovernmental solution was proposed, a wider Community, represented by heads of state and government, discovered the merits of the joint study programmes as platforms for Community policy in general (Stuttgart 1983, Milan 1985). This marked a political breakthrough for the Commission approach. Here was a problem that governments wanted to do something about at the symbolic level: how to attract the young to the European project. Here was the Commission with a potential solution in the shape of student mobility and exchange. There was just one element lacking: how could the pilot projects be turned into a Community programme without Community funding? That problem was in the political stream.

Drafting the Erasmus programme: the 1985 window

In the policy story of the Community institutions' formation of a higher education policy, it is possible to define moments at which the agenda changed because this represented a moment at which the problem, policy and political streams came together (Kingdon 1994). This section is based mainly on interviews with key players at different levels of the Commission and in some member states.

At the end of 1984 Jones and colleagues in the Commission had their solution ready, but the 'Grey Areas' difficulties still hung over them. They needed some dynamic from the political stream to transform the joint study programmes into a Community programme 'problem'.

That dynamic came with a sudden change in the political mood (Kingdon 1984). On 1 January 1985, Jacques Delors arrived as president of the Commission. He did not have on his agenda the problem known as the BBQ (the British Budget Question) which had ruined his predecessor's period of office. Delors' great project, announced in a speech within days of taking office, was to complete the single market by 1992. He also wanted successes. Delors' emphasis on the need to rebuild confidence in the importance of human resources and the skills of Europe's population was an element in the political stream. A further important element was that the education dossier was given for one year to Commissioner Peter Sutherland. He too was ambitious and entrepreneurial, and he was willing to listen to his cabinet's argument that he could do for education and training what a famous figure among the commissioners, Etienne Davignon, had done for technology, if he would agree to the Commission drafting programmes – the future Comett and Erasmus.

At the same time, the summit meetings were showing top-level political support for the idea of academic mobility and co-operation. The Commission education officials were confidently awaiting the publication of the report on a people's Europe, due to be presented to the summit in Milan in June 1985. They knew, because they had helped to write it, that it would recommend that the joint study programmes model be transformed into a Community programme.

The policy stream was reactivated with, this time, two policy entrepreneurs, representing a convergence of the Commission's political and policy interests. An important part of the action passed to Sutherland's cabinet level and the Frenchman, Michel Richonnier, recruited from the French Plan in advance of 1 January 1985, because of the forceful report he had produced on desirable Community policies. Richonnier's report had made play of the fact that it was politically essential to have a Community dimension to education in order to fight off popular cynicism about the Community and to combat unemployment. There was also Jones, whose persistence and policy vision, and whose key technical agency staff, had transformed the pilot projects for the structured co-operation into a technically feasible programme idea. It was Richonnier's responsibility to get agreement from Sutherland to support the drafting of one programme in the spirit of Delors' human resources strategy for the Single Market (Comett), and one, the future Erasmus, based on the joint study programmes. This was seen as a way of easing jurisdictional difficulties. The objective of improving technology transfer from universities to trainers in small business and industry seemed very '1992'. The Erasmus programme, it was hoped, could, jurisdictionally, ride on Comett's back. More difficult for Richonnier was the securing of provisional approval for a budget, numbered in millions rather than thousands of ecus. But that in itself was a product of Richonnier's vision: his motto was 'think big'. Jones's job was to get the programmes written within a year, while keeping development going, since Sutherland was due to hand over the education dossier at the end of the year when the Community was enlarged.

At the beginning, the jurisdictional strategy was to go for Article 235, the Article which allows member states to approve Community competence not specified in the Treaty but consistent with the objectives of the Community (Table 11.2). Then there occurred an event which was not entirely unforeseen but the timing of which was random (Kingdon 1984). On 13 February 1985, the European Court of Justice (ECJ) delivered the Gravier judgement (ECJ 1985, case 293/83). This, while confirming that education and training policies were matters for member states, ruled that national regulations on access to higher education could not, under Treaty law, discriminate between Community students on the grounds of nationality. Taking a lead from Article 128 of the Treaty and Regulation 1612/68 (Articles 7 and 12) and the Decision of 1963 on the principles of a common policy for vocational training (Table 11.2) the ECJ judged that 'education which prepares for a profession, trade or employment, or which provides the necessary skills and training for a particular profession, trade or employment, is vocational training, whatever the age, or training level of the pupils or students, or even if the course includes a part of general education.'

The immediate effect of the Gravier judgement on the Commission entrepreneurs was to make them change their jurisdictional strategy. Article 128, approved by a simple majority vote, offered a far more favourable base for Community development in the future. On 3 June 1985, the Council of Ministers (Education) were informed that the Commission was drafting two programmes. On 28 June 1985, at the European summit in Milan, heads of state and government accepted the report on a people's Europe, favouring a 'comprehensive European inter-university programme of exchanges and studies, aimed at giving this opportunity to a significant section of the Community's student population', and backed the development on a European academic transfer system.

In December 1985, Commissioner Sutherland presented the Erasmus Draft Decision to his fellow commissioners. Its features were a legal base in Article 128, and a mobility target of 10 per cent of the Community student population. On 3 January 1986, the Draft Decision was presented to the Council. It then took eighteen months and a renewed threat of Council breakdown, intervention by Community heads of state or government, member state mediation and negotiation among themselves, for the Erasmus Decision to emerge on 15 June 1987. The aim of the programme, as stated by the Decision, was to provide mobility for individual students and support measures for universities operating Europe-wide university co-operation networks, and additionally to offer a scheme for academic recognition, the European Credit Transfer system, and a network of national recognition and information centres (NARIC). The objectives of the programme were to develop an adequate pool of manpower, to improve the quality of education and training, and to promote interaction between EEC citizens. The aim was to provide exchange opportunities for 'significant' numbers of students, with recognition for periods of study and of 'broad and intensive cooperation' between EEC citizens.

Conclusion

In this account of Community policy formation my aim has been to show why the Community has been interested in higher education by unveiling the intrinsically political process in which the policy players, including national ministers of education, have been involved in creating a Community policy. The claim for this kind of process-based or processual (Barzelay 2000) account is that by showing how a policy process unfolds, we are providing an explanation of policy change. As suggested by the Kingdon model, the political process analysed here is not one in which there is an orderly process of planning, in which problems are identified, goals specified. Rather, as Kingdon suggests, for the attention of those in and around the policy process, 'problems [float] in and out, joined by fortuitous events or by . . . a skilful entrepreneur' (Kingdon 1995: 18). Over time, the underlying 'problems' change. The nature of the specifically higher education problems changed too. So did many of the political players. Yet over these years the policies advocated were extraordinarily similar and the periods of policy development were characterized by the presence of a policy entrepreneur.

This account takes us to something politically concrete, a long way from explanations of Community interest in higher education linked to such symbols as the medieval wandering scholars, the image promoted by the Commission and explicit in the name of the programme which commemorates the Renaissance humanist Erasmus of Rotterdam. Yet young people increasingly see themselves as European citizens; universities have roles as transmitters and interpreters of cultural values. What has been lacking is a recognition by national policy makers of the potential of the Erasmus idea to make mobility the norm for the majority of Europe's young citizens. Might not the national policy-makers take more interest in Community policy-making in higher education if they also saw an emerging European policy as the interaction of an idea and a process in which they could be much more ambitious players?

Acknowledgements

The author would like to thank Francisco Gaetani for comments on a first draft of this chapter.

Note

1. Naming policy: I use the term Community to mean the European Community in its different guises: EEC 1958–1992, EU thereafter. Following the practice of the European Commission I use higher education and universities interchangeably.

References

Barzelay, M. (2000) *The New Public Management: Improving Research and Policy Dialogue.* Berkeley, CA: University of California Press.

Baumgartner, F. and Jones, B. (1993) *Agendas and Instability in American Politics.* Chicago: University of Chicago Press.

Beukel, E. (1994) Reconstructing integration theory: the case of educational policy in the EC, *Nordic Journal of International Studies,* 29(1): 33–54.

Bousquet, A. (1999) *Education et formation dans l'Union Européenne.* Paris: La documentation française.

Cohen, M., March, J. and Olsen, J. (1972) A garbage can model of organisational choice, *Administrative Science Quarterly,* 17 March: 1–25.

Commission of ECs (1973) *Bulletin of the European Communities,* Supplement 10/73, For a Community policy on education (Janne Report). Luxembourg: Commission of ECs.

Commission of ECs (1974) *Bulletin of the European Communities,* Supplement 3/74 Communication from the Commission to the Council presented on 11 March 1974 'Education in the European Community'. Luxembourg: Commission of ECs.

Commission of ECs (1985) *Bulletin of the European Communities,* Supplement 7/85, A People's Europe: report from an *ad hoc* committee. Luxembourg: Commission of ECs.

Corbett, A. (n.d.) Explaining Erasmus (thesis in progress).

Council of the European Communities (1988) *European Educational Policy Statements,* 3rd edn. Luxembourg: Council of European Communities.

de Witte, B. (ed.) (1989) *The European Community Law of Education.* Baden-Baden: Nomos.

Field, J. (1998) *European Dimensions: Education, Training and the European Union.* London: Jessica Kingsley.

Gellert, C. (ed.) (1993) *Higher Education in Europe.* London: Jessica Kingsley.

Gellert, C. (ed.) (1999) *Innovation and Adaptation in Higher Education: The Changing Conditions of Advanced Teaching and Learning in Europe.* London: Jessica Kingsley.

Green, A. (1997) *Education, globalisation and the nation state.* London: Macmillan.

Green, A., Wolf, A. and Leney, T. (1999) *Convergence and Divergence in European Education and Training Systems.* London: Institute of Education, University of London.

Kingdon, J. (1984) *Agendas, Alternatives and Public Policies.* Boston, MA: Little Brown.

Kingdon, J. (1995) *Agendas, Alternatives and Public Policies,* 2nd edn. Boston, MA: Little Brown.

MacMahon, J. (1995) *Education and Culture in European Community Law.* London: Athlone Press.

Mény, Y. (1999) Les pilotes et la machine, *Le Monde,* 4 September, p.1.

Neave, G. (1984) *The EEC and Education.* Stoke-on-Trent: Trentham Books.

Scott, P. (1998) Massification, internationalisation and globalisation, in P. Scott (ed.) *The Globalisation of Higher Education,* pp. 108–29. Buckingham: SRHE and Open University Press.

Shaw, J. (1999) From the margins to the centre: education and training law and policy from 'Casagrande' to the Knowledge Society, in P. Craig and G. de Burca, *European Community Law: An Evolutionary Perspective,* pp. 555–95. Oxford: Oxford University Press.

Teichler, U. (1993) Structures of higher education systems in Europe, in C. Gellert (ed.) *Higher Education in Europe*. London: Jessica Kingsley.

van Craeyenest, F. (1989) La nature juridique des résolutions sur la coopération en matière de l'education, in B. de Witte (ed.) *The European Community Law of Education*. Baden-Baden: Nomos.

van der Wende, M. (1997) Missing links, in T. Kalvermark and M. van der Wende (eds) *National Policies for the Internationalisation of Higher Education*, pp. 10–41. Stockholm: National Agency for Education.

Wellens, K. and Borschardt, G. (1989) Soft law in European Community law, *European Law Review*, 14: 267–321.

Wildavsky, A. (1979) *Speaking Truth to Power: The Art and Craft of Policy Analysis*. Boston, MA: Little Brown.

12

Lifelong Learning in the Workplace: A Comparison of France and the UK

Yvonne Hillier

This chapter draws upon research exploring how work-based learning operates in England and France. A Socrates-funded staff mobility grant to members of departments involved in the continuing professional development of teachers and trainers of adults from City University, London, and the University of Tours, France, enabled the researchers to spend time in London and in Brittany to undertake a direct comparison of the practical features of work-based learning. One of the outcomes was an analysis of the cultural issues within which work-based learning was practised.

Visits in November 1998 to organizations in Rennes, Chinon and Tours comprised a series of semi-structured interviews with professionals who were involved in *formation continue*. As in the UK, adults in France are encouraged to develop their skills and knowledge to meet the demands of the technological society and the rate of change in skill requirements. However, the French system for undertaking accredited development is different from the UK system in its policy, funding and organization. Part of the interviews, therefore, involved identifying the ways in which *formation continue* was offered. The return visit to London and Northampton, in January 1999, explored further the issues arising from the interviews in France, particularly how higher education and lifelong learning policies both defined and encouraged the way in which work-based learning was practised.

The chapter discusses two themes: work-based learning and how it is delivered, assessed and contextualized in both countries; and the cultural differences, the milieu, in which the practice of work-based learning is located. It argues that it is not possible to analyse practices of work-based learning without addressing the cultural and political context in which this form of learning is undertaken.

Setting the scene: European policy on education and training

The European Commission's White Paper on education and training (Commission of the European Communities 1995) identified a need to address the 'upheaval' in its member states as a result of the dawning of the 'information society', the impact of scientific and technical developments and what could now be described as globalization. The objective of the White Paper was to develop broad-based knowledge, skills and aptitudes needed for employability (Leney 1999). It noted that some member states had begun already to address these three factors with a 'modern route' to education, training and learning whereby those 'rejected' by the formal system (of qualifications) would be encouraged to cultivate the skills they have (Commission of the European Communities 1995: 15). The paper therefore signalled the developments of work-based learning (WBL) and accreditation of prior learning (APL) which had already been created in the UK.

How have France and the UK responded to the objectives of the White Paper? As Leney (1999) notes, the European Commission has been influential in promoting research and policies in education and training but the role of subsidiarity forms an important part of what stems from its directives and policies. This chapter begins by considering how work-based learning is contextualized within the wider notion of lifelong learning and the learning society.

Work-based learning: lifelong learning in the workplace

There are different definitions of work-based learning and the knowledge that is developed as a result (see Eraut 1999), but it can generally be taken to mean learning which occurs through work rather than through study at a learning institution. Work-based learning comprises one aspect of learning which takes place after compulsory schooling has been completed and is a feature of lifelong learning. Such learning is integral to the notion of a learning society. The argument for a learning society encourages learning from work and education at 'either end of the lifecourse' (Schuller 1998) and incorporates the vision that all members of society should engage in learning activities. The central discourse of the learning society *is* lifelong learning.

Lifelong learning has been much debated in the UK. Three major policy and consultative documents on widening participation (Kennedy 1997), learning for the twenty-first century (Fryer 1997) and lifelong learning (Department for Education and Employment 1998) have created an agenda which has been widely discussed by providers of learning opportunities in all sections of the education and training communities. A central plank of this policy is the need to involve employees and employers in ensuring that people have the appropriate skills to help the country improve its economic viability, with a secondary aim of working towards social and personal benefits.

When considering work-based learning as a specific context in which lifelong learning can occur, the question of what constitutes learning arises. This learning does not have to be acquired by 'attending a training course' or a formal learning activity in a college or institution of further or higher education. This has been identified by Edwards as a blurring of the boundaries between learning as a dedicated activity and learning as an incidental activity (Edwards 1997: 79). Eraut (1998) suggests that learning must refer only to significant changes in capability or understanding, thereby excluding the mere acquisition of information which does not contribute to such changes. It is the deliberate thinking through of an experience in order to learn (Brennan and Little 1996) which defines learning.

Regardless of how learning in the workplace has occurred, what 'counts' as learning appears to relate to how it is accredited. There is a tension between identifying learning gained both formally and informally in the workplace and accrediting it. One of the themes explored in the visits in France and England was how individuals could develop and accredit their knowledge and skills and how well the policy framework encouraged this. As discussed below, the voluntary aspect of employer-sponsored training in the workplace in the UK contrasts with the training levy operating in France. However, neither system addresses the fact that people in employment are learning all the time; their knowledge and skills are simply not being assessed and accredited.

One consequence of the dominance of providers of education and training in the debates about lifelong learning is that the opportunities for appreciating informal learning are diminished. Thus, Ashton has noted that 'training is an infrequent activity but learning an everyday occurrence' (Ashton 1998: 3). This affirms the earlier view of Rogers (1997) that the term 'learning' is frequently used in a 'sloppy way' when it only applies to one kind of learning, i.e. formal learning, and ignores everyday learning. Researchers' interest in informal learning runs counter to the government's focus on accreditation of learning and the targets to increase the number of people in the workforce holding qualifications (Coffield 1998). One of the challenges to the discourse of lifelong learning argued by Edwards is that 'the very notion of "learning" is problematic, as learning for some is constructed as training and/or leisure by others' (Edwards 1997: 117).

The need to accredit work-based learning and the subsequent involvement by universities in this process formed the second theme for the researchers. In England, the Dearing Report (National Committee of Inquiry into Higher Education 1997) recommended that higher education equip its students with the necessary skills and knowledge to meet the demands of the workplace in the twenty-first century. As McNair (1998) argues, the ability of higher education institutions (HEIs) to offer a curriculum which allows adult learners to 'move in and out of formal learning throughout their lives' is questionable. HEIs play a key role in work-based learning through the accreditation of activities which equate with traditional degree and diploma programmes of study. They wield immense power over whom and what can be accredited. The analysis of the two systems, therefore, starts with the way in which access to higher education exists for those qualified to attend in each country.

Access to higher education

France

A notable difference between the French and British systems is how people gain access to higher education. In France, anyone with a *Baccalaureat* (Bac) has a right to university education. Higher education institutions in France confer the award of *diplôme* which covers three levels of award: *Licence* (Bachelors), *Maitrîse* (Masters) and *Doctorat*. There has been a trend in recent years to develop more professional *diplômes* including the *Diplôme d'études supérieures specialisées* (DESS). Each university *diplôme* in France requires a Bac plus a defined number of years of higher education. Entry by a portfolio of experience or competence is still exceptional.

Eighty per cent of young people in France gain the Bac. They do not have to undergo a selection process dependent upon grades to enrol on a course of their choice. This has resulted in large numbers of students enrolling on courses which must accommodate them if they possess the appropriate Bac and years of education. Students often find themselves in highly crowded lecture theatres simply because the university has to take them on. The system works initially through elimination by failure. Students can *redouble*, re-enrol, to repeat a failed first or second year, or enrol on a different course, up to a maximum of three enrolments. Only *Grandes Ecoles* operate in similar ways to the prestigious universities in the UK, where there is competitive entry (by *Concours*), following two years of preparatory course work (*les années 'prépa'*) which are open only to those students who have done particularly well in the *Baccalaureat*. The Instituts Universitaires de Technologie (IUTs) and the recently created Instituts Universitaires Professionalisés (IUPs) offer vocational courses and are more akin to a faculty within the management structure of universities (Davies 2000). These institutions are selective and take students with specific qualifications. The DAEU (*Diplôme d'accès aux études universitaires*) created in 1957, allows consideration for a university place for people without the Bac, without which individuals have no right of entry to higher education.

A second key factor for higher education provision in France is the influence of the state through its accreditation of diplomas and degrees. A university can only offer its own degrees/qualifications, subject to accreditation or *homologation* by the minister of education. Although all *diplômes* are awarded by the state, the HEIs have considerable autonomy in the actual content of their *diplômes*, particularly the professional DESS. This contrasts with the system in the UK where universities confer their own diplomas and degrees, although there is growing control through the Quality Assurance Agency (QAA) with its subject review of programmes.

Although a higher proportion of people have entry qualifications to the university system than in the UK, the university is still perceived as a place for young people and therefore does not attract adults who are entitled to study at this level. There is very limited provision for adults to re-enter the system and, until recently, such courses were not directly related to work.

In France, 85 per cent of those in work in 1997 possessed a higher education qualification, 73 per cent held the Bac (RERS 1998). With high proportions of the workforce thus qualified, the need to accredit learning gained through work may therefore be less pressing than in the UK. The qualification system confers rights upon the individual, not the institution (Davies 2000). The qualification also confers rights to certain conditions of service and salary scales in jobs, mainly in the public sector. The significance of the *diplôme* therefore extends beyond the education system into the world of work. Feutrie (1997: 92) suggests it is the 'spinal cord of the central nervous system of the social structure', which links the concept of citizenship with education, integral to the republican ideal (Davies 2000).

The UK

Despite the move towards government control over the education system in the UK through the introduction of the National Curriculum, the way in which *adults* reach qualification levels varies widely. People in the UK with qualifications similar to the Bac, National Vocational Qualifications (NVQ) Level 3, have not only gained them at eighteen: there is a policy towards encouraging the working population to gain Level 3 qualifications in the workplace if they have not already gained them during their schooling. The National Training and Education Targets (NTETs) continually revise targets (downwards) for numbers of young people and adults to possess qualifications. For 2002, the target is for 50 per cent to hold NVQ Level 3 and 28 per cent Level 4 (National Advisory Council for Education and Training Targets 1998).

In the UK, not only are people learning at work, they are studying purposively in further and higher education. Thus, over half the students in further education are over 21 years old and in higher education over half are more than 25 years old (Edwards 1997). The higher education system is now defined as a mass system which caters for young people and adults, offers opportunities to study both full time and part time and increasingly is moving towards a credit accumulation system so that students can study at times to suit their personal and work commitments. There are flexible modes of delivery within credits and units of study, including resource-based learning (RBL), distance learning (DL), negotiated programmes of study and accreditation of prior learning (APL).

Work-based learning in France and the UK

Accreditation of continuing professional development: the UK

In the UK, continuing professional development (CPD) is intrinsic to work-based learning although not all of this is accredited. The identification of the level of any developmental activity and its relationship to an individual's previously gained qualifications requires both horizontal progression (i.e. achievement of more qualifications at the same level) and the more traditional vertical progression (upward, linear) in the qualification system. Employees possessing qualifications at graduate level may develop skills and knowledge in a new context at a lower level, the prime example being use of information technology. Recent developments in the UK which enable the accreditation of skills and knowledge horizontally include the NVQ system, Credit Accumulation and Transfer Scheme (CATS), professional development portfolios and the National Record of Achievement (NROA). The introduction of WBL degrees and diplomas at Middlesex University has set a model for accrediting learning from work elsewhere in the UK (Brennan and Little 1996). Generally, people identify how their learning relates to particular learning outcomes which may be drawn from the criteria relating to CATS. This scheme enables 'modules' of learning to be accredited at either undergraduate levels 1 to 3 or at masters level.

The qualifications framework in the UK has been called a jungle (Ward 1997). The opportunities for employees to accredit their learning from work relies upon this qualifications framework. As Edwards (1997) notes, adult learners are dependent upon the institutions and departments to decide the type and amount of credit which can be recognized. Accreditation of learning from work is inextricably bound to the institutions and awarding bodies responsible for qualifications and their delivery.

Accreditation of continuing professional development: France

One of the developments of the accreditation system in the UK has been the adoption of competence-based systems of education and training, particularly in the use of NVQs. Although competence-based learning is in its infancy in France, it is gaining momentum. It is possible to accumulate accreditation of prior learning through the *validation des acquis professionelles* (VAP), but this tends to be in units which are a direct equivalence of modules from *diplômes*. There are developments in the Pas de Calais region where some employers and training agencies, mainly from management and commerce, are translating the British NVQ system for adaptation. There is funding through the European Union for analysis of accreditation of prior learning (APL), for example the Leonardo Project undertaken by Feutrie and Davies (Davies *et al.* 1997; Feutrie 1998).

The work of the Maison des Ressources Humaines (MRH) in Vannes aims to identify what skills people will need to meet the challenges of the next century. Here, a project funded by the European Union is attempting to encourage managers from small and medium-sized enterprises (SMEs) to identify the competences that their employees need in order to be commercially successful. However, identification of skills and knowledge which can be expressed as a *panier des competences* is only the first stage in the development and accreditation of these competences. APL, central to credit-based systems of learning, does not appear to be widely accepted by traditional higher education institutions.

Evidence from some of the agencies visited in Brittany suggests that practitioners in the field of education and training are aware of the need for, and the benefits of, accreditation of prior experience and learning. The strong emphasis in France on the status of knowledge-based qualifications, from the legacy of the Cartesian way of thinking which privileges cerebral, scientific and theoretical approaches, devalues practice and by implication competence which is other than academic. This is not dissimilar to the academic/vocational qualification divide experienced in the UK.

Funding training

Imperatives of new technology and the 'casualization' and fragmentation of the labour force have as much influence in France as in the UK (Ivanovsky 1998). The need to continually update, reskill and diversify is of concern to employers, employees and providers of education and training. A key influence on post-compulsory education and training in France is the levy imposed on employers, equivalent to 1.5 per cent of their salary costs. This ensures that training forms an important element of the work-related learning of employees. The levy is disaggregated to cover company training plans (0.9 per cent *le plan de formation*), young people's training funds (0.4 per cent *formation des jeunes en alternance*) employer/employee funds (0.1 per cent *le capital temps de formation*) and mutual funds (0.1 per cent *congé formation*). The last are organized by sector and individuals have a right to *congé* (sabbatical) where they can apply to undertake training with leave and/or fees covered by the fund. However, this part of the funding is not related to any strategic planning on the part either of employers or of the state. Larger organizations can and do invest a higher percentage of their funds in training, but SMEs do not have similar levels of resources either in time or in money.

In France, universities offer little work-based learning for employees from SMEs. *Formation Continue* is expensive and day release courses are often difficult for small employers to manage. The university is still largely offering knowledge- rather than competence-based learning, and such offers do not correspond to the demand from the workplace. There is an important and rapidly expanding market of training agencies/organizations in the private sector. These offer training, but not necessarily a formal qualification at the end. An exception is the CNAM (Centre National des Arts et des Métiers) which offers diploma courses for a largely adult population, and the ESCAE (Ecoles Supérieurs de Commerce et Administration des Enterprises), which offer some management programmes as part of their undergraduate business school provision.

In the UK, the role of employers from SMEs is seen as important in encouraging people to learn in the workplace. Fryer (1997), in particular, argues for all employees to have the opportunity to gain qualifications at Level 3 NVQs or their equivalent and that responsibility for this is a tripartite concern comprising employees, employers and the government. The voluntary approach to promoting learning at work is patchy, and particular effort needs to be directed to those working in SMEs and the self-employed.

The implementation of some policy recommendations has already started in the UK. The establishment of Learning Accounts of £150 for individuals has begun the process of encouraging the tripartite commitment to lifelong learning by individuals, employers and the providers. The launch of the University for Industry (now Learning Direct) in September 2000 will put individuals and employers in touch with providers of lifelong learning opportunities. However, Tight (1998) succinctly describes the underlying expectation that 'we will all be required to participate in lifelong learning . . . we will likely have to pay directly for that involvement as well (and, no doubt, be thankful for it)' (p. 484).

Key skills and accreditation: the disparity between development in the UK and lack of it in the French system

In the UK, there is a growing interest in the identification and development of key skills for students in the compulsory and post-compulsory sectors of education and for trainees undertaking any accredited programme of development. Although accreditation of key skills is comparatively new, particularly at higher levels, the interest being expressed by the government, the Qualifications and Curriculum Authority (QCA) and by awarding bodies indicates that key skills will become embedded in the qualifications framework. The key skills include transferable skills of 'problem solving' and 'working with people'. The domains described by the UK key skills may offer providers in the French system a means of developing the *panier de competences*.

In France, there are *référentiels* which define competences required of a list of different *métiers*, but the debate about core/key skills is quite recent, developing only in the past two to three years. In the *Diplôme d'études supérieures spécialisées* (DESS), a course of 'professional training', there is no single statement or objective which identifies professional competences. The need for competence is accepted, but a hierarchy of skills is far less evident. Many of the tutors are themselves products of a knowledge-dominated training and have not necessarily acquired competences and skills in their own specialist areas.

Participation, social exclusion and work-based learning

Socially excluded groups, not in employment, may not necessarily gain opportunities to learn, particularly in the use of technology. In the UK, Sargent (1997) has provided evidence that adults who have lower levels of educational achievement are much less likely to participate in formal learning. The practice of work-based learning as a means to equip the population for skills to meet new challenges will not enable those without work to become skilled. To some extent this serious issue of social exclusion cannot be addressed by practitioners of work-based learning who are attempting to encourage lifelong learning among a particular group, i.e. employees. Those without work remain outside this sphere of influence.

This problem has been echoed throughout Europe. Alheit (1999) cogently argues that western Europe and North America are experiencing a 'collapse of systemic integration and social integration'. Much of the policy-making of the European Union has been concerned with minimizing social exclusion, with funding objectives being reclassified from pure economic objectives to those which will combat social exclusion. The shift in policy from purely economic approaches to social and educational issues has occurred within the past decade (Hake 1999). An analysis of policies in the EU shows that there has been an incremental development towards education and training, but that the 1995 White Paper on education and training has created an agenda for lifelong learning where it is recognized that adults are able to learn continually both formally and informally throughout their lives. Yet, as with Green Paper *Learning Age* in the UK (Department for Education and Employment 1998), emphasis is placed on learning for work and 'employability' and a continued focus on young people. Thus:

> The White Paper is bereft of both original ideas and proposals which address the specific challenges faced by adults, whether they are adult learners or not, in the global information society which is their today rather than their tomorrow.
>
> (Hake 1999: 66)

All of the education and training providers in both France and the UK interviewed in the research discussed the increasingly polarized groups of people who were without access to training and lifelong learning. Their practices of dealing with social exclusion were inextricably linked to the political and cultural contexts within each country. The next part of this chapter looks at how cultural differences (and similarities) affect the way in which work-based learning is practised.

Cultural context

In many cross-cultural encounters there is often a cycle of awareness. First we look for and find points of resemblance, a certain commonality of understanding or experience that gives sense to the initial meeting. Without such mutual recognition, the encounter is, if not impossible, at least considerably more difficult (Lévi-Strauss 1955). Later, levels of difference reassert themselves and we become more aware of how we, or the other person or situation, are foreign, strange, unusual. Only beyond that phase, and at an entirely different level, do we appreciate the sharing of more fundamental values, expressions or actions.

The researchers lived through these loops of awareness: 'Yes, it is like that at home', or 'How peculiar, why do they do that?', 'What does that mean?', 'They seem to be behind us in Y', 'We used to do that'. They were faced with the seeming impossibility of comparing without judging, sometimes reacting in the same way to the same situation, sometimes reacting very differently. It was important explicitly to contextualize both the theory and the practice of education and training.

A second feature of the research, particularly in the second visit to England, was how words used by one researcher based in England had to be translated from 'English' to 'English' to explain the use of jargon which had changed the meaning of certain phrases. For example, the words 'key skills' no longer referred simply to important or necessary skills but to a specific set of competences which could be accredited. It became apparent throughout the two visits that something more than simple translation was vital to the shared understandings that were emerging from the study.

Equality, work and higher education

It was noted earlier that there is no selection for entry into university in France, a principle that is fiercely defended, notwithstanding that the government aims at an 80 per cent pass rate at the *Baccalaureat*, the equivalent of 'A' levels in the UK. This reflects the values of Republicanism, '*liberté, égalité et fraternité*', and the concomitant principle that all citizens are equal. There is, in this sense, a policy and a practice of equality of opportunity. It is perhaps this principle of mass education, aimed particularly at young people, that explains the absence in France of a vibrant and creative field of further education. There is a long tradition of *éducation populaire*, but this has never seen its role as providing alternative access to higher education for adult learners or return to learning within an ideology of lifelong learning.

Interpretation of this principle of equality, however, is not the same on each side of the Channel. In France, there is complacency because everyone is seen to be equal under the banner of '*liberté, égalité et fraternité*'; it is difficult to identify differences or inequalities that society should address or redress. The logic of affirmative action or positive discrimination is alien to this construction of society. Perhaps the reverse is true in the UK: equality for individuals stems from a notion that everyone is different. People who achieve are 'deserving' and win by 'merit'. Because there is a far greater tolerance of difference and individuality, because special needs of individuals and/or groups are recognized, it is all the harder to achieve social change through collective mobilization. Thus, in the UK, the complacency is not that we are all equal but that we are all different. Many social and cultural policies in both countries hinge on this dynamic of difference or non-difference, equality or discrimination (Todd 1994).

Because of the 'enforced' equality in France, the presence of the state takes on added importance. Not only is it a fact that one in five workers is a civil servant, including all teachers and lecturers from primary through to university level, but there is also a culture of assistance, which pervades both the world of work and academe. Subvention, state support and state control are endemic in the system, in sharp contrast to the enterprise culture of British universities and the overall insecurity of the UK job market. In Bollinger and Hofstede's (1987) categories, France is a very low-risk managerial culture. Citizens see themselves as members of this *état-nation*, nation state, and the presence or active involvement of the state is not only tolerated but even sought both in businesses and in the universities (Jobert *et al.* 1995).

One of the important paradoxes of French university/work culture is that, despite the insistence on equality, both the structure and the dynamics of relationships are marked by a far greater hierarchical distance than in the UK (Bollinger and Hofstede 1987). Status, role differentiation, and formal boundaries of responsibility and initiative are far more evident. One key factor on which such hierarchies are built is the rising scale of university diplomas. Britain may be stratified by class which does not wholly correlate with levels of education, but France is stratified by education, between the universities and the *Grandes Ecoles*, and between levels of qualifications: first, second or third cycle.

One consequence is that learner-centred programmes of education and training are rare, at least within the university. Within a Cartesian tradition and a classical hierarchy of disciplines, the universities are more concerned with teaching than with learning. Consequently, knowledge is not related to competence, and work that is manual is regarded generally as inferior to that which is intellectual. There is no place for alternative pedagogies based on self-directed learning. There is thus a clear demarcation zone between working and learning and the link, if it exists, is through preparing students

Table 12.1 Cultural and social differences between the UK and France impacting upon work-based learning

United Kingdom	France
Monarchy and meritocracy	Republic and oligarchy
Low hierarchical distances	High hierarchical distances
High-risk culture	Low-risk culture
Enterprise and autonomy valued	State assistance valued
Training and practice-based competence with education and theory knowledge	Education and theory knowledge
Elitist system of higher education	Mass system of higher education
Tradition of further and higher education	Tradition of higher education

(that is young students, 18–22 years old, rather than adult/mature students) *for* work.

The schema in Table 12.1 helps to identify some of the major cultural and social differences which were identified as having an impact on work-based learning. However, in both systems, there is movement along the continuum for the educational dimensions and the model is therefore fluid.

It may also be possible that the social and cultural construction of work is not the same in both countries. The root values and constructs of *travail* in French come from words that mean to torture or to suffer, and where work is usually hard and unrewarding. A day without work is a holiday, a day for feasting and relaxing, *un jour chômé*. Consequently, the unemployed are called *chômeurs*. To talk then of 'learning in the workplace' is to run head-on into a major cultural barrier. Only the training levy which gives employees access to *congé*, where they can take time from their work to undertake training, is acceptable, again because it is something provided for by the state through the levy.

Reflections on learning and control

The enterprise culture, as applied to the university in the UK, means that many departments are run as if they were businesses, as they have both financial and academic targets to achieve. Unlike their French counterparts who suffer from overall state control, but who have a very large local autonomy, British tutors and trainers are subjected to constant monitoring, evaluation and review.

It could be argued that the more that governments, approved training institutions or other training providers create, propose or impose a national structure of education, then the less place there is for the individual educator or student to define their own preferred learning outcomes. How much choice does an individual actually have in the learning/accreditation maze? The enthusiasm for student-centred programmes and the preference for identifying 'learning outcomes' rather than teaching/learning objectives needs analysis. It is always difficult to transfer one country's system to another. Ironically, the NVQ system in the UK, with its centralizing tendency, is counter-culture to France, where developments over the past fifteen years have been towards decentralizing education and training (Davies 2000). In particular, the discourse of lifelong learning in the UK, with its emphasis on learning for employment and economic success, demonstrates a policy direction which reaches across all sections of society.

In the French system, at the extreme, it would be easy to think that the university was concerned with education, and that private sector agencies in the workplace were concerned with training. In reality, training as *formation* cuts across both the university and the workplace, but it raises important issues about accreditation, qualification and the complex processes of professionalization.

The question today lies more in the creation of new working relationships, new job titles, and new definitions of key or core skills which serve not to define a given trade or activity but to identify transferable skills on which employment mobility, lack of job security and effective competition all depend. Alheit (1999: 78) draws attention to the need for realization that:

> informal learning in modern societies can unfold its quality only if the intermediary locations for learning (companies, organizations and educational institutions) change in parallel, if genuinely new learning environments and new learning publics come into being.

It will be interesting to reflect how, in France and in the UK, the university, its structure and status, react to these influences.

Concluding remarks

The French and British systems have different strengths. In France, more people get over the first hurdle in their race but do not necessarily manage to reach the finish line. In Britain, it is much harder, still, to get over the first hurdle, but once over it is possible to carry on. The UK has one of the most successful higher education systems in the world in terms of completion rates. The ideal would be where optimum numbers of people cross all hurdles. Yet simply to adopt the successful practices of one country without analysing the sociopolitical context in which such practices will be grafted is unlikely to meet with immediate success. The successful transfer of policy is more likely if the policy is consistent with the dominant political ideology in each country (Dolowitz and Marsh 1996).

The French are considering how to encourage their employees and socially excluded people to gain knowledge and skills which will be necessary for personal and economic life. They may not need a 'British' system of accreditation.

In the UK, England in particular, we still have far to go to overcome cultural opposition to vocational rather than academic qualifications and to encourage people to participate in accredited learning. The German model of training and qualifications is held as a shining example of how a state can successfully encourage its employees to gain initial qualifications and undertake vocational training. The divide between academic and vocational qualifications in the UK and elsewhere continues to haunt developments in both initial qualifications and lifelong learning.

The comparison of work-based learning in France and the UK distinguishes two very different cultures. Work-based learning in the UK is similar to that which has developed in most English-speaking western countries, particularly Australia and Canada. It may be that work-based learning has been given such a high profile in these countries because certain groups have not gained initial qualifications for entry to higher education.

One of the paradoxes of work-based learning is how its accreditation is seen to relate to prior learning, yet it is claimed to be a vital ingredient to the economic success of the nation. If people can already *do* and already *have* skills and knowledge, why are these countries deemed to be in need of qualifications in order to compete globally? It may be that in France, one of the reasons that little interest has been shown in the accreditation of work-based learning is that the sense of initial achievement through the Bac negates any need for further qualifications gained in later life, unless these are of a higher level.

Any discussion of work-based learning excludes those who are not in the workplace. In any system of mass education, particularly where it can be undertaken in increasing 'sites of learning', those who are on the outside become even more marginalized and excluded. Perhaps the challenge for both countries either side of the Channel is to consider how socially excluded groups can be encouraged to participate in lifelong learning which will provide 'useful' knowledge and skills for full participation in society in the much heralded twenty-first century.

As Coffield (1999) argues, accreditation without considering the 'learning' within the 'learning society' can lead to qualification inflation where people do not gain employment or improve their careers through study. He reminds us of the 'longstanding, brutal and awkward truth' that the roots of educational disadvantage originate from our social structures. European initiatives continue to aim for social inclusion within the context of subsidiarity. The lesson drawn from this study is that any European objective must consider the sociopolitical and cultural contexts of the member states if initiatives are to be both successful and to disseminate good practice.

Acknowledgement

This paper draws upon an earlier paper 'Learning by working, learning at work: a cross channel comparison', written with Dr Paul Taylor, University of Rennes, and presented at the First International Conference on Researching Work and Learning held at University of Leeds, September 1999.

References

Alheit, P. (1999) On a contradictory way to the 'learning society': a critical approach, *Studies in the Education of Adults*, 31(1): 66–82.

Ashton, D. (1998) 'Skill formation: redirecting the research agenda', in F. Coffield (ed.) *Learning at Work.* Bristol: Policy Press.

Bollinger, D. and Hofstede, G. (1987) *Les différences culturelles dans le management.* Paris: Editions d'organization.

Brennan, J. and Little, B. (1996) *A Review of Work Based Learning in Higher Education.* London: Open University Quality Support Centre.

Coffield, F. (1998) (ed.) *Learning at Work.* Bristol: Policy Press.

Coffield, F. (1999) Breaking the consensus: lifelong learning as social control, *British Educational Research Journal*, 25(4): 479–99.

Commission of the European Communities (1995) *Teaching and Learning: Towards the Learning Society.* Luxembourg: Commission of the European Communities.

Davies, P. (2000) Rights and rites of passage: crossing boundaries in France, *International Journal of Lifelong Education*, 19(3): forthcoming.

Davies, P., Gallacher, J. and Reeve, F. (1997) The accreditation of prior experiential learning: a comparison of current practice within the UK and France, *International Journal of University Adult Education*, 36(2): 1–21.

Department for Education and Employment (1998) *The Learning Age: A Renaissance for New Britain.* London: The Stationery Office.

Dolowitz, D. and Marsh, D. (1996) Who learns what from whom: a review of the policy transfer literature, *Political Studies*, 44: 343–57.

Edwards, R. (1997) *Changing Places? Flexibility, Lifelong Learning and a Learning Society.* London: Routledge.

Eraut, M. (1998) Learning from other people at work, in F. Coffield (ed.) *Learning at Work*, pp. 37–48. Bristol: Policy Press.

Eraut, M. (1999) Non-formal learning in the workplace: the hidden dimension of lifelong learning. A framework for analysis and the problems it poses for the researcher. Paper given at the First International Conference on Researching Work and Learning, University of Leeds, September.

Feutrie, M. (1997) Identification, validation and accreditation of prior and informal learning – France. Unpublished report for CEDEFOP.

Feutrie, M. (ed.) (1998) *Evaluer, valider et certifier les compétences professionelles, Tome 6, Rapport des Journées Internationales de la Formation.* Paris: Conseil National du Patronat Français.

Fryer, R. (1997) *Learning for the Twenty-first Century: The First Report of the National Advisory Group for Continuing Education and Lifelong Learning.* London: NAGCELL.

Hake, B.J. (1999) Lifelong learning policies in the European Union: developments and issues, *Compare*, 29(1): 53–69.

Ivanovsky, M. (1998) Espace innovation TPE. Développement économique des très petites enterprises en réseau, Vannes. Unpublished paper.

Jobert, A., Marry, C. and Tanguy, L. (1995) *Education et travail en Grande-Bretagne, Allemagne et Italie.* Paris: Armand Colin.

Kennedy, H. (1997) *Learning Works: Widening Participation in Further Education.* Coventry: Further Education Funding Council.

Leney, T. (1999) European approaches to social exclusion, in A. Hayton (ed.) *Tackling Disaffection and Social Exclusion: Education Perspectives and Policies*, pp. 33–46. London: Kogan Page.

Lévi-Strauss, C. (1955) *Tristes tropiques.* Paris: Plon.

McNair, S. (1998) The invisible majority: adult learners in higher education, *Higher Education Quarterly*, 52(2): 162–78.

National Advisory Council for Education and Training Targets (1998) *Fast Forward for Skills: A summary of NACETT's Report on the Future of National Targets for Education and Training.* London: NACETT.

National Committee of Inquiry into Higher Education (1997) *Higher Education in the Learning Society* (Dearing Report). London: NCIHE.

RERS (1998) *Repères et références statistiques sur les ensignements et la formation.* Paris: Ministère de l'éducation nationale, de la recherche et de la technologie.

Rogers, A. (1997) Learning: can we change the discourse?, *Adults Learning*, January: 116–17.

Sargent, N. (1997) *The Learning Divide.* Leicester: National Institute of Adult Continuing Education.

Schuller, T. (1998) Three steps towards a learning society, *Studies in the Education of Adults*, 30(1): 11–20.

Tight, M. (1998) Education, education, education! The vision of lifelong learning in the Kennedy, Dearing and Fryer reports, *Oxford Review of Education*, 24(4): 473–85.

Todd, E. (1994) *Le destin des immigrés: assimilation et ségrégation dans les démocraties occidentales.* Paris: Seuil.

Ward, C. (1997) Qualifications – the next eleven years, *EDUCA*, 172.

Part 3

The Future Community: Virtuality,
Reality and Liberal Idealism

13

Virtual Learning Communities and the Role of Computer-mediated Communication Conferencing: Practices and Problems

Ann Lahiff and Edwin Webb

This chapter looks at the notion of a community of learners in the context of computer-mediated communication (CMC), drawing upon both a sociological tradition and analyses which have been applied specifically to the context of computer-mediated virtual communities. The concept of a virtual learning community is explored through two principal dimensions: the interaction within a designated social (database) space, and that which takes place through the interactive learning space of the conference itself. The main evidences cited are derived from analyses of archives of several such CMC conferences operated within the University of Greenwich, London, conducted among groups of mature students following programmes of continuing professional development.

The CMC operations within these programmes employed a Lotus Notes system, providing the following key resources:

- an e-mail facility which allows both one-to-one and one-to-many communication: tutor to student(s), student to student(s);
- a 'conference' facility which allows all participants access to a common database where contributions are stored for all to read and respond to.

The analysis of the actual transactions which took place within the conference areas points to several issues which raise questions about the ways in which a group of learners (including their tutors) operate within this environment. In particular, we focus upon issues to do with the language of electronic discourse and the role of the tutor in managing CMC conferences. Together these reveal practices and problems which must be addressed if the learning group is to constitute itself as a co-operative community rather than as a collection of disparate individuals.

Notions of community

In the nineteenth century, the German sociologist Ferdinand Tönnies distinguished relations in communities which were characterized by such things as intimacy, longevity, a sense of 'communion' and kinship. These relations were constructed within the same geographical location. Tönnies (1955) described this societal structure as *Gemeinschaft* (community). He contrasted this with social relations constructed within *Gesellschaft* (society). In this social structure, relationships were impersonal, contractual and short-lived. Tönnies saw the development of *Gesellschaftlich* (social relations) as a consequence of the processes of industrialization and urbanization.

Tönnies lamented what he saw to be the 'destruction' of traditional society, and with it the potential for anomie and alienation. In Tönnies's work, great value is placed on the relations established within *Gemeinschaft* and the understanding engendered by his work led to an association of 'the concept of "community" with ideas of social support, intimacy and security' (Jarry and Jarry 1991: 98).

By the 1960s, sociologists generally accepted that a community is not necessarily location-dependent. Rather, it is dependent on 'networks of people'. Kinship studies (see, for example, Young and Willmott 1960) did much to inform sociological understanding and shift the focus from geographical proximity to the nature of social relations. Thus an emerging, more complex, understanding of the concept of community accepted that while community might refer to the nature of relationships which occur in any geographically confined location, it could also embrace relationships that were established at an abstract level – at the level of ideas – as in the notion, for example, of a 'research community'.

In more general usage there is at least one other way in which community is understood:

> a particular type of social relationship; one that possesses certain qualities. It infers [sic] the existence of a 'community spirit' or 'community feeling'.
>
> (Jarry and Jarry 1991: 99)

Advocating this type of social relationship as an ideal is typical of political discussions in the UK in the 1990s: the benefits of 'community' have been assumed; the possibilities of achieving it taken for granted.

Meanwhile, debates in modern social theory challenge the assumption that community is 'a good thing' *per se*. Those challenging the assumption, argues Knight Abowitz (1999), do so in part because there has been a tendency to construct community and human difference in opposition to each other. For community to operate, it is suggested, the 'erroneous assumption of shared subjectivity' (p. 147) must operate too. The image of an homogeneous group operating consensually dominates. Conflicts are discouraged; alternative views frowned upon in the community.

There are, perhaps, good reasons to disavow community: both in the past and present, communities have served to regulate desires, limit the growth of unrecognized or second-class citizens, and either erase ... or invent differences among persons ... in oppressive practices in political life.

(Knight Abowitz 1999: 148)

The solution for Knight Abowitz, however, is not to 'eradicate any meaningful use of the term' but to reclaim the concept of community. She suggests that social diversity/social difference, rather than undercutting an understanding of community, can be a feature of it. She argues that this is most likely to be the case in learning communities because it is in these that individuals from diverse backgrounds are more likely to be brought together. Identifying the processes by which participants interrelate thereby becomes the key to understanding how these communities function.

Community as experienced at the start of the twenty-first century can no longer be conceptualized only as having essential characteristics that focus on location and the 'sameness' or homogeneity of its members. Rather, to enable the concept to be operationalized in contemporary society, there is a need to embrace an understanding of community which, in the pre-cyberspace world, accepts that communities are:

- not necessarily bounded by location or geographical proximity
- composed of social networks and interrelatedness
- inclusive of social difference rather than 'sameness'
- dynamic rather than fixed.

The next section presents some of the discussions concerning the peculiarities of communities in cyberspace and identifies what might be considered to be the characteristics of 'cyber-communities.'

Community in cyberspace

Steve Jones points out that:

Critical to the *rhetoric* surrounding the information highway is *the promise of a renewed sense of community* and, in many instances, new types and formations of community. Computer-mediated communication, it seems, will do by way of electronic pathways what cement roads were unable to do. Namely, connect us rather than atomise us, put us at the controls of a 'vehicle' and yet not detach us from the rest of the world.

(Jones 1995: 11, emphases added)

Many writers suggest that it is this connectivity which is a central feature of computer-mediated communication (CMC). Rheingold's work (1993) is perhaps typical of those who argue, in a generic sense, that 'communities' can be created in the virtual world and are established because of a felt need for connectivity. He argues that, as informal social spaces dissolve in modern society, and with them the possibilities for establishing meaningful social networks, user-groups 'on-line' have increased. This, for him, has been as a result of the need that people have for a sense of community – and CMC offers the opportunity to re-establish social bonds in the modern world.

Jones (1995), in contrast, focuses on what the growth in on-line communication tells us about the postmodern world. The ways in which social contact is established in the CMC environments tell us a good deal about the nature of community formation in postmodern society. In Jones's portrayal of relationships in CMC, the image of the 'pick and mix' postmodern world is aroused: CMC allows us to customize our social contacts from fragmented communities (1995: 16).

Irrespective of why these groups are established, two linked questions remain for the purposes of this discussion. First, are groups that exist on-line really communities, or are they simply 'ephemeral, imagined communities, too fleeting, too superficial, and too "virtual" to warrant serious exploration?' (Thomsen *et al.* 1998: 2). Second, if communities can exist in cyberspace, what is their relevance to learning on-line?

In addressing the first question, Fox and Roberts (1999) and Thomsen *et al.* (1998) are particularly relevant. Although writing in very different contexts, both suggest that it is important, in virtual environments, to study the extent to which participants *believe* they are part of something that is special to them. Fox and Roberts cite Poster to illustrate:

> what makes a community vital to its members is their treatment of the communication as meaningful and important.
>
> (Poster 1995 cited in Fox and Roberts 1999: 664)

Fox and Roberts argue that participants' ongoing reflexive construction of social spaces and identities demonstrates that the participants in their CMC environment 'behave as if they are part of a community'. What leads them to such a conclusion includes the ways in which 'social order' is established – particularly through interaction and the nature of messages – and their (shared) context – in this case as general (medical) practitioners:

> Perhaps it is the collegiality of this group which leads it to invest their virtual interactions with features of community; a spirit of mutual trust, responsibility and on-going communication on the one hand; on the other, the petty spats and flaming which also mirror the tensions which arise in face-to-face engagements.
>
> (Fox and Roberts 1999: 666)

Thomsen *et al.* (1998) have little doubt that the user-groups which are the subject of their studies *do* form communities. But, following Cerulo (1997), they argue that on-line communities can only be studied as such if key analytic concepts used in studying 'real' communities are reconceptualized. An expanded social environment has been created by people's use of technological developments and therefore our tools to analyse it must also adapt. For them the central characteristics on which the definition of community turn include the nature and extent of social interaction the nature and extent of social bonding, and what they call 'empirical' (personal) experience.

Consequently, in the above discussions and others (Baym 1995; Jones 1995; Reid 1995) we are led to the conclusion that significant features of on-line 'communities' include:

- participants' perceptions that they are in fact part of a group/community
- high levels of social interaction
- relationship-building (social bonding).

Following Thomsen *et al.* (1998), we accept that an understanding of how these features might be articulated in cyberspace may differ from a 'terrestrial' or pre-cyberspace understanding.

Social spaces

From the discussions above, the transactions which create communities could be seen to be located in 'social spaces'. In traditional, pre-cyberspace communities, meaningful social relations can be established and developed at all times under all conditions, both face-to-face and at a distance (for example by telephone) simply by community members acting with each other. In electronic communication systems where people do *not* meet face-to-face, it is possible to create separate (virtual) zones of activity set aside for specific purposes. One such zone might be called a student common room.

For the purposes of research, one of the authors was given permission by contributors to enter one of these 'social spaces'. This particular common room area contained 387 entries over a six-month period. Students had been informed of the function of this space by the tutor who opened this social area with the message:

Here you can moan about things, exchange gossip and generally chat about the things you are interested in.

The tutor also alerted them to the fact that the area was a 'tutor-free zone'.

The entries range across wide and diverse activities, including swapping cake recipes, attempts for those living near to each other to make arrangements for a social get-together, the sending of birthday greetings to members of one of the study groups, and the exchange of jokes. All of these contributions and exchanges, with chit-chat and banter, clearly provided a sense of contact among participants, as well as offering some kind of light relief from the various pressures which the students were experiencing. Some students would simply 'drop in' from time to time to 'see what was going on' and then leave a note, as it were, on some matter which had caught their eye. Throughout the database as a whole, then, there is a sense that, at the very least, the facility provided a welcome diversion, somewhere to turn to, around the times that individuals had set aside to study. The personal pressures under which these distance students operate also find expression within this student common room. Such pressures were to do with the managing of study within full-time work and family commitments. The time recorded for some transmissions (very late evening and beyond midnight) was in itself an indicator of this. Some entries indicate that the patterns of domestic life and its established routines had to change to accommodate the demands of study.

These exchanges can be seen to serve three main functions and, simultaneously, lay the foundations for the establishment of a 'virtual' community. First, exchanging personal, circumstantial information about themselves enabled emotional support to be offered. As one student noted, learning that others were in similar circumstances and being able to 'talk' about these experiences – even when presented in an amusing fashion – provided essential emotional support. This emotional support was perceived by some as helping them to 'keep going.' Second, there is evidence of a sense of belonging together, of social bonding, among members, particularly in one of the study groups represented in the archive. After many weeks of collaborative work, one overseas member of this group (student A) withdrew from the programme. The news about student A is relayed to the common room by student B, with whom, it is evident, he has been in personal e-mail correspondence. The sense of loss felt by other members of the learning group is shown quite clearly:

> Thanks for letting us know . . . It is quite a blow to hear that one of 'us' has had to withdraw, but good to hear that [A]'ll be back when he can. I hope we didn't miss out something we could have helped with, although I think you kept well in touch . . .

> Thanks [B] for relaying [A]'s message. I must say it's a crying shame and when I read the message my heart sank.

> One small question . . . is/was there anything we could have done to keep him in the group? I get a really strong sense of defeat when this sort of thing happens, especially when he was so isolated overseas. Not asking for reasons, just that it's not failing on the communications front.

The sense of belonging is conveyed in these excerpts and it is interesting, in view of the discussions on the concept of community earlier in the chapter, that this belonging recognizes 'difference'; it is inclusive rather than being exclusive of others. Equally, all adopt the collective language of the first-person plural, as does [B] in response to these concerns:

> No, there wasn't anything to be done, we haven't been neglectful, don't worry. It's just pace of life and should settle down.

Third, to counter the assumption that physical co-presence is a key (determining) factor in judging 'the significance of a communication exchange' (Thomsen *et al.* 1998: 3), there are examples in the database of rich, quality interactions. For example, five months after the opening of the student common room, one student posted in this comment, spontaneous because it is unprompted by any earlier offering:

> Meeting (or virtually meeting) new people has been the best thing so far . . . what do you think?

In summary, from this brief overview of entries in one student common room alone there is evidence that where space is made available for students to 'create' communities of learners, they can and often do so. This does not mean that it will always 'just happen'. Our on-line learners share, for instance, a wider context-bound connectivity. They are drawn from a wider 'community' of professionals undergoing continuing professional development and this factor may enable them to interact and establish social relationships in more ready ways. Their membership of this wider context and the accompanying sense of common identity which it promotes, despite individual differences, enables them to transform a network of (potential) relationships into a shared community of learning founded on (presumed if not actual) shared experience. The differences which remain, together with the transacting medium itself, that of written communication and exchange for a collective learning experience, nonetheless must be made serviceable to all of the members of a conference group. Here, there are some particular matters to be resolved.

The language of electronic discourse

One of the major sets of problems confronting participants within CMC conferencing relates to the question of language. The problems are likely to be experienced most forcefully by first-time users of the conferencing facility, but can show themselves even within the meetings of more experienced users.

The first and most obvious point to note about CMC conferences is that they are conducted through a literary medium. All contributions to a conference have to be composed – and this, for most participants, tutors included, can create difficulties. 'Part of the problem here' observed Rowntree (1995: 213), 'is persuading students to give themselves permission to write notes rather than essays.' But there are powerful reasons why students especially find it difficult to give themselves that permission to write in reduced form. There is an anxiety, neatly expressed by this student response to an evaluation conducted by Murphy *et al.* (1998: 249): 'We tend to be careful of what we put down if it is saved and displayable for others to see.'

What is put down is meaning (in more permanent form than speech) within the language deployed. What one writes, therefore, could be subjected by others to exacting scrutiny, and the contributor found wanting both in terms of the value of the contribution and in relation to the adequacy of language. Whether or not any contribution would be subjected to that sort of demolition by any member of the conference is not the point here. The uncertainty remains. And it would be ingenuous to suppose that members of the CMC group do not form impressions of each other on the basis of what they read. The assumption that such a sharpened focus of attention will be given to one's written composition of language may inhibit contribution; perhaps especially within groups of practitioners sharing a profession, since to get something 'wrong' would call one's professionalism into question. How one appears, face-to-face, is represented in this new context of communication by how one 'looks' on the screen (or printed page). That such impressions are more permanent than the shifting images of face-to-face encounters – and may last the duration, at least, of the conference – perhaps reminds reluctant or nervous contributors that the language they compose composes also an impression of themselves.

There is a more specific reason why students will frequently find it diffi-cult to write in note-form their contributions to CMC conferences. To write in a reduced form of English is to risk reducing or distorting the meaning intended. Between persons with an established relationship, where much is known and can be assumed, the language of e-mailing may well show considerable variation:

> having a stylistic quality more like written speech than like conven-tional writing, something which its immediacy and speed allow and render seeming proper in its context.
>
> (Tweddle *et al.* 1997: 28)

What CMC conferences, within contexts of learning, call for in the main, though, is not spur-of-the-moment thinking but a *reflective consideration*. Further more, a reflective consideration which will be communicable to an actual (if virtual) audience, members of which might not be known to one personally. The language of composition therefore tends towards an *explicit* statement of meaning because little can be taken for granted. As meaning is driven towards explicitness, so it will move towards a form of language close to the conventions of standard English. This is especially so of the gram-matical construction of the language deployed. The form of language found in conference archives examined by one of the authors confirms very strongly this view. The variations of language do not, in fact, stray far from standard English, and the linguistic features observed may be called 'relaxed formal' (Webb 2000). An added advantage of CMC conferencing, therefore, is that it might be particularly well suited to developing contributors' abilities with the written mode of language itself.

There is another freedom within the electronic system which can directly damage learning. That is the freedom to compose in whatever form and to whatever length the individual wishes. Working to a common purpose, the members of a CMC conference have to work also towards a common set of practices as to how such a conference will be conducted, that is, how they will use its facility. The decentralization, or democratization of power, can mean that the members of an electronic conference spend a great deal of time working out how they intend to work together. This negotiation towards a set of common agreements then becomes the subject of the conference. Lally and Barrett (1999: 157) noted the following student report of her experience: 'I think we discussed having a discussion without really discussing anything.'

A tutor, in opening a conference, may well be clear as to its purpose, and may even make an explicit statement of it to all participants, as in this example from one of the archives examined:

> The purpose of having a conference is to **emulate classroom conditions** where peers are able to exchange ideas and opinions rather than just get the tutor's view.
>
> (Emphasis in original)

Once begun, however, the actual conduct of a CMC conference becomes the participative sum of its members, even where they all appear to have subscribed to an initial set of expectations. There can be occasions, however, when the form of contribution made by a member of the learning group can make it difficult for other students to contribute and can subvert the declared and agreed intention of the conference.

In the course of one conference, a male student [G] entered a lengthy, discursive, essay-type response. It was the first (and only) offering of this type within proceedings which, until then, had consisted of relatively short contributions. The same group of students moved on together to the topic of their next conference. Within this conference-topic there were then *several* lengthy essay-responses, some of greater length than G's original essay. This batch of essays came from G himself, and also from two other students: F (male) and A (female). This led student C (female) to interject:

> When I started work on this unit I believed that the purpose of the conference was to simulate the class discussion that would take place if we were not on a distance-learning course. While [F's] contribution is very impressive, it doesn't fit in with the spirit of this – being more like an assignment than a contribution to a class discussion. I haven't got the time or energy to write something along these lines for every activity. It put me off writing my own meagre contribution when it will be read alongside an entry like [F's] which is in a different league altogether. What does everyone else think?

The narrative of this electronic interchange bears a remarkable similarity to the progress of a face-to-face group discussion recorded by Johnson Abercrombie (1969) when one member of the group was taken to task by 'another member of the class [who] explained that the idea was not to debate with well-prepared speeches, but just to talk spontaneously' (p. 82). Self-regulation is an important requisite for the beneficial conduct of a CMC conference. Paramount here is learning to use the language of electronic discourse in ways which enable the group of learners to work co-operatively. Even given this convergence of practice, the role of the tutor in the management of CMC conferences remains critical.

Managing a CMC conference: the role of the tutor

The early experience of tutors involved in CMC conferences within the University of Greenwich was summarized by Hall:

> It took staff a while to work out the best way to lead conferences. Most began with an urge not to take too strong a lead in discussion but found themselves moving towards a more directive stance. The emerging preferred mode seems to be for the tutor to open a discussion by referring to something in the written materials, posing a question and asking for responses. The students then engage with the material – over quite a long period, perhaps a week. The tutor may maintain a watch on the discussion or may join in to urge it along or correct a misapprehension. The tutor often chooses to summarise the discussion before setting up the next one by raising some new issues . . .
>
> (Hall 1997: 56)

This account appears to reduce the tutor's role to a minimal operation, allowing students to engage freely, or not, with the subject of the conference. In this sense, once opened, the management of a CMC conference is itself 'open' – it will go the way, or ways, directed by individual contributions and any follow-up responses to such offerings. Equally, participants are free to ignore offerings made by contributors. The nature of a CMC conference – its asynchronicity and the dispersal of its contributors – changes the nature of control. Tella noted that, within the context of such a conference:

> Power is decentralised to the whole network area without an actual recognisable 'leadership centre' or 'leader'. Every participant possesses the potential power to take the initiative and independently respond or not to respond to messages received.
>
> (Tella 1995: 33)

One consequence of this decentralization is that individual participants are free to opt out of the proceedings, either substantially or completely (for periods of time at least). Such nominal participants have been described as 'lurkers' (Mason 1994). They may well 'look in' on a conference, but not actively contribute. Lally and Barrett (1999), in their evaluation project of CMC conferences, also identified such learners among their target groups:

> In the project evaluation, however, all but one of the students who hadn't contributed messages to the seminar events reported that,

although they hadn't contributed 'actively', they had enjoyed reading the contributions made by other people.

(Lally and Barrett 1999: 155)

Although there may be still some personal advantage to students who make no contribution to a conference, their 'absence' from the proceedings undercuts the notion of a working community of learners. In this respect, at least, it would seem that the tutors convening a conference need to monitor its proceedings and find means of encouraging all of its members to contribute, just as in face-to-face teaching a tutor will try to promote full participation. Whilst prompts to participate within live classroom discussions can be made directly, and unthreateningly, encouragements to specific members of the learning group to participate in a CMC conference are best transferred to the individual e-mail facility. The problem here is that one potential advantage of the CMC conference – the prospective sharing of control – when not adopted and actively implemented by all the participants, can be also its limitation. Thus, paradoxically, the 'democratization' of power conferred by the nature of a CMC conference requires a control function – as Tella (1995: 34) also concluded: 'The lack of firm leadership seems to be the main reason for failure in computer conferences'.

Ideally, one might argue, the control function of a CMC conference should operate through the autonomy of the learning group, the 'democratization' of the system worked co-operatively by its participants towards its stated outcomes. In practice, as Lewis *et al.* (1997) observed in their study of computer-mediated continuing professional development, 'conferencing in particular needed to be structured and directed, as the students seemed to be less independent and autonomous than had been expected' (p. 79). Although they thought that, in general, 'basic considerations regarding the conduct of classroom seminar discussions were still found to apply', they identified also the following distinct roles for the tutor in the management of CMC conferences:

Tutors should acknowledge every student's contribution to the debate, should draw out the tentative and control the garrulous, should help to structure and focus the issues under consideration, and should encourage students to interact with each other.

(Lewis *et al.* 1997: 79)

Detailed analysis of the archives of such conferences reveals that what tutors actually do in order to initiate and sustain control covers a wider compass of initiatives and strategies than those identified above by Hall (1997). They reveal also occasions when, within the development of a particular conference, an additional (or alternative) strategy would have helped to shape the conference more productively and to enhance the learning experience. Certainly, too, as tutors become both more experienced and more confident of their roles within a CMC conference, the evidence of the archives shows a greater preparedness to 'join in' as an equal partner in the matter at hand rather than just keep a watching brief.

Tutor activities in the management of CMC conferences

We supplemented our analysis of the CMC exchanges with discussions with tutors involved in CMC conferencing. From this, the following list of tutor activities emerged as guidelines for sound practice. Remember, these emerge from contexts to do with continuing professional development, and that this in turn assumes the model of the reflective practitioner.

- *Initiating the conference.* Practice here suggests that making explicit the expectations of the conference, including the anticipated way of working together, provides a useful sense of purpose to the event. In a way this is the CMC equivalent of a classroom statement of aims.

  > Throughout this Unit 5 conference we will make extensive use of the text and activities contained in the handbook. We are focusing conference entries on those activities which we feel will provide the most opportunities for the sharing and exchange of experiences and opinions. In most cases we have selected an activity from the unit handbook but in one or two instances we have either adapted them or created a new activity which will better facilitate a collaborative approach.
  >
  > We would encourage you to use the unit materials in preparation for working with your peers in the conference. Please feel free to comment on contributions made as you would in a traditional classroom. The unit conference is your opportunity to interact with peers and get tutor feedback . . .

- *Introducing the topic.* An obvious but essential requirement which sets the terms of reference for the ensuing conference. It may proceed from readings and activities within supporting printed materials or be freely composed. There may be occasions, as a means of 'getting things going', when the tutor might make a first offering on some aspect of the matter posed. In the archives examined, this appears not to happen, the tutors moving on immediately to the next stage of inviting responses (as Hall, above, noted) and waiting for participants to come in.
- *Inviting responses.* The essential thing here appears to be to state the nature of the responses sought in the opening stages of the conference. In one archive examined, the focus was provided by the question 'How would you define learning?' The framing of the question provoked responses which went straight to the language-conventions of definitions and their attempts at inclusiveness. Responses of a more personal nature, however, might have been invited, with examples of different kinds of learning experienced as a means of providing the first steps towards an exploration of their implications. That would have been more in keeping with the intended direction for the conference and the model of reflective practice on which it was founded. The responsibility for providing

direction within which individual entries can be 'shaped' would appear to
rest within the tutor's initial responsibility.
- *Intervening.* There would appear to be many occasions within a conference when a tutor might or should intervene for different reasons. One
is, as a member of the learning group, to make an individual contribution to the discussion. To do so requires deft judgement as to timing,
since the tutor would not want thereby to pre-empt contributions from
students within the group. Another form of tutor intervention is that of
challenge. Challenging is an essential part of the process of some learning, and if participants have not made a needed challenge then, arguably,
the responsibility for so doing rests with the tutor. In response to one
student's definition of learning, a tutor sent in the message: 'Thanks [D]
for that input – what have you based this definition upon?' That challenge prompted a much longer response from D, which in turn provided
details and matter with which others could engage. A tutor contribution
of another type might give a 'nudge' to the direction of the discussion.
Following several exchanges among participants, one tutor intervened with:

> Your contributions demonstrate very clearly the variety of approaches
> which students bring to the learning process, and of course we have
> to recognise that all learning is, in the end, individual. I liked [G's]
> comment that 'Some students seem to be able to interpret things in
> totally unexpected ways' . . .

The tutor here uses the contributions of others to act as a bridge to
matters of learning styles. The intervention brought about another batch
of useful contributions from students while at the same time enabling the
tutor to transfer thinking towards the next formal topic which had been
preselected for conferencing.
- *Collating.* Where opportunities present themselves for bringing together
two or more contributions for the attention of the whole membership,
the tutor may want to use the similarities or differences expressed to
reaffirm a matter central to the discussion – and possibly to stimulate
further responses to others. One good example reads:

> If you put [A's] and [L's] recent responses together you can get a
> good feel for what is behind Outcomes 2 and 3 of this unit . . .
> [A] has shown how he goes about trying to resolve cultural differ-
> ences between [different groups of people] when they meet as a
> group of learners. Many of you will have experienced similar sub-
> groups in your own classes . . .
> [L] describes the very different situations which arise when provid-
> ing learner support to individuals.
> Does anyone else have such experiences to share with us?

- *Redirecting.* There may be occasions within a conference when the target
for discussion becomes obscured, or even put to one side while other
matters are pursued. If a realignment of the discussion does not occur,

prompted by student contributions, then it is one of the duties of the tutor to effect such a redirection to the convened purpose of the conference. In one conference the proceedings veered into a lengthy (and ultimately helpful) discussion on the nature, length and style of contributions being made, their appropriateness as means of stimulating discussion, and the demoralizing effects which some contributions made on other participants. The tutors convening this conference allowed student offerings to proceed through such an airing of views before one of them posted a two-part offering of his own. The first part began: 'I'm glad you have sorted this out (sort of).' There followed a reformulation of the purposes of a CMC conference, together with a relating of this to participants' own experience of face-to-face teaching, challenging the students to explain their own resolutions of conflicting interests in the management of those circumstances. This part of the tutor's input represents a redirecting of the conference to general professional concerns. The second part of the contribution, however, is much more specific and directed. It opens:

> Back to the topic.
> The big issue here is whether we accept the Eysenck/Cyril Burt view that intelligence/ability is something that is more or less fixed . . .

The remainder of the contribution summarizes several student offerings made before the conference wandered onto its diversionary track, and concludes with an alternative statement of the conference topic for others to comment upon.

- *Summarizing*. Two kinds of summarizing appear in the archives of CMC conferences examined. There are those which summarize important points made during the course of the conference, such as the one cited immediately above. Such summaries identify the points made so far, and often employ this gathering of issues to direct attention to their further implications or applications. The purpose of these summaries is, therefore, to try to take things further. The second form of tutor summary appears at the end of the exchanges making up the conference. Thus, at the end of a conference on learning styles, one tutor's summary began:

> It was interesting that several of you have experienced administering the Honey & Mumford Questionnaire at intervals over a period of time, and have thus had the opportunity to observe that your successive scores have not exhibited much consistency. Apart from taking into account my earlier warning about the dangers of (self) labelling, there would seem to be three issues here . . .

The remainder of this entry summarizes the issues identified. The purpose of an end-of-conference summary appears to be twofold. First, it ensures that all participants recognize where they have been, the ground covered. Second, it 'values' the exercise and confirms its worth.

Another archive, a conference among health professionals, carried an interesting variation on tutor summarizing. In this case, the tutor split the participants into two groups, and asked the members of each group to prepare, and agree on, their own summary of an issue via e-mailing among themselves. Both group summaries were then to be entered into the conference area for comparison and evaluation.

What this review of tutor activities within CMC conferencing shows is a number of discrete functions in the management of participant interaction. In addition to such actual contributions, the tutor must maintain a watching brief on proceedings along the lines identified by Lewis *et al.* (1997), and seek to encourage all participants to contribute. If, as Tella (1995) concluded, the main reason for failure in computer conferences is the lack of leadership within an environment which, potentially, decentralizes power, then there is a paradox here. A CMC conference, as a learning device, must be coherent and display direction towards its intended purpose or outcome. In order to ensure that a conference does cohere, the tutor reclaims, as it were, that centralizing function if not by leading then by directing operations.

Conclusion

Learning communities *can* exist in cyberspace, though not without their acknowledged tensions, such as those identified in this chapter. Following Knight Abowitz (1999), such virtual learning communities would seem to accord more with her revised model of community than with traditional sociological descriptions. In part, the difference may be attributed to the power shift that the new technology operates by and employs. The potential democratizing of the system creates its own tensions. Given that each participant within electronic discourse may contribute to it at whatever length in whatever linguistic style, there is clearly a need to develop a tolerance of difference among participants. At the same time there may well exist an opposite urge, among some participants at least, either to impose or to negotiate a conformity across such contributions. As our examples show, such tensions may result in actual and declared conflict which then becomes a matter to resolve.

In order that the group of learners can consider themselves as a community, there needs to be a process by which they can arrive at a sense of cohesion. Individuals, left to themselves, might negotiate their way towards that sense of unity for the purpose of interactive learning. Failing that, it would seem that the tutor must be prepared to undertake the role of managing the learning event.

We have discussed some of the peculiarities which distinguish virtual learning communities from other forms of learning experience. Whilst the purposes of convening such communities remain unaltered, the radical shift in the means of communication challenges us to develop new ways of interacting towards a common goal. The nature of the complexity has been well summarized by Jones (1995) and ensures that we do not lose sight of the means at the centre of our discussion:

> CMC, of course, is not just a tool; it is at once technology, medium, and engine of social relations. It not only structures social relations, it is the space within which relations occur and the tool that individuals use to enter that space. It is more than the context within which social relations occur (although it is that, too) for it is commented on and imaginatively constructed by symbolic processes initiated and maintained by individuals and groups.
>
> (Jones 1995: 16)

References

Baym, N. (1995) The emergence of community in computer-mediated communications, in S.G. Jones (ed.) *CyberSociety: Computer-mediated Communication and Community*. Thousand Oaks, CA: Sage.

Cerulo, K.A. (1997) Reframing social concepts for a brave new (virtual) world, *Sociological Inquiry*, 67(1): 48–58.

Fox, N. and Roberts, C. (1999) GPs in cyberspace: the sociology of 'virtual community', *Sociological Review*, 47(4): 643–71.

Hall, D. (1997) Computer mediated communication in post-compulsory teacher education, *Open Learning*, 12(3): 54–7.

Jarry, D. and Jarry, J. (1991) *Dictionary of Sociology*. Glasgow: HarperCollins.

Johnson Abercrombie, M.L. (1969) *The Anatomy of Judgement*. Harmondsworth: Penguin.

Jones, S.G. (1995) Understanding community in the information age, in S.G. Jones (ed.) *CyberSociety: Computer-mediated Communication and Community*. Thousand Oaks, CA: Sage.

Knight Abowitz, K. (1999) Reclaiming community, *Educational Theory*, 49(2): 143–59.

Lally, V. and Barrett, E. (1999) Building a learning community on-line: towards socio-academic interaction, *Research Papers in Education Policy and Practice*, 14(2): 147–63.

Lewis, T., Gould, M. and Ryan, M. (1997) Computer conferencing and the continuing professional development of teachers in the post-16 sector, in J. Field (ed.) *Electronic Pathways: Adult Learning and the New Communication Technologies*, pp. 74–80. Leicester: National Institute of Adult Continuing Education.

Mason, R. (1994) *Using Communications Media in Open and Flexible Learning*. London: Kogan Page.

Murphy, K.L., Drabier, R. and Epps, M.L. (1998) A constructivist look at interaction and collaboration via computer conferencing, *International Journal of Telecommunications*, 4(2/3): 237–61.

Poster, M. (1995) Postmodern virtualities, in M. Featherstone and R. Burrows (eds) *Cyberspace, Cyberbodies, Cyberpunk: Cultures of Technological Embodiment*. London: Sage.

Reid, E. (1995) Virtual worlds: culture and imagination, in S.G. Jones (ed.) *CyberSociety: Computer-mediated Communication and Community.* Thousand Oaks, CA: Sage.

Rheingold, H. (1993) *The Virtual Community: Homesteading on the Electronic Frontier.* Menlo Park, CA: Addison-Wesley.

Rowntree, D. (1995) Teaching and learning on-line: a correspondence education for the 21st century? *British Journal of Educational Technology*, 26(3): 205–15.

Tella, S. (1995) *Virtual school in a networking learning environment*, volume 1. Helsinki: OLE Publications.

Thomsen, S.R., Straubhaar, J.D. and Bolyard, M. (1998) *Ethnomethodology and the Study of Online Communities: Exploring the CyberStreets* at http://sosig.ac.uk/iriss/papers/paper32.htm (accessed 26 July, 1999).

Tönnies, F. (1955) *Community and Society*. London: Routledge (first published 1887 as *Gemeinschaft–Gesellschaft*).

Tweddle, S., Adams, A., Clarke, S., Scrimshaw, P. and Walton, S. (1997) *English for Tomorrow*. Buckingham: Open University Press.

Webb, E. (2000) Making the virtual real: a computer application for apprentice writers? *The Use of English*, 51(2): 149–58.

Young, M. and Willmott, P. (1960) *Family and Kinship in East London*. Harmondsworth: Penguin.

14

The Virtual Learning Community: Informating the Learning Process with On-line Learning Environments

Kevin Brosnan

Although the adoption of on-line learning environments is now well established and has received significant attention in the Dearing Report (National Committee of Inquiry into Higher Education 1997), a whole range of dynamics has been unleashed that have the potential to change radically the fundamental nature of the relationship between student and teacher. In order to explore these dynamics carefully, this chapter employs the concept of 'informating' (Zuboff 1988) to illuminate aspects of the adoption process that have received little attention in the past. The chapter is structured as follows. First, the concept of informating is identified and examined, drawing out facets of it that are particularly relevant to on-line learning environments. Second, the informating facilities of modern, Internet-based, on-line, course management software are explored through an examination of one such system, WebCT. Third, the implications, both positive and negative, of these informating facilities for the student/teacher relationship are explored. Finally, some concluding remarks are offered about the need to acknowledge that it is the way in which technology is employed, not the technology itself, that offers opportunities for informating the learning process to the benefit or the disbenefit of the student/teacher relationship.

The concept of informating

In her seminal work, Shoshana Zuboff (1988) explored the way in which modern information technology shaped the nature of work in different organizations. She drew a clear distinction between the use of information technology to automate, i.e. 'replace the human body with a technology that enables the same processes to be performed with more continuity and control' (p. 9), and its ability to informate, which is where '[a]ctivities, events, and objects are translated into and made visible by information' (p. 10). It is through the informating capacity of information technology that it is possible to achieve 'a deeper level of transparency to activities that had been either partially or completely opaque' (p. 9). The use of technology to automate processes is now well understood and can be managed quite effectively, but the use of technology to informate is in its infancy and 'the consequences of the technology's informating capacity are often regarded as unintended' (p. 11).

One of the fundamental changes in the informated work environment is the shift from action-centred skills, where the worker relies on cues directly apprehended from the physical work environment, to 'intellective skills', where the worker relies on interpreting symbolic cues via a data interface, invariably in the shape of a computer screen. Intellective skill places new demands on workers as they must now engage in: 'sense-making based more exclusively upon abstract cues; explicit inferential reasoning used both inductively and deductively; and procedural, systemic thinking' (Zuboff 1988: 95). Effective performance in the informated environment requires that the worker is able to use the mass of data now available, to mentally visualize processes in order to experience 'the mastery, certainty, and control that was routinely available in the world of action-centred skill' (p. 80). One of the consequences of this shift from dependence on directly apprehended physical cues to interpretation of symbolic cues is what Zuboff calls the 'crisis of trust' (p. 80), where operators feel a sense of unease about what the symbolic cues actually tell them about the state of reality and they feel uncertain about their actions, which are now mediated through the symbolic interface.

A question must be posed about the applicability of Zuboff's insights to an entirely different context, namely universities, which offer courses that are either wholly or in part supported by networking technology. The work of a teacher in higher education requires a fundamentally different 'skill set' from that required of an operator in a paper mill. However, although there are clear and significant differences there is also common ground: higher education is becoming increasingly automated (a necessary precursor to informating) and, as pressure on resources grows, teachers in higher education have less opportunity for direct contact with their students. The opportunities for the use of action-centred skills, in an unexpected classroom situation, are receding, to be replaced by interaction mediated by various electronic media (e-mail, asynchronous computer conferencing, web pages and so on). The shift from action-centred to intellective skills in teaching in higher education has been noted by Jones (1998) in the context of computer conferencing when he observes that the 'application of computer conferencing and other new technologies may then be part of a process of making explicit and potentially codifiable what is currently craft or practice based knowledge in education' (p. 21). In order to explore this shift more fully, the next section examines the 'informating' facilities within WebCT, an Internet-based, on-line course management system.

WebCT and its informating facilities

World Wide Web course tools were originally developed at the University of British Columbia, Canada, but have now been sold to a commercial company, Universal Learning and Training. WebCT is an example of a growing range of software systems that provide a suite of integrated software tools for creating and maintaining courses that are offered either partially or entirely over the Internet using the Web protocols. Amongst the tools that WebCT provides for course management is a collection that allows for student tracking and monitoring. These tools allow the teacher, as course designer, to view:

- all students' accesses
- accesses of a subset of students
- an individual student's distribution of page hits
- the coverage of course pages accessed by an individual student
- the history of pages visited by an individual student.

A further tool, page tracking, allows the teacher to view how many times an individual Web page (containing course content) has been hit, the average length of time that students spent viewing each page and how many posts, to an electronic discussion forum, were made by students about a particular page. Screen shots of the 'All students' accesses' and 'Distribution of hits' output are shown in Figures 14.1 and 14.2.

The rationale behind these facilities is stated clearly by one of the principal designers of WebCT, Murray Goldberg:

> One common side-effect of the recent proliferation of WWW-based courses has been a loss of the ability to gauge a student's interest in, and progress through a course until an assignment or exam is given. This may be too late to help some students catch up. In a traditional lecture-based course it is relatively easy to determine whether a student has been attending classes. Likewise their level of involvement in lectures is immediately apparent through the questions they ask and their attentiveness during lectures. Unfortunately, WWW-based courses do not offer the same level of feedback. In delivering WWW-based courses at UBC [University of British Columbia] in the Department of Computer Science, our experience led us to realize the value of immediate and detailed knowledge of student progress through the course. Therefore, we designed and incorporated student progress monitoring tools into WebCT, our environment for building WWW-based courses. WebCT allows quick creation of WWW-based educational environments. The built-in student progress tracking tools facilitate timely determination of the progress of each student through the course material, as well as an overall determination of the level of use of each course component.

> (Goldberg 1996)

Figure 14.1 'All students' accesses' screen

Personal Information		Access Information			Articles	
Full name	Login ID	First Access	Last Access	Hits	Read	Posted
⌐∷	marty	Sep 18 13:03 97	May 8 16:20 98	11	0	0
⌐∷	april	Sep 18 14:25 97	Sep 18 14:57 97	2	0	0
⌐∷	teresa	Sep 18 13:22 97	Sep 19 10:05 97	3	0	0
⌐∷	henry	Sep 18 13:32 97	Sep 18 13:32 97	1	0	0
Fazal Karim, Salima						
⌐∷	tyler	May 26 16:43 98	May 26 16:43 98	1	0	0
⌐∷	murray	Sep 18 14:12 97	May 18 1:28 98	4	0	0
⌐∷	john	Sep 18 13:07 97	May 20 18:10 98	77	0	0
⌐∷	anita	Sep 18 13:22 97	Sep 18 13:22 97	1	0	0
Ogg, Ryan						
⌐∷	sasan	Sep 6 22:11 97	Sep 23 22:24 97	78	3	2
⌐∷ \	heather	Sep 18 15:48 97	Sep 18 15:48 97	1	0	0
⌐∷	paul	Sep 18 15:50 97	Sep 18 15:50 97	1	0	0

Figure 14.2   Distribution of hits for Parker

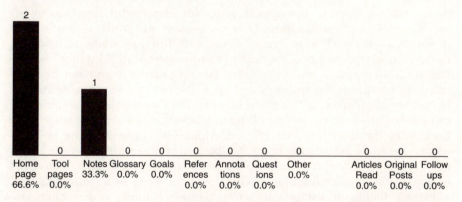

| Home page 66.6% | Tool pages 0.0% | Notes 33.3% | Glossary 0.0% | Goals 0.0% | References 0.0% | Annotations 0.0% | Questions 0.0% | Other 0.0% | Articles Read 0.0% | Original Posts 0.0% | Follow ups 0.0% |

The student and page tracking tools enable the teacher to generate explicit data about the ways in which students are using the resources within the system and how students are interacting with each other. In short, these tools have 'informed' the learning environment, providing the teacher with a set of symbolic cues, which now replace the rich set of sensory data available within a traditional face-to-face classroom setting. The teacher must now bring to bear a set of 'intellective skills' as well as (or instead of) the tacit action-centred skills they employ within the traditional classroom. Just as the workers and managers studied by Zuboff experienced profound, and unsettling, changes in the nature of their work, it is likely that students and teachers will have similar reactions to the pervasive growth of on-line learning environments which informate, as well as automate, the learning process. However, where the mill workers experienced a crisis of trust in the ability of the technology to replace their previous, direct and physical understanding of a manufacturing process in the academic community, the crisis of trust associated with on-line learning technology is likely to be much more profound. What is at stake is at the very heart of the learning process: the relationship between the student and the teacher, a relationship that rests upon a degree of mutual trust. The student/teacher relationship in higher education is under increasing strain for a number of reasons (see, for example, Furedi (1999) on the formalization of the student/teacher relationship in the light of complaints procedures) so a pertinent question is, can the informating facilities of on-line learning technology serve to improve this relationship or will they lead to its impoverishment? The next section explores this question.

For better or worse? Informating the learning process and the student/teacher relationship

As student numbers increase, and more students take paid work to fund their academic careers, the opportunities for meaningful engagement between student and teacher (and between student and student) continue to diminish. As Bates (1995) suggests, 'even with full-time students, it will be difficult to categorise them as either "campus-based" or "distance" education students within a few years.' This blurring of the distinction between full-time, campus-based students and 'at a distance, part-time students' has been noted by Turoff (1997) when he observed that increasing numbers of campus-based students were enrolling to take distance learning course units because of the flexibility they offered. Although on-line learning environments can easily provide for more flexible forms of learning they are much more difficult to design in order to offer the kind of interaction that occurs in a good face-to-face learning environment. In terms of encouraging and effectively managing useful interaction between student and teacher, student and material, and student and student, any data that allow the teacher greater insight into how students are using the on-line environment must surely be a step in the right direction.

Leidner and Jarvenpaa (1995) discuss the use of technology to 'informate up and down and ultimately transform the educational environment and processes' (p. 265). According to them, 'informating up' in an educational environment entails 'giving the instructor feedback concerning student understanding of class material in a timely fashion so that the instructor could clarify misunderstandings and misinterpretations' (p. 275). By using the informating capacity of on-line environments, teachers can now overcome, to some extent, the lack of the familiar, direct, sensory data associated with the traditional classroom and which they would use (almost without thought) to guide their classroom practice. Instead, they can now turn to the detailed, symbolic data provided by the system in order to effect change.

This shift from the (implicit) use of direct, physical cues to the (explicit) use of abstract symbolic ones is not easy to deal with, at least initially. A key skill that will be required of the teacher in a highly informated learning environment is that of visualization, as 'the act of visualization brings internal resources to bear in order to soften the distance, disconnection, and uncertainty that is created by the withdrawal from a three-dimensional action-context' (Zuboff 1988: 87). However, the mere provision of data about learning processes to the teacher (informating up) is the least effective aspect of informating. Informating down is a more radical use of technology, involving 'the provision of information to students to allow them to critically analyse information or discuss issues among a set of peers' (Leidner and Jarvenpaa 1995: 276). In this respect, the data from, for example, WebCT's student tracking tools, could easily be made publicly available to students allowing them to compare their patterns of interaction with those of other students which can then serve as the basis of a reflective dialogue. Further 'added value' could be offered by analysing the relationship between particular usage patterns and the results obtained in quizzes, tests or other forms of assessment. This use of the technology means that 'events and the relationships among events can be illuminated and combined in new ways. As surrounding events and processes become the objects of disengaged awareness, they become susceptible to examination, comparison and innovation . . . the technology not only frees individuals "from" but also frees them "to"' (Zuboff 1988: 180–1).

Viewed in this light, and with a skilled and imaginative teacher, the informating facilities of on-line environments would appear to offer considerable potential to enhance the student/teacher relationship. However, as well as the potential to enhance, the informating facilities of on-line systems can also offer considerable scope to impoverish or damage the student/ teacher relationship. It is the capacity of this technology to offer means of surveillance (of both students and teachers) that threatens the integrity of the student/teacher relationship. As Noble (1997: 7) has observed, 'the technology also allows for much more careful administrative monitoring of faculty availability, activities and responsiveness.' If students and staff are aware that their on-line activities are being monitored, recorded and used for purposes of which they are unaware, it is inevitable that the nature of the interaction between them will be affected. This type of self-conscious, guarded behaviour was noted by Zuboff in her study of the use of computer conferencing to support work activities: 'everyone agreed that the new emphasis was one of formality, self-consciousness, and self-protection' (p. 384).

In order to illuminate the informating potential of technology to offer sophisticated and unobtrusive means of surveillance, Zuboff draws upon Bentham's panopticon. The panopticon is described in some detail by Foucault:

at the periphery is an annular building; at the centre, a tower; this tower is pierced with wide windows that open onto the inner side of the ring; the peripheric building is divided into cells, each of which extends the whole width of the building; they have two windows, one on the inside, corresponding to the windows of the tower; the other, on the outside, allows the light to cross the cell from one end to the other. All that is needed, then, is to place a supervisor in a central tower and to shut up in each cell a madman, a patient, a condemned man, a worker or a schoolboy. By the effect of backlighting, one can observe from the tower, standing out precisely against the light, the small captive shadows in the cells of the periphery . . . Full lighting and the eye of a supervisor capture better than darkness, which ultimately protected. Visibility is a trap.

(Foucault 1977: 200)

The panopticon encapsulated principles of discipline, control and power that had been developing throughout the seventeenth and eighteenth centuries and were being applied to working-class housing estates, hospitals, asylums, prisons, schools and military camps. With the growing emphasis on surveillance and monitoring, Foucault noted:

A whole problematic then develops: that of an architecture that is no longer built simply to be seen (as with the ostentation of places), or to observe the external space (cf. the geometry of fortresses), but to permit an internal, articulated and detailed control – to render visible those who are inside it; in more general terms, an architecture that would operate to transform individuals: to act on those it shelters, to provide a hold on their conduct, to carry the effects of power right to them, to make it possible to know them, to alter them.

(Foucault 1977: 172)

The ability of information technology to embody the principles of the panopticon has been noted by Zuboff when she refers to the 'information panopticon'. According to Sewell and Wilkinson (1992), the 'electronic panopticon' creates an environment where 'a disembodied eye can overcome the constraints of architecture and space to bring its disciplinary gaze to bear at the very heart of the labour process' (p. 283). Ultimately, in the context of total quality control systems, Sewell and Wilkinson observe how the use of information technologies as an electronic panopticon can subvert the delegation of responsibility to workers:

the development and continued refinement of electronic surveillance systems using computer-based technology can provide the means by which management can achieve the benefits that derive from the delegation of responsibility to teams while retaining authority and disciplinary control through ownership of the superstructure of surveillance and the information it collects, retains, and disseminates.

(Sewell and Wilkinson 1992: 283)

Does the increasing use of on-line learning environments represent the start of a slippery slope towards the 'learning panopticon' where the human relationship, based upon mutual trust and respect between student and teacher, is replaced by one based upon data collected through sophistic-ated surveillance and codified in detailed procedures? Warning voices are beginning to make themselves heard. Perhaps the most vociferous is David Noble through a series of articles ironically appearing in an electronic journal (Noble 1997, 1998a, b). In the first, Noble quotes Robert Heterich, the president of an organization called Educomm (which is attempting to develop open standards for electronic learning resources): 'the potential to remove the human mediation in some areas and replace it with automation – smart, computer-based, network-based systems – is tremendous. It's gotta happen'. Clearly, this quote can be held up as a 'straw man' representing an easy target for arguments against the march of on-line learning environ-ments. But Noble provides more sophisticated evidence to underpin his argument:

> In Canada, for example, universities have been given royalty-free licenses to Virtual U software in return for providing data on its use to the vendors. Thus, all online activity including communications between students and professors and among students is monitored, automatically logged and archived by the system for use by the vendor . . . Thus, all students once enrolled are required to sign forms releas-ing ownership and control of their online activities to the vendors. The form states, 'as a student using Virtual U in a course, I give my permis-sion to have the computer-generated usage data, conference transcript data, and virtual artifacts data collected by the Virtual U software . . . used for research, development, and demonstration purposes'.
>
> (Noble 1997: 10–11)

He goes on to quote an administrator from the University of California at Los Angeles, who stated that, 'student use of the course Web sites will be routinely audited and evaluated by the administration'. Finally, Noble offers this reflection:

> Marvin [sic] Goldberg, designer of the UCLA WEB-CT software ac-knowledges that the system allows for 'lurking' and automatic storage and retrieval of all online activities. How this capability will be used and by whom is not altogether clear, especially since websites are typically being constructed by people other than the instructors. What third parties (besides students and faculty on the course) will have access to the student's communications? Who will own student online contribu-tions? What rights, if any, do students have to privacy and proprietary control of their work? Are they given prior notification as to the ultim-ate status of their online activities, so that they might be in a position to give, or withhold, their informed consent?
>
> (Noble 1997: 11)

Noble's views have not gone unchallenged (White 1999), but his observations about the increasing collection, storage and retrieval of data about student (and teacher) activity in on-line learning environments are difficult to refute. However, even though there are increasing volumes of data about on-line activities available for use, it does not necessarily follow that usage of these data must always be to the detriment of the student/teacher relationship:

> There are forces at work that are going to reshape the practice of distance learning and higher education in the United States. Technology only enters as an opportunity to channel these forces in very different directions. The channelling process is really that of administrative and management practices and policies that govern the utilization of educational technology and methods. While there are desirable futures possible it is becoming evident that many current practices and related economic forces can result in a future that is quite analogous to the 'darkside' of the force.
>
> (Turoff 1997)

Concluding remarks

The availability of increasingly sophisticated, flexible and reliable on-line learning environments is welcomed by many academics. These environments offer the opportunity to provide a learning experience that goes some way to compensating for the lack of personal contact that is a corollary of the modern high-volume, low-resource university. Under such circumstances, the growing use of on-line learning environments will shape our notions of 'learning communities' (Lahiff and Webb, this volume) and the relationships within those communities in ways that we are barely aware of at the moment. If on-line learning environments are to fulfil their potential in higher education, considerable attention must be given to the ways in which they shape the social interactions that are at the heart of the learning process. Perhaps Green (1999) offers a balanced view of the future:

> despite some dire predictions on both sides of the issue, the real future of technology in higher education is not about a winner-take-all competition between high touch and high tech. Rather, what's ahead for most faculty and most students is some kind of hybrid learning experience in which technology supplements, not supplants, both the content and the discourse that have been part of the traditional experience of going to college.

References

Bates, A.W. (1995) *Technology, Open Learning and Distance Education.* London: Routledge.

Foucault, M. (1977) *Discipline and Punish* (trans A. Sheridan). London: Penguin.

Furedi, F. (1999) When trust slips, *Times Higher Education Supplement*, 12 November.

Goldberg, M. (1996) *Student Participation and Progress Tracking for Web-based Courses Using WebCT* at: http://www.webct.com (accessed 5 October 1999).

Green, K. (1999) *Campus Computing Survey* at: http://www.campuscomputing.net (accessed 5 October 1999).

Jones, C. (1998) Context, content and cooperation: an ethnographic study of collaborative learning online. Unpublished PhD thesis, Manchester Metropolitan University, UK.

Leidner, D. and Jarvenpaa, S. (1995) The use of information technology to enhance management school education: a theoretical view, *Management Information Systems Quarterly*, 19(3): 265–91.

National Committee of Inquiry into Higher Education (1997) *Higher Education in the Learning Society* (Dearing Report). London: NCIHE.

Noble, D. (1997) *Digital Diploma Mills: The Automation of Higher Education* at: http://www.firstmonday.dk (accessed 5 October 1999).

Noble, D. (1998a) *Digital Diploma Mills. Part II: The Coming Battle over Online Instruction* at: http://www.firstmonday.dk (accessed 5 October 1999).

Noble, D. (1998b) *Digital Diploma Mills. Part III: The Bloom is Off the Rose* at: http://www.firstmonday.dk (accessed 5 October 1999).

Sewell, G. and Wilkinson, B. (1992) 'Someone to watch over me': surveillance, discipline and the just-in-time labour process, *Sociology*, 26: 271–89.

Turoff, M. (1997) *Alternative Futures for Distance Learning: The Force and the Darkside* at: http://eies.njit.edu/~turoff (accessed 5 October 1999).

White, F. (1999) *Digital Diploma Mills: A Dissenting Voice* at: http://www.firstmonday.dk (accessed 5 October 1999).

Zuboff, S. (1988) *In the Age of the Smart Machine: The Future of Work and Power*. New York: Basic Books.

15

Culling Community from Conceptual Conflict: A Comparative Analysis of Prospects for Building Higher Education Communities in the Twenty-first Century

Eric Gilder

The higher education community is in a conceptual crisis as we enter the twenty-first century. In the 'affluent' western societies (that have taken what Inglehart (1995) has called the 'postmodern shift'), the very purpose of higher education is being undermined from within by the banalization of formerly 'elite' discourses of deconstructionism and postmodernism. Hence, the very notion of an authoritative 'authorial' voice of expertise (the *raison d'être* of universities' existence in times past) has come under increasing fire within academe.

Seeing this epistemological disarray in an academic community that they have previously had so much faith in, government officials have set their gunsights also upon academe, reducing funding to institutions of higher education and insisting on increased accountability. Add to this showdown a fast-changing jobs market that has required higher education graduates cynically to search for their best 'positional advantage' in the marketplace by pursuing mere degrees (and not by pursuing liberal learning), one can easily see why the traditional triad of teaching, learning and research is on the defensive. Thus, nowadays it is 'every institution for itself' in the current higher education market: a situation that, however successful for individual colleges and universities, weakens the whole social fabric of the academic community.

This chapter searches for grounds for a new, wiser community of scholarship for the twenty-first century in both likely (the Republic of Korea) and less likely (Romania and Liberia) territories. By detailing initiatives in these countries that attempt to rebuild academic communities within a 'scarcity' reality/value system, the study encourages higher education policy planners in wealthier countries to consider different ways of creating an ethical collegiate community that truly serves its society and people.

A handmaiden of division and control or a 'universal watchtower': the function of higher education in a globalized world economy

> The world is getting smaller, as people like to say, but is not coming together. Indeed, as economies are drawn closer, nations, cities and neighborhoods are being pulled apart. The processes of global economic integration are stimulating political and social disintegration. Family ties are severed, established authority is undermined, and the bonds of local community are strained. Like cells, nations are multiplying by dividing.
>
> (Barnet and Cavanagh 1994: 13)

Reviewing such phenomena and its multiple effects under a telling heading of 'inhuman globalization', John Urry (1999: 4–5) argues that globalization is rapidly undermining the ability of the nation-state to manage its own affairs, whether as an imperial power or as an 'organized capitalist' state. Whatever their other shortcomings, western European welfare societies and the United States had been able, for a time in postwar history, to reasonably posit a relatively stable conception of what it meant to be a human being, and what a 'good life' for such an entity should be. Globalization processes, he argues, have disrupted this stability of definition of what it means to be human in the (rapidly dissolving) nation-states of the world. Globalization has been conceived in a variety of forms; he states, among them:

- As ubiquitous flows of cross-border information, which then impinge upon national policy formation processes.
- As a controlling ideology, by which transnational corporations can override national interests in the name of profits, and frustrate subsequent efforts of any social-democratic *polis* to control its reach.
- As a device of political-economic mobilization, particularly as used by environmental organizations, media organizations, advertisers and political actors, especially those in international non-governmental organizations.
- As a 'new medievalism', defined by overlapping, competing institutions (political, corporate, regional trading blocs) free to go their own way, thanks to the lack of any single major threatening political power to upset the status quo.

Higher education has been much affected by globalization in all these forms, but it could be argued that while the two first analytical variants noted by Urry have had either mixed or negative effects on the higher education community, the last two variants of globalization hold possibilities for academic communities to resist commodification and to build authentic communities. In the first instance, for example, while the exponential growth of digital technology and the computer revolution it begat over the past quarter-century has made wordprocessors, the Internet and true distance learning possible, it has also encouraged rank commercialization of formerly private spaces and threatened the end of residential undergraduate education for all but a small elite. The second analytical variant of globalization that Urry notes has been almost uniformly negative upon the higher education community. Rampant neo-liberal ideological attacks on state-sponsored higher education systems that dare to attempt escape from the incessant 'market modeling' desired by 'captains of industry' are commonplaces in the current policy literature (see, for example, CEPES 1999; Gray 1999). Jan Sadlak of UNESCO reminds us, however, that while universities are less 'a *reflection* of social, cultural and economic' relationships in a newly globalized world, but they are, more hopefully, 'a *determinant* of such relationships' as well (1998: 106).

Embracing this elemental fact, that the words that policy-makers employ to discuss what is even considered possible in the sector's structure and future policy direction, the past director-general of UNESCO, Frederico Mayor, has purposely used the metaphor of 'the university as watchtower' in discussing how universities can and should lead us to a 'less asymmetric' world in this hypertext age:

> We face a dilemma: higher education must respond to and interact with the globalization of communications, of the market economy which appears to dominate today's world. It should do so not just out of necessity, but as a stimulating and creative challenge. However, if we create market universities, run purely on market principles with a market vision, they may be *of* their age but will not *transcend* their age. If they only adjust or adapt to circumstances, rather than fulfil an anticipatory role, they will not be able to help *shape* the future. If they simply allow events to prevail, they will not be able to guide future generations, as they have guided us, with the timeless values that serve as an ethical and intellectual touchstone.
>
> (Mayor 1998: 250, original emphasis)

In this light, the last two analytical variants of the globalization process that Urry notes offer some hope to those who seek to rebuild academic communities in often less than ideal environments, particularly given that, as Peter Scott (1998: 109–13) has persuasively argued, much of university policy-making remains firmly grounded in local and national concerns despite all the present-day talk of globalization.

Whither community? Higher education in the advanced West and the loss of shared meaning

The higher education 'project', in Western thought at least, has, throughout its history, been plagued by multiple confusions over the 'nature' of knowledge, the proper role of the teacher of that contested knowledge, and the sense of the student's own being. Drawing from the American example, Rouner observes that academe is becoming a more lonely place, despite great advances in communication technology:

> Our campuses increasingly reflect this general cultural loneliness. Loneliness is not a new phenomenon in the academy – academic research, writing, and the grading of term papers have always been done by working long hours alone with the door closed. In the past, however, this solitude was relieved by a collegial sense that faculty members and students were involved in a common endeavor, and that this common life was structured according to an agreed-upon set of values. Now, changes in institutions, in scholarship, and in the culture of the academy at large make it more and more difficult to identify a shared set of values.
>
> (Rouner 1997: B4)

Add to this philosophical and pragmatic confusion of community in the university the ever-growing global 'economic imperative', and the epiphenomenal 'quality imperative' it has borne in a capitalist consumer society driven by the philistine thought of business interests, and one is inevitably led to either the abject intellectual poverty of mere 'competence and skill' training that passes for much higher education today, on one hand (in which any search for humane meaning is seen as irrelevant to the requirements of the preprogrammed syllabus), or to the vapidities of supposedly high-minded consumerist postmodernist critique on the other (in which any search for core human understandings are defined away at the start). Following the rediscovered lead of Aristotle, what is required, Barnett and Griffin argue, is for academics to become 'practical epistemologists' (1997: 170). How can one, however, best understand the social context which governs, in part, whether specific academic communities can achieve this call? This writer suggests first considering the results of a comprehensive World Values Survey conducted by Ronald Inglehart and colleagues (Inglehart 1995), in which over 70 per cent of the world's population in 43 nations was sampled in 1990–91 to obtain a solid analytical grounding for such an understanding.

As Inglehart argues, societies can best be analysed today as being governed either by 'scarcity values' or 'security values,' rather than merely analysed by the traditional developmental categories of being either (traditional) 'pre-industrial' or (modern) 'industrial.' Vitally for any serious consideration of higher education and its purposes, Inglehart's work reveals that there now exists in the advanced countries a 'postmodern shift,' partially transplanting the earlier modern shift. (The modernization shift, Inglehart argues, encompassed the well known forces of change – urbanization, industrialization, occupational specialization, secularization, the rise of mass education and media, among others – in its much-heralded 'march' through the nineteenth and first half of the twentieth century.) As the 1960s drew to a close, however, the forces of modernization became an issue of political discussion (via the ecology movement) in the capitalist West, and then the modernist paradigm came to be questioned in the socialist East as well, leading, in part, to the dramatic events in Europe of 1989. The grand March of Progress had been interrupted.

As a result of this 'interruption' of technological modernism via a political 'postmodern shift' in mentality, Inglehart (1995: 383–8) claims that communal authority has been shifted away from *both* religion and the state, and *towards* the individual. This social shift leads to five 'winds of change', affecting mindsets of scholars and their communities the world over:

- A move from 'scarcity values' towards 'security values'.
- A move away from social respect towards bureaucratic authority.
- A move away from individual belief in ideologies of whatever colour.
- A move away from willing submission to social responsibilities (duties) and towards celebration of individual rights and freedoms.
- A move away from rationalism towards emotionalism, thereby leading to widespread doubt about the ability of 'science' to solve increasingly complex problems.

This writer posits that while Inglehart perhaps provides a compelling structure by which to argue why scholarly communities in the advanced western countries have lost their faith and purpose, one should not necessarily think thereby that other countries' scholars have also lost theirs. As Inglehart's analysis suggests, countries holding 'scarcity values' should hold different visions of what higher education properly is and what it can become. In the following section, the search for practical social knowledge by members of academe in three very diverse 'scarcity value' countries (the Republic of Korea, Romania and Liberia) are detailed, thus demonstrating how the liberating aspects of the globalization process noted by Urry (political action and 'medieval' associationalism) operate in specifically local community contexts.

University community in less secure places: virtues of scarcity (either imagined or real)

Case study 1: Still believing in the project of progress – Korea and the communal role of modern higher education

In the West and even in the European East, one can now easily find much discourse that questions the very notion of progress. Since the 1960s, one has heard voices (both cynical and sincere) pondering the implications of a society wedded to progress as its penultimate value, a value that united elites in both the Soviet bloc and its western competitors. From the armament and science races of the immediate postwar period to Chernobyl in 1986, dominant interests in both blocs shared the same faith in science and rationality to solve human problems. Today, given personal and social dissatisfaction of for ever 'keeping up with the Joneses' in the 'secure' world, given the ever louder critique of lopsided development projects in the third world, and given the increasingly effective political role of the ecological movement in Europe and America, progress as an ideal has, nevertheless, been dethroned.

This is not the case, though, in much of Asia, and certainly not in the Republic of Korea. Teaching here, one can see an almost blind faith in the best the West, particularly the United States, can offer. Many professors and students look forward to studying in America, and the higher educational structure in Korea shares many of its 'traditional' modernist structures and assumptions. Indeed, the author often gets the feeling that he experienced in Korea a confidence in positivistic science and ideological solidarity that United States higher education possessed from the late 1950s to the early 1960s. For example, even with (and probably because of) the recent economic crisis in Asia, Korea has embarked on an ambitious plan of reconstructing its higher education system, dubbed Brain Korea 21. This audacious plan is of particular interest because, unlike discussions of higher education in 'security value' countries, it is a plan marked by an almost unbounded optimism and faith in the high modernist formation of schooling (Son *et al.* 1999, but see Lee 2000, on the controversy raised by its planned adoption for 'non-elite' Korean universities).

Kyonggi University, a comprehensive private university of about 16,000 students located in Suwon and Seoul, likewise shows such optimism in its own expansion plans. Its educational mission and vision statement eagerly embrace all the latest technologies, happily partaking of globalization's benefits (while seemingly not fearing its dark consequences), always seeking to extend academic co-operation with the outside world, and so on (Kyonggi University 1998). As similarly posed above, the question arises as to why Kyonggi University specifically, and Korean higher education institutions generally, are not afraid of the future despite the real challenges ahead for the Korean economy and society.

The answer lies in the fact that Korea still is, in many ways, a feudalistic/modernist composite society, thus still embracing (and benefiting from) the 'scarcity values' beyond the term of their actual necessity. Faith in family and community is still strong, despite strong empirical evidence that these institutions are under stress. This 'faith' is predicated upon a national ideology of largely Confucian principles, buttressed by the ongoing cold war with North Korea (Kim 1999).

For Kyonggi University, its operative values, its ideology are defined by a core commitment to *jinsongae*, the pursuit of truth, sincerity and love. As detailed by Hyun and Gilder (1998: 222), the 'best intellectual community is a tensioned combination of [imagination and locale], wherein any individual's intellectual vistas opened by IT [information technology] are socially grounded in the security and caring of . . . Korean community and culture'.

As the ASEAN countries such as Korea, strong in their embrace of scarcity values and a corporatist ethic, gladly embrace an updated model of

1950s positivistic science as their basis for the university of the future, what of intellectual communities, large or small, who, to avoid the problem of career credentialism and/or the vapid corporate banality that often goes with it, *wish* or, because of a lack of sizeable funds or infrastructure, *must* establish their universities on another basis? To answer this question, the author will detail two additional educational initiatives, one in Romania, the other in Liberia. In these countries, neither of which possesses the resources or mind to build corporate campuses, it is ennobling to note that a higher educational community, properly conceived, can be begun in almost any situation, and then grow with the resources available. One does not have to wait for resources to build a new campus equipped with all the modern technology, good though that undoubtedly is, to teach basic humanistic and theoretical curricula. Indeed, the converse is true as well: having the best infrastructure does not guarantee a vibrant university community. Two specific examples will suffice here: the experience of the author teaching (without knowing it then) in a truly 'invisible college' in Romania over three years, and the prospects of a destroyed college's rebuilding itself and its curriculum in post-civil-war Liberia.

Case study 2: From bottles to bursaries – the invisible college model in Romania

The author is privileged to have spent over six years living, teaching, researching and serving a community of scholars in Romania, a unique nation whose tormented recent history has paradoxically, in his mind, produced thinkers who are fearless in envisioning their own new world order, without undue homage to the political/economic allures of East or West (cf. Gilder (1995) for a discussion of this experience). A Romanian philosophy colleague, Ana Liţa, now at Bowling Green State University, Ohio (USA), states the charge facing the universal community of scholars in the 'post-ideological' era thus:

> If we are to think philosophically, existentially, about this second 'after-time', the question must be modulated from utopian considerations to ethical ones. For we all, both East and West, are so confused about both means and ends that we need to start with more modest questions. What is the best way to view the *ethos* of the newly invoked 'end of history' in liberal democracy and the free market? What may be an *ethics* responsive to this second 'after-time'? The question is not any more 'What *is* going to happen?' but rather 'What *may* happen?' and, then, in view of that, 'What should we, together, do?'.
>
> (Cristea and Gilder 1997: 180, original emphasis)

Liţa goes on to argue that the still-extant, albeit hidden, polarizations between East and West, between Marxism and liberalism, between command economies and consumerist 'relaxation' economies, make the ethical task of thinkers, of philosophers, pondering these elemental questions more difficult – but not impossible. Through initially informal initiatives such as the Bucharest Reading Group, and the Romanian National Reading Group it fostered, the author and colleagues were able to form a nascent 'invisible college' of young social scientists who sought together to answer truthfully these basic questions, and are thereby now 'making their mark' in the world as thinkers committed to sustaining a moral community of scholars worldwide.

How can one best describe such an invisible college? Basically, it is little more than an informal reading circle with a structured plan to promote subsequent collaborative research work among the participants. As described in Gilder *et al.* (1996: 138), an invisible college is defined by its Socratic methodology, best described as including 'a communal ideal to know; committed professors and students; lively talk; and, it must be admitted, the sacrificed contents of a few bottles of wine and beer.' From such private Dionysian beginnings, much of public worth was created, including two years (1994–96) of nationwide reading groups co-chaired by Sorin Anthoi of the University of Bucharest and the Central European University, Budapest, with attending authors such as Anthony Giddens, Slavoj Zizek, Krishnan Kumar and Bernard Paqueteau.

The most notable effort along similar pedagogical lines has been the establishment in 1994 by Professor Andrei Pleşcu and colleagues of the New Europe College (NEC) in Bucharest upon the basis of a 1993 award given to Dr Pleşcu by a consortium of six international institutes for advanced study. It is a seminar-based humanistic postgraduate college that seeks to keep Romanian scholars in country and in academe, by the provision of individualized scholarships and communal intellectual support. Although a small programme (20 scholars a year participate as fellows) such has been its success that it was awarded the prestigious Hannah Arendt prize in 1998 (Agovino 1999; New Europe College n.d.). The core of the NEC curriculum is a weekly series of lectures and discussions, given both by the fellows and by selected Romanian and international academics in varied humanistic specialities. Also of importance to the fellows are the ready availability of modern research and communication facilities, funding for books and journals, and an extensive research visit abroad for each fellowship recipient.

The basis of success of these ventures lies in the fact that they embody the best example of 'academic trust', lost in the West in recent decades amidst increased educational access and decreasing institutional resources. How do these innovative programmes maintain their freedom from intrusive accountability and assessment measures used elsewhere in the world? Simply by being relatively low-budget academies unapologetically meritocratic (even elitist) and individualized in their conception, not high-budget educational factories driven to promote *both* universal access for incoming students *and* a high job-preparedness 'quality' of outgoing graduates. However odd it might sound to 'politically correct' western ears, such an out-spoken elitist policy is not a necessarily a bad choice for nations with limited funds for postgraduate humanistic education to pursue, *if the selection process is seen as fair and above-board by all.* Perhaps such an approach for rebuilding a true academic community could best come from a state where, not too long ago, barely literate peasants and workers were artificially promoted into university studies for political reasons.

Case study 3: Building for a practically spiritual university community after civil war in Liberia

West Africa faces a rather more desperate problem with higher education: the sector is barely functioning. Years of civil unrest (still ongoing in parts) have largely destroyed the limited infrastructure that existed before 1990. Thus, the problems that Dore (1976) discussed concerning the challenges of higher educational provision in developing countries are even more dire now. Consider the following case of Cuttington University College in Liberia as a sombre, yet hopeful, instance of a community seeking both to reclaim, and to build anew from the ashes of war, an historic institution of higher learning.

Cuttington University College, founded in 1821, is considered the oldest 'coeducational, four-year, degree-granting institution in sub-Saharan Africa'. Called by some the Amherst of Liberia, it has had a long and venerable history as an 'elite' higher educational institution in the region. An Anglican Church college, it had offered courses of study in both the liberal arts and technical studies. Forced to close in 1929, it was reopened in 1948 at its current site, 120 miles outside the Liberian capital, Monrovia (Cuttington University College 1999a).

The 1960s to the late 1980s were the heyday of the 'old' Cuttington. Both the Rockefeller and Ford Foundations supported the college's programmes with substantial funds in the 1960s, and the American Schools and Hospitals Abroad (ASHA) programme donated funds from the late 1970s to 1989 for health projects and a hospital. A Rural Development Institute was begun in 1978, from a United States Agency for International Development (USAID) grant of us $5.5 million, which over the years developed into the Center for Agriculture and Rural Development, also funded by USAID. Peace Corps and Fulbright scholars came regularly to teach, do community service and perform research.

Most poignantly, with the celebration of its centennial in 1989, the old Cuttington's days were numbered. A ruinous civil war began in Liberia in late 1989 and the college was forced to close in May 1990. In that the college was an attractive target for warring troops, its infrastructure was largely destroyed during the conflict, and its student and professorial community either scattered or killed (Cuttington University College 1999a).

In June 1991, a 'Cuttington in Exile' was established at a sister Anglican (Episcopal) College in Virginia, USA: St Paul's College. After the end of the civil war in 1996, Cuttington University College reopened in October 1998, albeit on a small scale, while reconstruction funds are being raised by the Episcopal Church of the United States and the Colleges and Universities of the Anglican Communion. The vital point to note is that, even in the midst of war, the vision, the hope of the university remained and the community lived on.

Concerning the educational mission of the new Cuttington University College, while it is still under revision, there already exists a consensus of what it should *not* be: a re-creation of the old Cuttington with the horrors of the immediate past war. To borrow a phrase of architect Rem Koolhass, 'the past is too small to inhabit' there, even if one could (Cuttington University College 1999b). John and Judy Gay are American teachers, researchers and missionaries with over thirty years of experience in Africa, many of them in Liberia and Cuttington. Contrasting the academic outcomes of the old Cuttington with the new educational realities, they restate Dore's (1976) thesis of the counterproductive results of much development thinking in vivid terms, referring to the outcome of an advisory meeting at the college:

> We knew what we wanted, namely, a place where the needs of the rural community would be foremost. We realized at that time that the old Cuttington had become too much of an elite establishment, too much a breeding ground for the technocracy, too much a springboard for graduates to get jobs in Europe or America. Cuttington had been a great success in that sense, but had to a serious extent failed in making life better for rural Liberians. Even those rural Liberians who entered Cuttington by and large ended up succeeding either in Monrovia or, more likely, in the United States. We hoped at those planning meetings to build a new environment, where the curriculum was developed and the classroom teaching carried out in relation to the needs and problems of post-war Liberia. We hope that environment can be created and sustained. It will require serious work to change the mind-set of ambitious young people toward Christian service to their brothers and sisters in rural Liberia as opposed to instant movement into the wealthy elite. This cannot be done, moreover, by western-oriented exhortation and sermonizing. It must arise from a deep realization of the trauma that Liberia (and so much of Africa elsewhere) has suffered.
>
> (Gay and Gay 1999)

Hence, the Gays forcibly argue that the curriculum of the new Cuttington 'cannot be simply a repetition of the western-oriented curriculum that we relied on and to a serious extent imitated in the pre-war period'. As examples they say that the nursing curriculum must 'reflect the horrors of war, both the physical and the spiritual horrors'. Economic theory courses at the new Cuttington must deal not with the 'wonders of globalization, but with its losses and shortages for Africa, and the survival tactic of improvization' (Gay 1997).

Conclusions

In a survey of the international academic scene today, Philip Altbach clearly suggests that the higher educational community needs to find its voice if it is to save itself from further decline:

> This is not an especially happy time for higher education worldwide. Academe is under attack everywhere. University leaders have been unable to defend the institution successfully from its critics and from governments committed to cutting budgets and shifting governmental priorities. The academic community does not speak with a united voice. Indeed, in general it does not speak at all. The contemporary university must present a vision of its role in the future and defend its past contributions to knowledge and to society.
>
> (Altbach 1998: 356)

While the dreams of true liberal and liberating higher education are under stress in an economically-obsessed western-oriented world as Altbach claims, despite noted efforts of some colleges to 'buck the trend' as shown by Nussbaum (1997), it is surprising to find that in countries not 'blessed' by security values, spiritual dreams of a humane education are being enacted, often despite severe hardships. By their very different embodied examples, Kyonggi University of Korea, the New Europe College of Romania, and Cuttington University College in Liberia clearly demonstrate that 'community' is an ideal that can be lived freely, if only we can first think through the essential conceptual conflict that faces all higher educational institutions today, that is, how do you measure success, and by which values?

References

Agovino, T. (1999) Romanian fellowship program helps academics beset by economic stress, *Chronicle of Higher Education*, 30 April. Website search under 'New Europe College', www.chronicle. com (accessed 9 December 1999).

Altbach, P.G. (1998) Comparative perspectives on higher education for the 21st century, *Higher Education Policy*, 11: 347–56.

Barnet, R.J. and Cavanagh, J. (1994) *Global Dreams: Imperial Corporations and the New World Order*, New York: Simon & Schuster.

Barnett, R. and Griffin, A. (1997) *The End of Knowledge in Higher Education*. London: Cassell.

CEPES (European Centre for Higher Education) (1999) *The Entrepreneurial University: How to Survive and Prosper in an Era of Global Competition*, special issue of *Higher Education in Europe*, XXIV(1).

Cristea, L. and Gilder, E. (1997) Social implications of the opportunities for Romanian higher education in the new world order, *Higher Education in Europe*, 22(2): 175–82.

Cuttington University College (1999a) *Cuttington's History* at: http://www.cuttington.org/cuchist.htm (accessed 2 December 1999).

Cuttington University College (1999b) *Plans for the Future* at: http://www.cuttington.org/cucfut.htm (accessed 2 December 1999).

Dore, R. (1976) *The Diploma Disease: Education, Qualification and Development.* Berkeley: University of California Press.

Gay, J. (1997) Proposal for a research institute at Cuttington University College (Liberia), 3 December, internal document.

Gay, J. and Gay, J. (1999) Comments on meeting of academic advisory committee for Cuttington University, Liberia (personal communication, 26 October).

Gilder, E. (1995) Turning personal experiences into social reality: communication as a 'third-culture-building' tool in the Romanian classroom, in F. Casmir (ed.) *Communication in Eastern Europe: The Role of History, Culture, and Media in Contemporary Conflicts,* pp. 197–222. Mahwah, NJ: Lawrence Erlbaum Associates.

Gilder, E., Mitrea, A. and Vasi, B. (1996) Communicating across cultures and disciplines: the Bucharest Reading Group as embodied social knowing, *Higher Education in Europe,* 21(4): 127–38.

Gray, H. (ed.) (1999) *Universities and the Creation of Wealth.* Buckingham: SRHE and Open University Press.

Hyun, C.M. and Gilder, E. (1998) The *telos* of information technology in a transitional culture: implications for the globalization of Korean higher education, *Higher Education in Europe,* 23(2): 217–26.

Inglehart, R. (1995) Changing values, economic development and political change, *International Social Science Journal,* 47(1): 379–403.

Kim, W.B. (1999) Are Asian relations harmful for economic development?. Paper presented to the International Conference on Universal Ethics and Asian Values, Seoul, 4–6 October.

Kyonggi University (1998) *Kyonggi University's Educational Mission and Vision.* Seoul and Suwon, Republic of Korea: Kyonggi University.

Lee, G.E. (2000) Brain Korea 21: a development oriented national policy in Korean higher education, *International Higher Education,* 19: 24–25.

Mayor, F. (1998) The universal university, *Higher Education Policy,* 11: 249–55.

New Europe College (n.d.) Prospectus 1994–1998. Bucharest: New Europe College.

Nussbaum, M. (1997) *Cultivating Humanity: A Classical Defense of Reform in Liberal Education.* Cambridge, MA: Harvard University Press.

Rouner, L.S. (1997) Social solipsism and moral loneliness in the intellectual community, *Chronicle of Higher Education,* 3 October: B4–B5.

Sadlak, J. (1998) Globalization and concurrent challenges for higher education, in P. Scott (ed.) *The Globalization of Higher Education,* pp. 100–7. Buckingham: SRHE and Open University Press.

Scott, P. (1998) Massification, internationalization and globalization, in P. Scott (ed.) *The Globalization of Higher Education,* pp. 108–129. Buckingham: SRHE and Open University Press.

Son, C.K., Hyun, C.M., Sung, T.K. and Gilder, E. (1999) From terminal threats and exacting exchanges to innovative integration: can higher education (re)weave the knowledge web? Paper presented at the 3rd International Conference on Technology Policy and Innovation, The University of Texas at Austin, USA, 30 August–2 September.

Urry, J. (1999) Contemporary transformations of time and space, in P. Scott (ed.) *The Globalization of Higher Education,* pp. 1–17. Buckingham: SRHE and Open University Press.

Appendix

Papers to SRHE Annual Conference 'Higher Education and its Communities', Manchester, 1999

The academic community

The business community

The regional community

The European and international communities

Index